NOV 2 8 2018

McGraw-Hill Education

Police
Officer
EXAMS

McGraw-Hill Education
Police Officer
EXAMS

Second Edition

MICHAEL J. PALMIOTTO, Ph.D.
Professor Emeritus of Criminal Justice, Wichita State University

MICHAEL L. BIRZER, Ed.D.
Professor of Criminal Justice, Wichita State University

ALISON McKENNEY BROWN, J.D.
Criminal Justice Instructor, Prosecutor, and Legal Adviser

New York   Chicago   San Francisco   Athens   London   Madrid   Mexico City
Milan   New Delhi   Singapore   Sydney   Toronto

1 2 3 4 5 6 7 8 9   LHS   22 21 20 19 18

ISBN   978-1-260-12101-8
MHID   1-260-12101-1

e-ISBN   978-1-260-12102-5
e-MHID   1-260-12102-X

McGraw-Hill Education books are available at special quantity discounts to use as premiums and sales promotions or for use in corporate training programs. To contact a representative, please visit the Contact Us pages at www.mhprofessional.com.

Contents

- Hostage Negotiations Teams
- Bomb Squad Officers
- Warrant Officers
- Airport Police
- Housing Police
- Port Authority Police
- Transit Police

PART II: BECOMING A POLICE OFFICER

- Memorization
- Visualization
- Spatial Orientation
- Verbal or Written Expression

  Vocabulary terms

  Grammar/Sentence Structure/Spelling

  Sequencing

  Ability to Provide Information Clearly and Concisely

  Investigative Report Writing
- Verbal, Reading, or Written Comprehension

  Applying Learned Information

  Understanding Information
- Problem Sensitivity

  Following a Procedure or Directions

  Eyewitness Descriptions

PART I

ALL ABOUT POLICE WORK

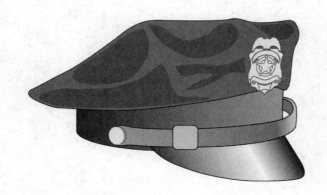

CHAPTER 1

Understanding the Role of the Police Officer

> ### Your Goals for This Chapter
> - Learn about the different kinds of law enforcement agencies.
> - Find out what police officers do.
> - Explore the structure of police departments.

There is always a need for highly trained and highly skilled law enforcement agents. Today too, all policing agencies are finding that rapidly changing technology not only provides law enforcement with new ways to investigate crime, but also provides criminals with new tools to commit crimes. As a result, law enforcement agencies are constantly seeking to hire and train new policing candidates who are able to work well with the public, maintain high ethical standards, work independently, use common sense, and act as a positive role model for the community. Today's police officer also needs to have well-developed communication skills. Communication skills are important because police officers are expected to communicate in one-on-one situations with citizens from all walks of life, especially in conflict resolution and mediation situations.

To evaluate each candidate's potential for civilian law enforcement, agencies have developed an assortment of written, psychological, and physical tests. It is very possible, even encouraged, to prepare for the written portion of these tests. Once candidates are aware of the ability areas that the tests attempt to evaluate and the testing methods agencies typically use, they can begin to sharpen and improve the necessary skills.

If you are interested in a law enforcement career, you should begin by educating yourself on the various law enforcement agencies with which you may wish to seek employment. Factors such as the size of the agency, the area of the country, and the population density may all be important issues when you are determining what agency or agencies to apply to.

After choosing an agency or agencies, the second step is to prepare for the compulsory tests that every law enforcement agency uses to evaluate candidates. Candidates for police positions are expected to communicate well both verbally and in writing. These candidates are also expected to demonstrate an ability to perform basic mathematical processes, read and understand legal information, and reason through large amounts of seemingly unrelated information to find clues or connections. While the process of preparing for written law enforcement exams is not easy, it will seem well worth the effort when you are notified that you have been selected for an important and exciting career as a police officer.

OVERVIEW OF POLICE DEPARTMENTS

Policing in the United States (U.S.) is divided into four broad categories: federal, state, county, and municipal agencies. There is no real hierarchy between these categories. Each branch of law enforcement has been created to enforce a specific set of laws within a specific geographical area. This means that the key to understanding which law enforcement agency has the authority to respond to a crime is two-fold. First, one must determine which governmental unit prohibited the act. For example, homicide is an act that is prohibited at the state level. So, as a general rule, only law enforcement agencies with authority (jurisdiction) to enforce state laws may investigate the crime of murder. Second, one must look at the place (venue) where the criminal act occurred. If the murder occurred in Alabama, the Alabama authorities would be responsible for investigating the crime. Thus, if you are primarily interested in becoming a homicide detective, you would most likely be interested in applying to a state or local policing agency rather than to federal law enforcement agencies.

The following overview of law enforcement agencies is intended to provide a brief understanding of the various categories of police departments in the United States. Use this list as a starting place for determining which type of law enforcement agency seems the most interesting to you. Then, contact that agency directly to seek information concerning the application process. Much of this information may also be available on the Internet. A list of many state agency Web site addresses is included in the materials of this book. In addition, federal and local agencies are also likely to have information available on the Internet. To find a local agency, look up the city's Web site and you will usually find a link to the police department.

Public expectations for police officers often seem immense. The public expects the police to prevent crime and make arrests. In addition, the police are expected to perform numerous other duties: including operating detention facilities, search and rescue operations, business licensing, supervising elections, staffing courts, and chauffeuring officials. Since the terrorist attacks on New York City and Washington D.C., the police have also been given the responsibility of monitoring for signs of possible terrorism at the municipal level.

Still, most police departments, regardless of their size, provide the same types of services to their communities. Although modern television dramas have created the impression that police officers race from one murder scene and arrest, to the next, police officers do much more. They investigate crime, enforce traffic regulation, maintain social order, provide emergency services, rescue animals and vulnerable people, patrol to deter crime, and work to keep the peace. They may also report potholes in the roads, malfunctioning streetlights, or children that appear in need of social service intervention. In short, police do whatever is necessary to allow people to continue living and working together in a safe and healthy environment.

A brief review of the specific responsibilities of the different levels of police agencies follows.

Federal Law Enforcement Agencies

Police officers that work for the national government are generally called federal police officers. These police officers enforce criminal federal laws that are passed by the United States Congress and signed into law by the President. They have the authority to arrest anyone who commits a violation of federal criminal laws within the specific area they are hired to protect.

Police agencies that hire federal police officers include the White House Police, Capital Police, Supreme Court Police, and Park Police. Each of these police agencies has specific responsibilities. For example, the Park Police enforce federal criminal laws in the nation's parks. Those individuals who would like a position as a federal police officer are required to take a federal police examination for that position.

In addition, there are federal law enforcement agencies designed to protect the rights and privileges of all U.S. citizens. While these agencies have not been created with a particular hierarchy of power, each has been created to enforce specific laws or address certain specific situations.

The Federal Bureau of Investigation (FBI) is probably the best known of the federal law enforcement agencies. The FBI is a branch of the United States Department of Justice (DoJ). This agency is not a police agency; instead it investigates matters involving violations of federal law including civil rights violations, espionage, treason, bank robbery of federally insured institutions, serious crimes that cross state lines, and terrorism. The FBI is estimated to have more than 13,000 agents employed primarily in the United States.

The United States Marshals Service is the nation's oldest federal law enforcement agency. Marshals serve to protect federal judicial officials, maintain security in federal courthouses, and protect the safety of those witnesses in federal trials who are endangered by testifying. U.S. Marshals also track down fugitives from justice from across the world, transport federal prisoners who need to be moved across jurisdictions, and maintain detention facilities for unsentenced prisoners.

Other federal agencies are designed to enforce specific federal laws. The Secret Service has two primary missions: protecting all living current and former U.S. Presidents and their families and controlling counterfeiting. The Bureau of Alcohol, Tobacco, Firearms, and Explosives assists in controlling the sale of untaxed liquor and cigarettes, illegal firearms, and explosives. The Drug Enforcement Administration (DEA) is the federal agency that enforces federal drug laws. Agents of the DEA primarily carry out their responsibilities by assisting local and state authorities in investigating illegal drug use and drug trafficking. They also work with foreign governments to reduce the amount of illegal drugs entering the United States, as well as operate independent investigations into drug crime.

State Law Enforcement Agencies

All 50 states have state police agencies. Generally, there are two models of state police agencies. Some states like New York, Pennsylvania, and Michigan have a single State Police Department that is responsible for both traffic and criminal investigative responsibilities. These state level policing agencies are divided into two primary units. One unit is responsible for patrolling state turnpikes and highways. The second unit is responsible for investigating criminal offenses.

The second model of policing used by state agencies has been adopted by states such as California, Florida, Georgia, and Kansas. These states have two separate state police agencies. One agency is called the Highway Patrol. The Highway Patrol monitors state turnpikes and highways. The second state level policing agency is assigned the responsibility for state level criminal investigations. The names of these agencies are varied and include the Florida Department of Law Enforcement, Georgia Bureau of Investigation, and Kansas Bureau of Investigation.

In addition, state law enforcement may be responsible for running state law enforcement training academies, providing emergency medical services, maintaining a crime lab, and providing other services that are needed to support local level law enforcement efforts.

County Law Enforcement Agencies

The third level of policing occurs at the county level and typically involves an elected sheriff and appointed deputies. A few states may forego the title of sheriff and maintain a county police department.

The duties of a sheriff's department vary according to the size and population of the county. Nearly all sheriffs' offices provide basic law enforcement services to areas outside incorporated municipalities. These duties include routine patrol, responding to citizen calls for service, and investigating crimes. They are authorized to enforce state law within their county as well as enforcing county-level laws including traffic enforcement and, in many counties, animal control.

In addition, sheriffs' departments are usually responsible for the county jail or detention facility. Although some states still maintain separate local detention facilities in every city and town, most have consolidated this function into a single county area facility utilized by all municipalities within the county. Detention duties may be rotated among all appointed deputies, or deputies may be hired for the single purpose of staffing and monitoring the detention facility.

Finally, the sheriff's department is typically assigned duties associated with court services. These duties include serving civil court summons, providing court security, providing courthouse security, and dealing with criminal warrants.

Municipal Law Enforcement Agencies

Municipal law enforcement agencies are those police departments created to serve an incorporated city, town, village, or borough. The greatest opportunity for those interested in policing is at the municipal level because most policing occurs at the municipal level. There are about 17,000 municipal police departments in the country; more than 70 of those police departments employ in excess of 1,000 police officers, and 83 police departments employ 500 to 999 police officers. The majority of municipal police departments, however, employ 10 or fewer officers. In the United States 75 percent of police officers are employed by departments that serve communities with a population of fewer than 10,000 residents. This means that although there are large police departments like New York City, Chicago, Houston, and Los Angeles, the vast majority of police departments and the vast majority of police officers are found in smaller communities.

The primary reason municipalities establish a police department is to maintain order. For example, it is important that all drivers follow traffic regulations to reduce the likelihood of accidents or injuries. Most drivers occasionally ignore traffic regulations without concern for the danger they are causing to others. Police officers enforce the traffic regulations to remind drivers of their responsibility to drive in a manner that is safe for the entire community. This may not seem like a critical policing task, but protecting the communities' health and safety by preventing vehicle accidents is a primary goal of all municipal law enforcement agencies.

The American Bar Association (ABA) outlines the functions of the municipal police officer to include a broad range of activities. Municipal police officers are expected to:[1]

- Identify criminal offenders and criminal activity and where appropriate, to apprehend offenders and participate in subsequent court proceedings.
- Reduce the opportunities for the commission of some crimes through preventive patrol and other measures.
- Aid individuals who are in danger of physical harm.
- Protect constitutional guarantees.
- Facilitate the movement of people and vehicles.
- Assist those who cannot care for themselves.
- Resolve conflict.
- Identify problems that are potentially serious law enforcement or governmental problems.

- Create and maintain a feeling of security in the community.
- Promote and preserve civil order.
- Provide other services on an emergency basis.[1]

POLICE ACTIVITIES

So what do police actually do? Studies of police activities indicate that most police work involves activity that is non-criminal in nature. Many non-criminal calls are considered service-related. Primarily police activities involve:

- Handling domestic issues
- Working traffic accidents
- Finding missing persons
- Directing traffic
- Filling out paperwork

However, one of the key tasks assigned the police is to respond to calls regarding criminal conduct. When a citizen telephones the police to report a crime or disturbance, the police dispatcher assigns a patrol unit to handle the call for service. After a police officer arrives at the scene and begins an appropriate investigation, the officer may determine that a violation of law has occurred. Then, depending on the seriousness of the offense and departmental rules and regulations, the officer can either make an arrest or handle the incident less formally.

It is important to remember that while state and local police are concerned with predatory crime, including murder, rape, burglary, and theft, they do not have authority over every type of crime. They may not have the authority to investigate economic crimes, violations of civil rights laws, or labor law disputes. Those types of crimes usually involve a violation of a specific federal law that must be handled by a specific federal agency. State and local police officers are limited to responding to those criminal acts and behaviors prohibited by either state or local laws.

STRUCTURE OF POLICE DEPARTMENTS

American police departments are organized as a bureaucracy along semi-military lines and structured into ranks based either on the army or navy rank structures. The rank structure of police departments varies between police departments, depending upon the size of the department and the needs of the community. Generally, big city departments have a much more complex rank structure than smaller city departments and rural police departments. For example, the rank structure of the New York City Police Department with approximately 36,000 police officers is much more complex that of than Scarsdale, New York, a department of about 45 police officer in suburban New York.

---

[1] American Bar Association, *The Urban Police Function*, (New York: American Bar Association, 1, 1973).

The rank structure of a police department forms a hierarchy with *patrol officers* at the bottom of the rank structure, *sergeants* at the second level, *lieutenants* at the third level, *captains* at the fourth level, and the *police chief* at the top of the hierarchy. The rank structure allows for the patrol officers to report to one supervisor, generally a sergeant. This concept is known as a *unity of command*. It is recommended that in a police department each individual report to one boss. This method eliminates problems within the organization when more than one person supervises a patrol officer.

The police hierarchy generally holds that a sergeant should supervise about five police officers. This concept is known as *the span of control*. The idea behind maintaining a span of control is that a supervisor can only effectively serve a specific number of employees. Similar to the unity of command principle, the span of control principle seeks to reinforce the chain of command inherent in a structure based upon rank.

As a semi-military organization, police departments require that officers wear uniforms, carry firearms, wear badges, and display nameplates. Police officers are expected to maintain the chain of command by obeying the orders and following the directions of their immediate supervisors. Police officers who do not follow orders or directions can be suspended or dismissed, depending upon the seriousness of their violation and the amount of disruption their behavior imposed upon the department as a whole.

It should be noted that any individual hired as a police officer serves a probationary period from several months to one year. During this period, officers are often termed *probationary officers* or *probies* for short. The exact length of the probationary period depends on the requirements of each individual police department. It is important that police officer candidates understand that the goal of the probationary period is to evaluate their ability to perform on the job and to fit into the department. Probies may be dismissed during the probationary period without cause and no reason needs to be provided. Damaging a police vehicle, a single incident of excessive use of force, violating the chain of command, or making negative comments about superior officers may all demonstrate that a probie is not the right fit for a department's needs.

Once a police recruit successfully completes the probationary period, more workplace protections are acquired. Generally, following the probationary period, law enforcement officers are given civil service status. The actual rights and protections associated with this status differ from municipality to municipality and from state to state, but they will always provide at least a few rights that are missing during the probationary period.

Big City Police Departments

The entertainment and news media have created the impression that policing primarily occurs in very large municipalities, such as Los Angeles and New York City. While it is true that every state has one or more cities large enough to employ more than a hundred police officers, the vast majority of cities are small enough to require 25 or fewer officers. So, the majority of policing positions will be available in smaller police departments.

However, it should be recognized that big city police departments provide opportunities not usually available in smaller departments, such as the ability to specialize in a certain area of law enforcement.

The number of crimes that arise in larger police jurisdictions allow police departments in such cities to create areas of specialization, such as crime prevention, crimes involving children, community policing, crime scene investigation, and drug education. Very large departments like New York City, Kansas City, Denver, and Seattle are also able to have a few units specifically assigned to a single crime, such as their homicide units. Additionally, many of those knowledgeable about policing believe that the opportunities for promotion are greater in a big city department like New York as compared to a smaller department like Scarsdale, New York.

Small Community Police Departments

The majority of police agencies are categorized as small city or rural police departments, although the concept of *small* may be based on perception. For example, those individuals living in medium-sized cities such as Wichita, Kansas, may think their 700 member police department is big. However, that number of officers would seem small to residents of Los Angeles, California. Clearly, individual departments often define themselves as large or small depending upon the needs of their community, their proximity to other communities, and the size of the actual urban area in which they are located.

Generally, small police agencies do not have personnel to investigate homicides or other serious crimes. These agencies have to obtain assistance from the state police. Officers in small agencies often are not as well educated or trained as officers in bigger cities due to being exposed to less crime on a less regular basis.

However, the best reason for joining a smaller police department is that police officers in small departments know the citizens in their communities. They know most of the history and issues, both community-related and family-related, which evolve over time to require police intervention. They can settle complaints in an informal manner rather than through a more time consuming and costly criminal justice process.

The duties in smaller departments are often more varied and interesting that the limited areas assigned in larger departments. Often, small police departments encourage their officers to spend the majority of their time on patrol and interacting with the public. A typical day for an officer in a small police department may involve: controlling animals running at large, visiting with the kindergartners about the role of police in their community, issuing a few traffic citations, taking a report of a theft from the local convenience store, and arresting an individual for domestic violence. While murder may be a rare event in small cities, protecting the health, safety, and welfare of citizens remains an important service to the community.

CHAPTER 2

Police Careers and Opportunities

Your Goals for This Chapter

- Explore your reasons for wanting to become a police officer.
- Learn what duties police officers perform.
- Discover opportunities for women and minorities.
- Learn about all the different assignments available to police officers.

Police work offers an opportunity for a satisfying and rewarding career. Before you apply, you will want to find out everything you can about what police officers do on the job. You will also want to learn about all the different assignments available to police officers. Which one is right for you? To answer that question, think about your reasons for wanting to become a police officer.

WHY BECOME A POLICE OFFICER?

Why a person should become a police officer is a question each potential recruit must ask themselves. Some people become police officers because they want job security. Police officers have a steady job, with a steady paycheck, and a limited chance of being laid-off. Some people become police officers because they want to work outdoors for a few years before changing to an indoor job. Still other people become police officers to avoid close supervision, while others become police officers because they want to help others or give something back to their community. You must determine for yourself what your career goals are and whether or not entering law enforcement will allow you to achieve those goals.

The authors of this book recommend that those who are interested in entering the police field attend a Citizen's Police Academy and become an auxiliary police officer or reserve officer in their community to get a better understanding of police work. They can also request to do volunteer work for their police department. The more a person knows about a career in policing, the better position that individual will be in to make the decision that a career in law enforcement is the right choice.

DUTIES OF A POLICE OFFICER

In some states, state laws specifically explain the duties of police work, while in other states, each police department is allowed to define the scope of its responsibilities. For example, the State of Missouri defines policing for the police departments of St. Louis and Kansas City (MRS Section 84.090) specifically spelling out the duties of municipal police officers. The job description defined by the State of Missouri provides an excellent example of both the expectations for Missouri police officers as well as for police officers everywhere. The statutory duties for a municipal police officer in St. Louis and Kansas City are to:

- Preserve the public peace.
- Prevent crime and arrest offenders.
- Protect the rights of persons and property.
- Guard the public health.
- Preserve order at every public election, and at all streets, alleys, highways, waters, and other places.
- Prevent and remove nuisances on all streets, alleys, highways, waters, and other places.
- Provide a proper police force at fires for the protection of firemen and property.
- Protect transients at public wharves, airports, and railway and bus stations.
- See that all laws relating to elections and to the observance of Sunday, and relating to pawnbrokers, intemperance, lotteries, policies, vagrants, disorderly persons, and the public health are enforced.
- Suppress gambling and bawdyhouses, and every other manner and kind of disorder and offense against law and public health.
- Enforce all laws and ordinances which have been passed or may be subsequently passed.

OPPORTUNITIES FOR WOMEN AND MINORITIES

Since the 1970s the opportunities for women and minorities in policing have increased substantially as law enforcement agencies have begun to recognize the importance of ensuring that the police force they hire resembles the public it polices. Today, police departments do not have a sufficient number of women and minorities applying for policing to meet that goal. For this reason, many police departments are actively recruiting women and minorities because they would like the opportunity to hire them. In today's policing environment, both women and racial minorities who meet the criteria and qualifications to be police officers have unlimited opportunities.

AFFIRMATIVE ACTION/EEOC

Affirmative Action is a part of the civil rights laws that has been implemented through the Equal Employment Opportunity Commission's (EEOC) attempt to enforce programs established by Congress. EEOC is an independent federal agency that oversees federal civil rights laws. EEOC is the agency that investigates cases of discrimination and takes action to eliminate discrimination when they locate it. Affirmative Action policies and federal law make it a crime to discriminate against any person because of race, national origin, religion, gender, age, or sexual orientation. This means that a person cannot be discriminated against in the hiring process, promotional process, or in wage determinations.

ASSIGNMENTS FOR POLICE OFFICERS

In the field of policing, there are a wide variety of positions that police officers can hold during their careers. Many factors influence whether an individual police officer will hold one position throughout their career or many different positions. The leading factor influencing a police officer's career is the desire of the officer to achieve the skills necessary to be placed in a new position. Additionally, factors such as time in rank and the size of the police department impact the opportunities available to police officers. Following is an outline of the many positions available within law enforcement.

Automobile Patrol

The most common method of patrol for decades has been the automobile. The patrol vehicle offers mobility and covers a large geographical area or beat. The automobile offers a fast response in emergency situations and can carry important equipment like fire extinguishers, additional ammunition, computers, radar units, and informational manuals. The patrol vehicle is also helpful for pursuing suspects in vehicles and for transporting prisoners. Finally, it should be noted that the automobile provides protection for the officer from both crime and inclement weather.

Foot Patrol

Foot patrol officers are useful for special events, such as parades and dignitary protection, and for public relations (PR). They are also useful for patrolling shopping malls, beaches, apartment complexes, schools, and areas where a motorized vehicle cannot gain access. Officers on foot can observe more than officers in vehicles. They can use their sense of smell and sense of hearing to identify problems. In addition, foot patrol can improve communication between the police and community. Foot patrol officers can function as community organizers and dispute mediators and be important links between social agencies, law enforcement, and members of the community in need of specialized assistance.

Traffic Officer

Many cities have a traffic division with a team of police officers assigned to monitor traffic. The traffic officer's ultimate goal is to minimize serious and fatal collisions. To achieve this goal, these officers are responsible for the enforcement of traffic laws and for investigating serious automobile accidents. Accident reconstruction is also a common responsibility of the traffic division. This responsibility involves reconstructing the scene of serious accidents to determine the cause or causes of the collision. Often, a skilled traffic investigator will be able to determine if any changes to the roadway, signage, or enforcement procedures could be applied to prevent further tragedies in the same area. Occasionally, it is information forwarded by law enforcement to the appropriate manufacturers, educators, engineers, and legislators that initiates changes necessary for the improved health, safety, and welfare of the entire public.

Bicycle Patrol

Bicycles have been used by police officers since someone thought they provided a good way to chase down horse-drawn vehicles. Today, bicycles continue to be an effective transportation tool because they offer police officers more speed, mobility, and flexibility than they have on foot. They are useful for patrolling college campuses, parks, beaches, housing areas, and congested downtown areas. Bicycles are a good PR tool and an effective mechanism for controlling crime in the downtown areas of cities.

Motorcycle Patrol

Motorcycles have been traditionally used for traffic enforcement and control. A few cities also use them for escort services for funerals or for parades. The motorcycle has maneuverability and can move through crowds of people or traffic more easily than a conventionally sized vehicle. However, their popularity with policing agencies seems to rise and fall with the price of fuel because of the obvious safety problems associated with motorcycles. Police officers often drive in dangerous situations, and motorcycles offer little protection from weather, other traffic, or situations involving crime.

Horse Patrol

Horse patrol units are often developed because they are excellent PR tools. They also provide important services to law enforcement. The mission of mounted patrols is to provide high visibility patrol to the busiest sections of urban areas. Mounted patrols are also used for crowd control tactics and formation riding and to assist with non-mounted police tactics. Finally, mounted patrols are often seen participating in both urban and rural search-and-rescue operations because they are able to access areas that foot patrol, bicycle patrol, and policing vehicles have more difficulty accessing, such as heavily wooded areas or areas around ravines.

Marine Patrol

In addition to drug smuggling along America's coastlines, predatory crimes occur on rivers, lakes, and the ocean. For this reason, agencies with authority to police waterways often develop marine patrols. The marine patrol has three main functions: rescue and recovery, agency assistance, and law enforcement. Police respond to calls for assistance from boaters, kayakers, or anyone else on the water in distress. They assist other agencies, such as the United States Coast Guard, United States Customs, or other marine patrol units, who need back up or are too far away to respond to a call. The marine patrol can also be used to transport police or fire personnel to places that are easier reached from the water. For special events, the marine patrol can be used to enforce no-wake zones, speed restrictions, no-access areas, and general safe boating,.

Aircraft Patrol

Many police departments are developing aircraft patrol units. These units provide aerial support to ground-based units in traffic law enforcement. They detect speeding and reckless drivers from surveillance overhead. They are also used to assist other enforcement agencies by providing air support for such things as drug activity surveillance, covert surveillance, tracking of criminal suspects, VIP escort support, searches for missing persons and downed planes, aerial photography, and emergency organ transport.

Helicopter units provide many of the same services as patrol planes, but they may be called on to provide additional types of assistance. Helicopter units may be needed to assist with firefighting efforts, to transport severely injured accident victims, or to assist with ground mapping efforts.

Juvenile Officer

Many medium-sized and large police departments assign police officers to units designed to address issues with juveniles. It is also not unusual for small police departments to have at least one officer devoted to issues surrounding juvenile offenders if sufficient juvenile problems exist in the area. The laws relating to juvenile offenders differ from the criminal laws for adults because juveniles are not usually considered criminals: they are considered offenders. States have adopted specific laws and procedures for the dealing with juvenile offenders. Because state laws deal with juveniles in a non-criminal manner, officers assigned to deal specifically with juveniles require specific training on the procedures, laws, and methods for speaking to, investigating, and detaining juveniles.

Canine Officer

The primary purpose of the police canine unit is to improve law enforcement while reducing the jeopardy to human police officers. The canine functions as a psychological deterrent to the law violator while at the same time serving as an effective PR tool. Police officers are selected to serve with canine officers based on their willingness and ability to work with a dog. Officers selected for the canine unit receive specialized training. Officers and their dogs are used for search and rescue operations both inside buildings and in the wilderness. They may be trained to respond to the presence of drugs or explosives without the requirement of a search warrant. They may be sent to bring down a suspect who is able to outrun a human police officer or be trained to stand guard and protect vulnerable human beings. The uses for canines and their human police companions within law enforcement is rapidly expanding and becoming a very critical tool in effective law enforcement.

Crime Scene Investigator

Several medium-sized and large police departments have crime scene investigators whose job is to collect evidence. Police officers assigned to this position usually receive training on how to investigate a crime scene. This position often requires a bachelor's or even master's degree in criminal justice, forensics, or biological sciences. The job of the crime scene officer is to take all necessary precautions when dealing with crime scenes, especially those relating to health and safety regulations. Crime scene officers are expected to keep abreast of new technical developments in forensics and in analyzing the crime scene.

Crime Prevention Officer

Many police departments have a crime prevention officer who has the responsibility of educating the public on crime prevention. This includes performing surveys for businesses and for residences, both houses and apartments. The crime prevention officer is expected to give talks to professional and social organizations on crime prevention. In addition, the crime prevention officer works with patrol officers and detectives in developing and implementing crime prevention strategies.

Community Policing Officer

Community policing has become the philosophy for today's police officer. Medium-sized and large police departments assign officers to community policing beats. The community-policing officer interacts with the community and participates in neighborhood functions and events. The community policing philosophy is that the community policing officer should function as a problem-solver. Community policing officers are expected to identify community problems, find solutions to the problems, implement those solutions, and then evaluate the effectiveness of those solutions.

Hostage Negotiations Teams

In the last several decades it has become increasingly common for criminals and terrorists to take hostages. Today, police officers are needed to negotiate with criminals and terrorists who have taken hostages. Generally, police officers with several years of experience are selected to receive training as hostage negotiators. It has become the job of the hostage negotiator to work to obtain the safe release of hostages without giving in to terrorist demands.

Bomb Squad Officers

There are individuals who telephone schools and other public buildings claiming that a bomb has been planted in the building. Sometimes these telephone calls are a hoax, but they are always taken seriously. Usually, the building will be cleared until a determination can be made that no bomb exists in the building. It is the job of the bomb squad officer to check out the building and to verify that no bomb exists. If there appears to be a bomb, it is the job of the bomb officer to detonate the bomb in a safe location or to diffuse it. Bomb squad officers receive special training on the detection, handling, diffusion, and detonation of bombs. Today, the bomb squad officer is an important component of mid-sized and large departments. Police officers must volunteer for this dangerous work and successfully pass a vigorous course.

Warrant Officers

Police officers are often given the responsibility to serve warrants. Municipal police officers serve arrest warrants upon suspects wanted for a criminal offense. They also serve bench warrants for individuals who have not shown up for a hearing or court case. Warrants can also be served on individuals violating a court order.

Airport Police

Many cities have airports. Therefore, it is not surprising to learn that municipalities often assign police officers to maintain a presence at airports. Airport police will monitor traffic concerns such as parking in front of the airport or disturbances within the airport. In addition, if serious matters arise, they are already on scene to respond and to evaluate if back up, or a larger police response is necessary in any given situation.

Housing Police

Many mid-sized cities and large cities have public housing. Because of the large number of people housed in public housing units, it is not uncommon for crime to occur there. To deter crime before it happens, and to provide the fastest possible response time after crime happens, municipal police officers are assigned to patrol public housing complexes. It is not unusual for police departments to have a mini-station located in a public housing apartment complex, with officers specifically assigned to the public housing complex. These officers are often trained much like community policing officers. They are encouraged to get to know the residents of the area they patrol and be aware when they are in need of assistance.

Port Authority Police

A port authority can include a pier, a bus terminal, a train terminal, a tunnel, bridge, or an airport. In large cities and sometimes in mid-sized cities, police officers are specifically assigned to these locations. Crime can occur in all these locations and police officers are expected to maintain order in all public areas of public transportation.

Transit Police

In large cites with public transportation and city-operated buses or subways, it becomes the responsibility of the police to develop an effective method of patrol. As subways, train cars, and buses are constantly moving, specially trained units are assigned to monitor these areas. Transit police are now authorized to check individuals and their carry-on bags for any explosive devises that could be carried onto public transportation. The transit police also have the responsibility for maintaining order and preventing crime on city buses.

PART II

BECOMING A POLICE OFFICER

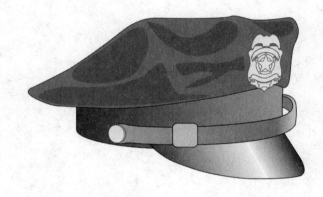

CHAPTER 3

Qualifications and Opportunities for Police Officers

Your Goals for This Chapter
- Find out the general requirements for becoming a police officer.
- Learn about the normal probationary period.
- Explore promotion opportunities and benefits.

If you've set your sights on a police career, you need to know the requirements for becoming a police officer. You also need to know the typical procedure for applying for the job.

GENERAL REQUIREMENTS

Specific requirements for being accepted to a law enforcement training academy vary from department to department. The general requirements are that the applicant:

- Is a U.S. citizen
- Is at least 21 years of age
- Has at least 20/20 vision uncorrected; (or 20/20 corrected by glasses)
- Is able to distinguish colors
- Is physically and mentally healthy

Applicants who have served in the military must have been honorably discharged and furnish a copy of their Department of Defense "DD 214" form. The DD 214 is a certificate of release or discharge from active duty in the United States Armed Forces. Applicants may not have been convicted of driving while intoxicated and must hold a valid drivers license for at least three years prior to application and have a good driving record. Applicants should have no criminal convictions, although some misdemeanor crimes may not bar applicants from a law enforcement position. All applicants are expected to be free from drug use, be of good moral character, and have personal integrity. No applicant should have any history of criminal or improper conduct, have a poor employment record, or have an irresponsible financial history. Generally, applicants should at least have a GED equivalency or a high school diploma; however, some departments, such as that in Dallas, Texas, are requiring 60 or more hours of completed college coursework.

NOTICE FOR EXAMINATIONS

Generally, police departments will announce the dates of pre-employment examinations and require that an applicant complete an application to take the examination. Announcements are often published in the local newspaper, on the local cable network, on the Internet, and in announcement bulletins posted in the police department. Information may also be available through the city's human resources department or the applicable state's employment office. Other common sites for finding information about law enforcement agencies that are preparing to hire a new recruit class are bulletin boards in local colleges and municipal and state office buildings.

PROBATION PERIOD

When a candidate receives an appointment to the police department, the candidate must then successfully complete recruit training, which can last from several months to more than a year, depending on the training requirements of the police department. Once the recruit has successfully completed the training academy, the recruit then usually receives field training under the supervision of seasoned officers. Upon the successful completion of the field training, the officer is considered eligible to be on their own.

Police recruits are on probation during the entire period of training and usually are on probation for a period of time after they have completed their training. The length of time that a recruit serves on probation varies from department to department. The purpose of the probationary period is discussed in the previous chapter, but it should be noted that officers will not generally be eligible for a promotion until the probationary period is successfully completed.

OPPORTUNITIES FOR PROMOTION

Opportunities for promotion vary from police department to police department. The size of the department plays an important role in opportunities. Larger departments are likely to have greater opportunities for advancement and a wider variety of areas of specialization available to officers.

BENEFITS

Applicants who are successfully employed as police recruits will immediately receive health, dental, and life insurance, long-term disability, and a pension. They also may receive holiday pay, sick days, and shift differential. Benefits vary from city to city.

CHAPTER 4

The Screening Process

Your Goals for This Chapter

- Learn the steps in the police officer screening process.
- Find out what is required at each step.

The screening process differs in relation to the needs and size of the specific department being applied to. However, screening processes tend to be similar between departments of the same size. The following list provides an overview of the typical screening process.

- Individuals must apply for a police officer position by completing the required application for the police department. Generally, police applications are very detailed and require that specific information be provided.
- A written examination is required for all police departments in medium-to-large cities. The type of examination can vary from an essay examination to one that has reading comprehension, mathematics, and memory skills. Medium-to-large cities are likely to have in-depth written examinations, while smaller agencies may substitute essay exams, video exams, oral interviews, or in-depth background checks.
- A police candidate who successfully passes the written examination is then required to take a physical abilities/agility test. The physical abilities test is an obstacle course designed to simulate obstacles that an officer may encounter during a typical tour of duty.
- A police candidate who successfully passes the physical abilities/agility test is then given a date to take a pre-employment polygraph examination. Candidates are given a polygraph examination administered by a qualified polygraph examiner. The polygraph examiner will ask the candidate specific questions concerning criminal activity, drug usage, truthfulness, integrity, and employment history.
- A candidate who successfully passes the pre-employment polygraph examination must then undergo a background investigation. The background investigation can be very detailed and cover educational background, work history, and criminal and traffic records. Individuals knowledgeable

about the candidate, including school teachers, neighbors, friends, and acquaintances are interviewed to assist in determining the character of the candidate.

- A candidate who successfully passes the background examination is then given an oral interview. During this process, the candidate is asked a series of questions to assess ability to deal with people, solve law enforcement-related problems, communicate effectively, demonstrate initiative, and tolerate stress. In some police agencies the oral board interview is scheduled before the background investigation. The order will vary among police agencies.

- A candidate who successfully passes the oral examination is then scheduled for a psychological examination. A certified psychologist gives the candidate a battery of psychological tests and interviews the candidate to determine that he or she is not suffering from emotional problems and meets the psychological criteria for a career in policing.

- A candidate who successfully passes the psychological examination is then scheduled to take a medical examination. The medical examination determines if the candidate is physically fit to work as a police officer.

- A candidate who passes all the previous examinations may be asked to participate in a final oral interview with the police chief, the head of the training academy, or police command staff to determine whether the candidate should be offered a police position in the department.

Understanding the Written Exam

A written examination is required for almost all police departments in medium-to-large cities. The type of examination can vary from an essay examination to one that has reading comprehension, mathematics, and memory skills. Medium-to-large cities are likely to have in-depth written examinations, while smaller agencies may substitute essay exams, video exams, oral interviews, or in-depth background checks. This chapter focuses on the most commonly given examination: the written multiple-choice exam. A brief explanation of the video test and essay-type examination is provided in the next chapter.

PREPARING TO TAKE THE WRITTEN LAW ENFORCEMENT EXAM

When preparing to take a written law enforcement exam, remember that the main objective of the exam is to test your ability to memorize and to solve problems. Usually, the test is timed to prevent you from thinking too long on any given question. While timing the test is an effective way to simulate the stress under which law enforcement officers must make most of their daily job-related decisions, it creates an additional problem for test takers: the need to read and decipher quickly.

Many of the questions on law enforcement exams present a large amount of information that must be read and then sifted to find the appropriate answer to the question. The information may be relatively technical, or it may seem straightforward, yet require you to recognize minor details. With unlimited time many of the questions might be worked out and seem almost easy, but under strict time constraints, the questions are more likely to seem long and difficult to understand.

There are two critical steps that you can take to minimize the stress and difficulty of taking a law enforcement written exam. First, you should contact the agency or agencies to which you are interested in applying. Most law enforcement agencies will provide applicants with a packet of pretest materials. The packet informs the applicant of the specific ability areas tested and of a few potential testing formats that are used on that agency's exam. It may also provide pretest materials that must be studied prior to taking the written exam. In addition, the pretest materials include any information that the testing agency needs applicants to know prior to taking the written exam. These materials should be obtained from the agency as soon as possible after they become available.

Second, you should sharpen your test-taking skills. Most law enforcement exams focus on the same general ability areas: memorization, visualization, spatial orientation, verbal or written expression and comprehension, problem sensitivity, mathematics, deductive reasoning, inductive reasoning, and information ordering. While pretest packets provided by law enforcement agencies provide a list of the specific ability areas that are tested, the materials do not provide examples of every potential question format that is used to test those ability areas. Although it may not be possible for a candidate to know every potential format that a question may be presented in, it is possible to prepare for more formats than are presented in the agency's pretest materials. Learning to recognize the ability area being tested and the common question formats used in that ability area can help you become quite comfortable with the law enforcement testing process.

To help you achieve this goal, the authors of this book provide a description of each of the ability areas commonly tested and include a broad range of the question formats that may appear on different agency's written law enforcement exams. Some tips for answering the different types of questions associated with each ability area are also included.

Applicants should review every practice test included in this book to become familiar with the wide variety of methods that are used to test each ability area. Remember, preparation and practice are the best ways to ensure a higher score on this type of exam.

GENERAL TIPS FOR TAKING EXAMINATIONS

Before learning about the details of the written examination, you should review some general tips on taking the examination.

- Rest appropriately the night before the exam.
- Eat breakfast before the exam. Avoid foods that make you sleepy or provide a quick burst of energy but then leave you feeling drained.

- Bring several sharpened No. 2 pencils with you, as well as any additional tools that were listed as permitted in the pretest materials, such as scratch paper or calculators.
- Read all directions carefully. Sometimes the skill being tested is the ability to read and follow directions.
- Listen to directions concerning the answer sheet.
- Keep track of your time.

  ○ If you find you have less than five minutes left and too many questions to answer within that time, begin guessing. Leaving a question unanswered guarantees an incorrect answer. Guessing provides at least a chance of a correct answer.
  ○ If you have time remaining, make sure that your answer sheet shows that you have answered the correct number of questions. It is not uncommon to skip a line on an answer sheet and find that there is one more or one less answer than is necessary. This is easily corrected if it is noticed in time.

- Ask questions immediately if you are unable to hear or understand any of the directions.
- Determine if you will be allowed to mark in your testing materials, if scratch paper is allowed, or if all work must be done in your head.
- Use basic testing strategies. Begin by answering all the questions for which you feel confident about the answer. Then, in your remaining time, go back to the more difficult questions and eliminate all the answers choices you know are wrong. Then, make the best possible choice from the answer choices that are remaining.
- Use the answer sheet carefully. Most questions on law enforcement exams are presented in a multiple-choice format with four possible answers. A sample answer sheet used to mark responses to multiple-choice questions has been provided for you to review. Remember to fill in the answer circle completely without going outside the lines. These forms are graded by a machine that may misread answers if the circle is not completely filled in, or if stray marks go outside an answer circle.

ABILITY AREAS AND ASSOCIATED TESTING FORMATS

A law enforcement examination typically assesses a range of ability areas:

- Memorization
- Visualization
- Spatial orientation
- Verbal or written expression (spelling, grammar, sentence structure, sequencing, providing information clearly and concisely, investigative report writing)
- Verbal, reading, or written comprehension
- Problem sensitivity
- Mathematics
- Deductive reasoning
- Inductive reasoning
- Information ordering

Memorization

Memorization is the ability to observe and recall. Although memorization is a straightforward skill, *it is the area where law enforcement examinations most differ*. Clearly, all agencies use a memorization section to assess an applicant's ability to remember street names, people, geographic areas, business layouts, and other details that a police officer is constantly required to recall.

To assess memorization ability, law enforcement examinations provide pictures or drawings of scenes that could occur in any neighborhood and require the applicant to recall the information provided. These pictures may be provided in the pretest materials packet or in the examination itself. When the pictures or drawings are provided as part of the pretest materials, you will be expected to memorize the scene prior to arriving for the exam. Then, the first portion of the exam will cover your ability to recall the details of the picture(s). It is not unusual for pictures provided in advance to be accompanied by short explanatory paragraphs that provide additional information to clarify the scene. You are required to memorize and recall this information as well.

When the pictures or drawings are provided as part of the exam itself, the process of memorization is slightly different. Typically, you are given a 5- to 15-minute period to study the picture (*the study period*). You are not allowed to make any marks on the picture, use scratch paper to make notes about the picture, or do anything else during the study period. At the completion of the study period, the pictures are turned back in to the proctor. This is followed by a 5- to 15-minute period during which you are to retain the information (*the holding period*). Again, you are not allowed to use scratch paper or make notes of any kind during this period; rather, you are expected to sit and mentally review the information in preparation for answering any questions. After that, you are given the questions associated with the picture.

One technique for memorizing the details provided in a scene is summarized in the acronym EASE. The EASE method encourages an organized process of memorization, beginning with recognizing the broad theme(s) of the picture and then working down to the details of the picture.

E—Events: Begin by determining what event or events are being presented in the scene. Do not focus on a single event or person, but rather determine all the events being depicted. Use your fingers to assist in tracking the number of events occurring. This provides a tactile means of assisting your memory. Finally, if possible, put the events you see in some order of occurrence.

A—Ask yourself: Who, what, when, where, and how many?

- Determine *who* is in the picture: police officers, fire fighters, pedestrians, criminals, children, etc.
- Determine *what* is in the picture: buildings, cars, dogs, street signs, streets, trees, businesses, etc. Signs, such as the name of a street, the place where the scene is occurring, or a number pattern, are often used to provide clues.
- Determine *when* the scene is occurring: Look for clues about the time of day and the time of year.

- Determine *where* the scene is taking place: a neighborhood, inside a home, on a busy city street, etc. Also, orient in your mind where in the scene each person or thing is in relation to other people or objects. Determine *how many* of each object or person are represented in the picture. For example, how many cars were involved in the collision, how many law enforcement officers are at the scene, or how many apartment doors are visible. Again, use your fingers to track the number of each item.

S—Section the scene: Divide the picture into three or four smaller sections and study each one separately. It is usually easier to remember seven or eight details associated with four small scenes, than 28 details associated with one large scene.

E—Express yourself: In addition to using your fingers to provide a tactile method of assisting your memory, say the information to yourself either quietly out loud or in your head. Do not confuse saying the information to yourself with merely thinking about or perceiving the information. Actually forming words about the detail and saying those words to yourself forces your brain to directly focus upon that detail.

Memorization questions may be primarily information, such as the picture and information provided on a "wanted" poster. This information tends to be quite detailed and will usually be presented in a pretest packet to give you adequate time to familiarize yourself with the information so as to be able to recall it quickly.

Memorization questions are typically in multiple-choice format.

EXAMPLE 1

SKETCH OF SUSPECT

NAME:	Jerry Balducci	Eyes:	brown
Alias:	Jason Winters	Hair:	brown
Age:	23	Height:	5'10"
		Weight:	165 lbs.

Identifying characteristics: 1. Missing front tooth, 2. Snake tattoo on left forearm.

Wanted for: Suspected auto theft

FIGURE 5-1:

Which of the following characteristics DOES NOT describe the suspect?

(A) Brown eyes
(B) Black hair
(C) Age 23
(D) Height 5ft 10in

The correct answer is B. The poster clearly states that the suspect's hair is brown.

Visualization

Visualization is the ability to observe and use information. Typically, law enforcement exams will test this ability by providing an *original* person or item to be studied and then providing a group of similar items or people. You must choose which of the four similar items or people matches the original picture. The match of the original will have been changed in some manner, such as putting a topper on a pick-up, or painting a vehicle, or putting a hat and glasses on a face. You need to see through the disguise.

An effective technique for approaching this type of question is to focus on those details that will not change. You may assume that the disguised features have not been changed by surgery or major reconstruction. For example, a short- bed pick-up may be disguised by changing the paint or adding a topper, but it will never turn into a long-bed pick-up. Similarly, a woman's face may get glasses, but the shape of the woman's features will not change.

In the following drawings of a suspect and four similar individuals, it is possible to quickly determine which of the four similar individuals is most likely to be the suspect. Focus on the shape of the eyes, mouth, and nose. Eyebrows, hairstyles, jewelry, and clothing will change to confuse you. One feature, such as the eyes, may be the same in all the drawings, but at least one of the main three facial features will differ in the drawings.

EXAMPLE 2
Which of the four drawings on the right most closely matches the suspect on the left?

FIGURE 5-2:

The answer is D. The face of person D is the only one that has the same nose and mouth.

Spatial Orientation

This ability area involves understanding one's own location in relation to the surrounding area. It involves understanding the space one is in or is about to enter. It could be the interior of a building, an open area, a street network, or a city. Questions testing this ability often use a full-page map of an area and then ask a series of questions requiring you to be aware of a direction of travel and also of limitations on travel, such as traffic rules or large furniture. Some exams provide these maps in advance and require that you memorize them, in the same way that all law enforcement officers must memorize the geographic areas of their patrol.

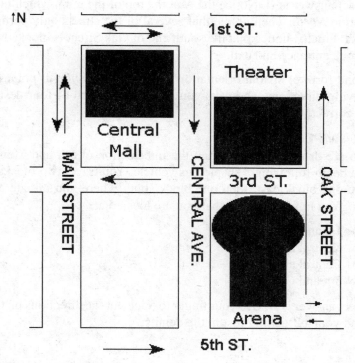

FIGURE 5-3:

When responding to a spatial orientation question, begin by determining which direction is north, south, east, and west. Then, look for identifying characteristics such as street names and buildings. Finally, note any impediments to travel such as one-way streets or dead ends.

These types of questions are multiple-choice questions and usually come in two different forms. The first form places you at point A and asks how to reach point B by the shortest route without violating traffic regulations.

You then choose which of the four routes provided is the shortest and does not violate any laws.

EXAMPLE 3

You are at the intersection of 5th and Main when you receive a call to an emergency at 3rd and Central. Which of the following is the shortest route you can take without violating any traffic laws?

(A) One block north on Main Street to 3rd Street, then one block east to Central Ave

(B) One block east on 5th Street to Central Avenue, then one block north to 3rd Street

(C) Two blocks north on Main Street to 1st Street, then one block east to Central, then one block south to 3rd Street

(D) Two blocks north on Main Street to 1st Street, then two blocks east to Oak Street, then one block south to 3rd Street, then one block west to Central

The correct answer is C. Notice the *N* at the top of the map, which indicates the direction *North*. Then notice that several of the streets only permit one-way travel. Finally, notice that the south end of Oak Street is blocked off due to the Arena entrance and exit.

The second form of spatial orientation question places you at point A, provides driving directions, and asks you to identify which of four destination points is correct.

EXAMPLE 4

You are driving north through the intersection of 5th and Main when you begin following a suspicious vehicle. You travel two blocks north, then one block east, then one block south where you initiate a traffic stop. You notify dispatch that you are located at:

(A) 1st and Oak

(B) Central and 3rd

(C) Central and 5th

(D) 5th and Oak

The correct answer is B. Use your finger to trace out the directions on the map if you find yourself getting lost in the details.

Verbal or Written Expression

This ability area encompasses several different question formats. Each question format is geared toward assessing your ability to use language and includes knowledge of vocabulary, grammar, and sentence structure.

VOCABULARY TERMS

Some law enforcement exams provide a list of vocabulary terms with the pretest materials. You must familiarize themselves with the terms and the definitions provided, and you should be able to use the terms correctly in a sentence. You are not allowed to take the vocabulary list—or other pretest materials—into the exam. You must rely on your ability to recall information about the terms provided.

You should be careful to learn the definition provided and not rely on your own understanding of the term. Often these vocabulary words are **terms of art**, meaning that they are defined by the profession that uses them.

EXAMPLE 5

Code: A body of law covering one general subject that is established by the legislative authority of a governmental body, such as a state or local government.

Officer James consults the codebook. He is most likely looking for:

(A) A signal flag pattern
(B) Codes currently utilized by spies
(C) The definition of a crime
(D) A Morse code pattern

The correct answer is C. It is the answer that most closely meets the definition provided.

GRAMMAR/SENTENCE STRUCTURE/SPELLING

Grammar and sentence structure questions attempt to assess your ability to convey ideas using written language. Some agencies provide a list of rules of grammar with their pretest materials and then require you to correctly apply those rules on the exam. Other agencies do not provide any particular list of rules, but ask questions that require a general mastery of basic rules of grammar and sentence structure.

EXAMPLE 6

Which of the following is correct?

(A) Officer Jones took they're shoes away.
(B) Officer Jones took there shoes away.
(C) Officer Jones took their shoes away.
(D) Officer Jones took theirs shoe away.

The correct answer is C. It is the sentence that uses the correct form of *their*.

SEQUENCING

A third type of format used for verbal expression questions asks you to put a list of sentences in the order that makes the most sense.

EXAMPLE 7

1. Mrs. Peterson took her cat home.
2. The cat had been in the tree for days.
3. Mrs. Peterson thanked the fire department.

4. The fire department was called.

5. The fire department rescued the cat.

Which of the following is the most logical order for the above sentences to appear?

(A) 1, 2, 3, 4, 5
(B) 2, 4, 5, 3, 1
(C) 2, 4, 1, 5, 3
(D) 5, 4, 3, 2, 1

The correct answer is B. You may not see the sentences placed in the order you would like to see them placed, but you must choose the best arrangement presented. However, you should look for sentences that must be in a certain order and then rule out any answers that do not follow that order. For example, the fire department must be called before they can rescue the cat. Therefore, D is clearly wrong because sentence 4 must come before sentence 5.

ABILITY TO PROVIDE INFORMATION CLEARLY AND CONCISELY

Another type of question that analyzes your ability to express yourself is one that requires you to determine the best method of conveying information. Typically you are given some information and then asked to select a sentence that best conveys that information. Answering this type of question requires the ability to recognize conclusions, opinions, biases, or judgments that have been attached to the original information.

EXAMPLE 8

As Officer Parker arrived at the scene of an accident involving a bicycle, he saw a white sedan leaving the scene.

Which of the following statements best conveys Officer Parker's information?

(A) A white sedan hit a bike.
(B) A white sedan hit a bike and then left the scene of the accident.
(C) A bicycle hit a white sedan.
(D) A white sedan left the scene of an accident involving a bicycle.

The correct answer is D. All of the other answers draw conclusions that have not yet been proven.

INVESTIGATIVE REPORT WRITING

A few exams require you to write reports and complete forms. Generally, information about the reports is provided in the pretest packet. You must memorize the instructions for filling out the form or forms prior to taking the test. Then, on the day of the exam, you are given a short scenario and then asked to fill out the appropriate report form based on the instructions that you learned earlier.

EXAMPLE 9

Instructions for Completing a Form		
Box 1	Date offense started	Enter the month, day, and year on which the offense occurred.
Box 2	Time offense started	Give the exact time that the offense started. Use military time (add 12 hours to all P.M. hours). The offense starts at the time the law is actually broken.
Box 3	Location of offense	Provide the street name and address of the offense. If no actual address at site, use closest approximation of address preceded by *appx*.

The police officer is asked to complete a form concerning the following incident:

On July 11, 2006, at approximately 9:00 P.M. Patty Smith walked into the Super-Mart, located at 502 E. 69th Street N.

Date Offense Started	Time Offense Started	Location of Offense	Date of Report
1	**2**	**3**	**4**
Date Offense Ended	Time Offense Ended	Number of Victims	Victim Injuries
5	**6**	**7**	**8**

What information should be placed in box 2?

(A) 9:00 P.M.
(B) 900 hours
(C) 2100 hours
(D) 9 A.M. appx.

The correct answer is C because the directions state that all time should be noted in military time.

Verbal, Reading, or Written Comprehension

Questions in this ability area are designed to assess how well you understand language. There are two question formats that are designed to test this ability: applying learned information and understanding information. Both begin by requiring you to read a long passage of information, typically one-half page to a page and one-half. The information relates to law enforcement.

APPLYING LEARNED INFORMATION

In this testing format, after you finish reading the passage provided, you are asked a few questions requiring you to apply the information to a specific scenario. For example, you will read a passage about departmental arrest procedures and then read a short scenario about an arrest. Then you will be asked to evaluate the arrest described in the scenario using the information learned from the preceding reading passage.

The best approach to these questions is to read the questions first and then go back and read the passage. That way you will be looking for the information you need as you read. Then, review the first question and seek the correct answer in the passage. There will be a huge amount of information, but most of it will not be necessary to answer the question.

UNDERSTANDING INFORMATION

In this testing format, you will read a long passage filled with details. The questions will require you to recall those details and then recognize that same information when it is presented using slightly different words. For example, after you read a passage about a robbery, the questions may require you to recognize what level of disorder is described in the passage, for example, if the robbers searched for something specific, took everything of value, or took a single item and left.

Problem Sensitivity

This ability area is designed to assess your skill at recognizing when a problem exists. Although questions in this ability area do not require you to solve the problem, they are aimed at determining if you can sort through the information to find clues that suggest a problem exists. Clues may include flawed written information, a faulty eyewitness description, or an error in a procedure. Two types of questions—questions about following a procedure or directions and questions about eyewitness descriptions—are used to assess this ability. Both involve the presentation of a large amount of information.

FOLLOWING A PROCEDURE OR DIRECTIONS

In this question format you are given a list of procedures, rules, directions, or policies. Then you read a scenario and answer questions determining where there is an error in applying the procedures or policies.

EXAMPLE 10
The detention facility has the following procedures that all law enforcement officers must follow when booking a suspect into custody.

1. Drive your vehicle into the rear garage unit. Wait for the garage door to close completely before leaving your vehicle.

2. Remove your suspect from the vehicle and walk together to the entry doors.
3. State your name and agency into the intercom unit. After visual verification, you and your suspect(s) will be buzzed into the secure holding area.
4. Wait for the interior guard to permit you and your suspect(s) out of the holding area. No other suspects or officers will be allowed into the holding unit until you have been released to enter the detention facility.

Officer Smith was transporting two suspects from the scene of their arrest to the detention facility. He drove his vehicle into the rear garage unit, parked, got out, and went to the intercom. He said his name, badge number, and agency name. Then he walked away from the door to retrieve his suspects from his vehicle. Which of the following procedures did Officer Smith violate?

(A) Drive your vehicle into the rear garage unit.
(B) Remove your suspect from the vehicle and walk together to the entry doors.
(C) State your name and agency into the intercom unit.
(D) Upon visual verification, you and your suspect(s) will be buzzed into the secure holding area.

The correct answer is B. There is no information about whether or not Officer Smith violated D. He did perform the requirements set forth in answers A and C.

EYEWITNESS DESCRIPTIONS

This type of question requires you to read a list of eyewitness descriptions and then determine which description is most likely the most correct.

EXAMPLE 11

Police Officer Huang interviews four witnesses to a murder that occurred outside of a carwash. Each of the witnesses was present at the time of the shooting. They described the perpetrator as follows:

Witness No. 1: She had short black hair, a tattoo on her neck, and a baggy shirt and jeans. She was barefoot.

Witness No. 2: He was short with black hair, a loose fitting button up shirt hanging open over a white t-shirt. He had baggy blue jeans on and raggedy old tennis shoes.

Witness No. 3: She was average height but dressed like a boy. She had black hair and really tanned skin. She had on a short-sleeved button-up shirt over a white t-shirt and baggy blue jeans. She had a tattoo on her neck, which was clearly visible because her hair was so short.

Witness No. 4: She was average height and was wearing baggy clothes and old tennis shoes. Her hair was pulled up into a bun so a big bruise was visible on her neck.

Based on the descriptions provided, which of the four witness statements is most likely to be correct?

(A) Witness No. 1's statement
(B) Witness No. 2's statement
(C) Witness No. 3's statement
(D) Witness No. 4's statement

Answer C is most likely correct, because when all the details from each of the witness's descriptions are compared, witness No. 3 had no details that directly conflicted with those observed by the other witnesses. Witness No. 1 saw a barefoot person, witness No. 2 saw a male, and witness No. 4 saw hair pulled back in a bun and a bruise instead of a tattoo.

	Hair	Height	Sex	Clothes	Marks
No. 1	Black, short		F	No shoes, baggy shirt and jeans	Tattoo on neck
No. 2	Black, short	Short	M	Baggy jeans and old tennis shoes	
No. 3	Black	Average	F	Short-sleeve shirt, white t-shirt, baggy jeans	Tattoo on neck
No. 4	Black in a bun	Average	F	Baggy clothes and old tennis shoes	Bruise on neck

Mathematics

Mathematics may be included on an exam as its own section, or it may be part of the deductive reasoning section of the exam. Regardless of where it is placed within the exam, law enforcement exams that test your ability to perform mathematical processes generally limit the questions to problems involving basic addition, subtraction, multiplication, and division. These questions will be in numerical format and presented as word problems involving mathematical situations that a law enforcement officer is likely to encounter.

EXAMPLE 12

The members of the traffic control unit issued the following citations during a recent seven-day period.

Officer Maxim issued 36 citations.
Officer Mendosa issued 107 citations.
Officer Carosa issued 39 citations.
Officer Hussein issued 27 citations.

How many citations were issued by the two traffic control officers writing the most citations for this time period?

(A) 143
(B) 75
(C) 134
(D) 146

The answer is D. $107 + 39 = 146$.

Deductive Reasoning

Deductive reasoning is the ability to apply general rules to a specific situation. The three most common types of questions involving the use of deductive reasoning are applying verbal rules/procedures, applying quantitative rules, and interpreting laws.

APPLYING VERBAL RULES/PROCEDURES

This type of question is usually presented as a list of rules or procedures or classifications followed by a scenario. The applicant must choose the rule that best fits the scenario.

EXAMPLE 13
Emergency Equipment Use

No emergency equipment: Reporting to the scene of a non-injury accident. No traffic laws should be violated, but the officer should go directly to the scene.

Lights: Initiating a traffic stop.

Sirens: Warning the community about bad weather approaching.

Lights and sirens: Responding to the scene of a possible injury accident. Traffic laws may be broken to a degree that such action can be taken safely. Speed should not be more than 10 mph over the posted limit.

Officer Parker has been dispatched to the scene of an accident with a possible injury. What level of emergency equipment use is procedurally permitted?

(A) No emergency equipment
(B) Lights only
(C) Lights and sirens
(D) Sirens only

The correct answer according to the procedures is C.

APPLYING QUANTITATIVE RULES

This type of question is usually presented as a numerical word problem.

EXAMPLE 14
Fees for exceeding maximum speed limits:

1–10 miles per hour (mph) over the limit, $30

11–20 mph over the limit, $30 plus $6 per mph over 10 mph over the limit

21–30 mph over the limit, $90 plus $9 per mph over 20 mph over the limit

31 and more mph over the limit, $180 plus $15 per mph over 30 mph over the limit

Officer Maxwell has issued a speeding citation for 45 mph in a 30 mph zone. If mandatory court costs are $50, which of the following equations will provide an accurate amount of the total cost of the citation?

(A) $30 + 50$
(B) $30 + (6 \times 5) + 50$
(C) $15(45 - 31) + 30 + 50$
(D) $15(15) + 30 + 50$

The correct answer is B. The citation was for 15 mph over the posted speed limit. The rule states that the fine is $30 + $6 for every mile over 10 mph, which is $15 - 10 = 5$ miles. So $30 + ($6 \times 5) +$ the court costs ($50).

INTERPRETING LAWS

This type of question involves reading the definition of a law or a series of similar laws. Then you will be given a scenario. The question will ask you either to determine if the act described in the scenario matches the definition provided, or to match the act described in the scenario to one of a list of criminal definitions.

EXAMPLE 15
Theft: A person commits the offense of theft if he unlawfully appropriates the property of another with intent to permanently deprive the owner of the use of the property.

Which of the following scenarios best represents an example of *theft*?

(A) Tara takes her neighbor's lawn chairs without asking to use during her dinner party.
(B) Tara takes her neighbor's child because she wants one of her own.
(C) Tara finds a $100 bill lying on the sidewalk near her house. She picks it up and keeps it.
(D) Tara finds her neighbor's poodle that has wandered into Tara's backyard. She brings the poodle into her house and keeps it.

The correct answer is D. Answer A does not involve intent to permanently deprive, Answer B does not involve taking property, and Answer C does not involve unlawfully taking or appropriating the property of another. Therefore, the answer is D, in which Tara takes the poodle into her house and keeps it.

Inductive Reasoning

Inductive reasoning is the ability to reason from the specific to the general. For example, a police officer must often look at a specific situation, rule, or concept and see the similarities to a group of other situations or concepts. For this reason, law enforcement tests seek to assess your ability to find a rule or concept that applies to a specific fact pattern.

EXAMPLE 16

Police Officer Ludwig received three reports of home break-ins that all occurred in the same neighborhood during the week of June 15–21. Each report included a description of a suspect(s).

Report No. 1 (June 16): Two white males in their late teens. One was 5ft 10in, 150 lbs, with strawberry blond hair cut short. The other was 6ft, 200 lbs, and wearing a ball cap which covered his hair. They both wore jeans, tennis shoes, and t-shirts.

Report No. 2 (June 18): One Hispanic male in his early twenties. He was 5ft 11in, 165 lbs, long dark hair held back in a short ponytail. He was wearing dark work pants and a white tank top. He appeared to have a tattoo on his right forearm.

Report No. 3 (June 19): One white male, about 18-years-old. He was tall and heavyset with very short dark brown hair. He wore jeans and a t-shirt.

On June 22nd another report of a home break-in was received. In this case, however, the four young men living in the house surprised the suspect, tackled him to the ground, and held him there while they waited for the police to arrive. Police found items from the young men's home in the suspect's car. The description of the suspect in this break-in is:

Report No. 4 (June 22): One white male, about 18-years-old, 5 ft 11 in, 160 lbs, with short blondish hair, and no visible tattoos.

Based on the description of the suspects in the first three reports, the suspect in Report No. 4 should also be considered a suspect in:

(A) Report No. 1, but not report Nos. 2 or 3
(B) Report No. 2, but not report Nos. 1 or 3
(C) Report Nos. 1 and 3, but not report No. 2
(D) Report No. 3, but not report Nos. 1 or 2

The answer is A. The suspects in reports No. 2 and No. 3 do not match the description of the individual in report No. 4.

Information Ordering

This ability area requires you to apply rules to a factual situation in order to determine the correct or best order to resolve that situation.

EXAMPLE 17

Upon arrival at the scene of a building with an activated burglar alarm, the officer should:

- Note any open doors or windows and note whether the rooftop would be a possible point of exit. Maintain radio connection to dispatch.
- Note any people visible in the area and any suspicious behavior. But do not disregard individuals acting in a non-suspicious manner.

- When all evidence suggests that the burglar(s) are still at the scene, a determination should be made as to whether civilians are in danger. If the burglars are visible, dispatch should be provided with a physical description. If no civilians appear to be in danger, the officer should plan a strategy to block any escape, including disabling an apparent getaway vehicle.
- Wait for back-up before entering any structure unless a civilian is clearly in danger and you have a real opportunity to assist without unnecessary danger to yourself or others at the scene. It is preferable for the burglar to exit the building and leave rather than for the officer to enter an occupied building and possibly create a hostage situation.
- While waiting for back-up, place yourself in a position that provides you the greatest possible view of the interior and exterior of the building, and any possible points of entrance or exit.

Officer Lutz arrives at the scene of a building with an activated burglar alarm. She can clearly see through the front windows of the building that two individuals are removing money from a damaged cash register. What should Officer Lutz do next?

(A) Fire her service weapon through the front of the building at the suspects.
(B) Plan a strategy for blocking an escape.
(C) Enter the structure with her service revolver drawn.
(D) Approach the front of the building and call out to the suspects to surrender.

The answer is B according to the procedures set forth above. Officer Lutz discovered two suspects in the building that she could watch without entering the building. No civilians appeared to be in immediate danger.

CHAPTER 6

Understanding the Oral Interview Board

> ## Your Goals for This Chapter
> - Preparing for the oral interview board
> - Expectations during your scheduled oral interview board
> - Learning the types of questions the oral interview board might ask
> - Preparing to answer questions asked during the oral interview board

An important part of the police officer selection process is the oral interview board. The following overview provides a snapshot of what to expect during the oral board interview and a few tips to help you perform better.

In many police agencies, the oral board interview is a pass or fail stage in the selection process. Applicants not passing the oral board are disqualified from continuing in the selection process. The purpose of the oral interview board is to assess several basic things: 1) the applicant's appearance and demeanor; 2) the applicant's communication and interpersonal communication skills; and 3) the applicant's problem-solving skills. From the moment the applicant walks into the interview, the first impressions are noted, and assessment begins.

To start, an interview panel will ask a series of general questions. The answers given to those questions are rated and scored by the panel. There are usually three to five members who serve on the oral interview board. Two or more board members are usually from the police agency, and it is increasingly common that one or two citizens from the community serve on the board. In some departments, a member of the human resources department may serve on the board. Generally, the oral board interview should last between

20–30 minutes. During your interview, you can expect the panel members to write down notes as you answer their questions and you should not be concerned if this happens.

PREPARING FOR THE ORAL INTERVIEW BOARD

For many police applicants, the mere thought of the oral interview board can invoke a fair amount of unwanted anxiety and nerves. This is good. You should be a little nervous. With preparation comes recognition that you are being queried on your initial fitness to serve in a very important position. Chances are, if you enter the oral board prepared, this will build confidence and reduce some of your anxiety. Effective preparation is critical to doing well on the oral interview board. As a start, you should learn as much as you can about the police agency. In an age when information is readily available with the click of a computer mouse, much of your preparation can be done on the Internet. Explore the police agency's website. It will be beneficial for you to learn about how the police department is structured, the size of the department, and any initiatives the department is undertaking, such as community policing or other crime reduction strategies; and if you do not know, learn the name of the chief of police and some of the command staff. In addition, talk to other officers, if possible. Some oral interview boards ask applicants if they know the name of the chief of police. If you have properly prepared, you will shine as you confidently recite the chief's name. This also demonstrates to the oral board that you have done your homework and that you take the selection process seriously.

It is also important that you learn about the community served by the police agency. This is especially beneficial for applicants applying for police positions in other states other than their own. Do an Internet search in order to learn the demographics of the community in terms of population, race, ethnicity, and specific segments of the city. It may also be helpful to learn the crime rate and other issues the community may be experiencing. Some oral boards ask what applicants know about the police department and community.

The day before your scheduled interview, get a good night's sleep. Ensure that your grooming standards are appropriate. Grooming standards include neatly styled hair, and for men, make sure to shave the morning of the interview. For women, a nicely groomed pantsuit, skirt and jacket, or a dress worn at the oral interview board is appropriate. For men, wearing a suit is recommended, but at a minimum, wear a coat and tie. If you do not own a blazer or sports jacket, visit the local secondhand store. Secondhand stores sell clothing at a low cost, which will be good enough to get you through the interview. Attire such as blue jeans, t-shirts, athletic wear, and tennis shoes should never be worn to the interview. It is very important for you to remember, the minute you enter the interview room the oral board members forming an initial impression of you. A good first impression can go a long way in your ability to stand out among other police applicants. You do not necessarily have to dress in expensive designer clothing, but you should dress appropriately. Some police departments actually have an "Appearance" category for scoring as part of the oral interview.

If you have visible tattoos, make sure they are covered. Some police agencies have policies prohibiting police officers from having visible tattoos. If you have visible body piercings, such as nose or lip rings, it is wise to remove them before your oral interview board. Avoid wearing distractive jewelry. This last tip may seem like trivial, but remember to turn off your cell phone prior to your oral board. The last thing you want to happen is for your cell phone to ring a few minutes into your interview.

WHAT TO EXPECT

When you are called into the interview room, you will be instructed where to sit. Usually you will be seated across the table from the interview panel. The interview panel will introduce themselves. Smile and make eye contact with each interview panel member during the introductions. If the opportunity presents itself, extend a firm handshake to each panel member. It is okay to greet each panelist with a simple "hello" or "nice to meet you" during the introductions. As you will learn, police agencies are para-military in structure. This means that they use a military rank system. If you know the rank of the police personnel serving on your oral interview board, refer to them by rank title. For example, "Sergeant Jones" or "Lieutenant Harris." After introductions, a member of the interview panel will explain the instructions for the interview.

It is natural to experience anxiety prior to and during the oral board interview; however, it should not dominate your performance. We all exhibit certain behaviors unconsciously while under stress, such as fidgeting with change in our pocket, thumbing around with a pen or paper clip, tapping a foot, or excessively clearing our throats. One way to minimize some of these unconscious distracting habits is to sit with your hands loosely clasped on the table. This will minimize the potential of fidgeting with items in your pocket or items that may be within reach on the interview table. Keep both feet on the floor as opposed to crossing your legs, sit up straight, and maintain good posture during the interview.

GENERAL QUESTIONS

The questions asked of police officer candidates during the oral interview board will vary among police agencies. The first set of questions are open-ended and focus on your motives and preparation for becoming a police officer. Questions focus on your motives and preparation to become a police officer. General questions may query what you know about the department, why you want to work for the police department, the jobs you have held, your strengths and weaknesses, and your educational attainment.

Examples of General Questions (While all of these questions might not be asked during the oral interview, you should give much thought into how you would answer each one of them. These types of questions are often asked.)

1. Why do you want to want to work in law enforcement?
2. Why do you want to work for this department?
3. Describe your employment history in chronological order, starting with your first job. *(If you have held several jobs over a short period of time, be prepared to explain why the jobs were held for a short period of time and the reason for leaving them.)*
4. Tell us about your education.
5. What specific things have you done to prepare for a job in policing?
6. What do you know about the police department?
7. If you are hired, tell us about your short- and long-term goals on the police department.
8. Are you currently an applicant for any other law enforcement agencies?
9. What is your greatest strength and your greatest weakness?
10. Please describe a problem that you experienced in either your personal life or in the workplace and tell us about how you solved it.

It may be beneficial to practice answering these questions in front of several friends. Have your friends serve as interview board members, where they take turns asking you each of these questions. For the best results, make it as real as possible. Wear what you would wear to the interview and have a mock oral board around a conference table or similar table.

HYPOTHETICAL QUESTIONS

The second set of questions examines your judgment and ability to make decisions. These questions are often called hypothetical or situational, and present the police officer candidate with a fact-based hypothetical situation that the candidate negotiates. Hypothetical questions give the oral board an opportunity to observe how candidates organize their thoughts, how they articulate a reasonable resolution to a hypothetical situation, and how they maintain their poise and bearing. In some cases, board members ask several follow-up questions. Keep in mind, hypothetical questions tend to intensify the interview. There are generally one or two hypothetical questions asked during the oral board interview.

As the interview board member reads the hypothetical question, be attentive and listen carefully. If there is any part of the question that you do not understand, ask the oral board member to repeat that part of the question. Try not to take an overly excessive amount time to begin your answer. Taking a few seconds to process the question and organize your thoughts before answering is okay. Keep in mind, police work involves making important decisions, some of which have to be made in a matter of seconds with little time to think about it. Many decisions police officers make have the potential to greatly impact on public safety and human life. If you struggle to answer a hypothetical question, it may leave the oral interview board with the impression that you have difficulty making decisions.

Answer hypothetical questions in a coherent and organized order. Do not skip around or change your answer several times. Your answer should not give the oral board the impression that you are unbalanced. For example, if the question pertains to how you would handle a disorderly person who refuses to leave a local park after hours, do not reply that you would take out your expandable baton and begin to deliver blows until the person leaves. If you answer in this manner, you will not pass the oral board, and rightly so. We offer the following five tips to incorporate into your answers where appropriate:

1. If a hypothetical question involves the use of force, use only the minimum amount of force necessary to resolve the situation. For example, if asked how you would handle an upset traffic violator who curses at you because you just issued him a traffic ticket, do not reply with "I would yank him out of the car, deploy my Taser, and take him into custody." That is an unacceptable answer and constitutes excessive use of force. By the way, if all the violator did was curse at you after receiving a traffic citation, one way to handle it is to explain to the violator that he can contest the traffic ticket in court, point out the number for him to call, and then end the traffic stop.
2. Follow the chain of command. For example, if you are asked what you would do if you observe another officer using excessive force on a citizen, the proper response is that you would report it immediately to your supervisor.
3. Never answer a hypothetical question with an unethical solution. If you are asked what you would do if you saw another officer stealing items from a grocery store while investigating a burglary, do not reply that you would overlook it the first time because you have never known the officer to steal anything. The proper reply, of course, would be that you recognize this is a crime and would immediately report what you saw to your supervisor.
4. Answers to hypothetical questions should never create a liability for the police agency or the local governing authority. Always keep the best interest of the police department in the forefront.
5. Incorporate the use of effective communication and de-escalation skills into your answer whenever possible. If asked how you would handle two people arguing loudly in a crowded shopping mall, do not say you would threaten to zap them with your Taser if they did not calm down. An appropriate reply is that you would first try to de-escalate the problem by using communication skills in an attempt to resolve the problem and disperse the two people.

EXAMPLE OF HYPOTHETICAL QUESTIONS

Question 1

You are a police officer assigned to a second-shift patrol. One afternoon as you are preparing for work, Officer Smith, whom you have worked with for several years, calls and asks if he could catch a ride to the police squad room because his car will not start. You agree and tell him as soon as you finish putting on your uniform you will head in his direction and pick him up. After you pick up Officer Smith, you make a stop at a local convenience store to grab a cup of coffee, something you have done regularly for the past year. As you prepare your coffee, you notice that Officer Smith asks the store clerk for a pack of cigarettes. The store clerk, while handing the pack of cigarettes to Officer Smith, jokes, "Cigarettes are bad for your health." They both laugh, and Officer Smith engages in small talk with the clerk for about a minute or so. Officer Smith, who is in full uniform, then places the pack of cigarettes in his shirt pocket and walks out of the convenience store without paying. You have never known Officer Smith to do anything like this in the past. There are several customers standing around who saw what just occurred. They turn and look at you. What would you do?

Possible Answer to Question 1

This question presents an ethical dilemma of sorts that you have to negotiate. What should you do in the case of a fellow officer who walks out of a convenience store without paying for a pack of cigarettes? You could simply pay for the cigarettes and then bring it to the attention of Officer Smith that you saw that he did not pay for the cigarettes. However, this does not resolve the issue that Officer Smith in fact left the convenience store without paying for the cigarettes. If this was done intentionally, is a crime. It may be that Officer Smith forgot to pay for the cigarettes—an honest, forgetful oversite. However, an important fact remains—the citizens and convenience store clerk's perception of what happened. They may believe the police officer stole a pack of cigarettes. The police department's reputation has to be considered above all else in handling this situation. Within this framework, you have little choice in how you should handle such a situation. Summarized below are some things to consider when responding to this hypothetical question:

- Point out in your answer that you recognize that Officer Smith's actions have the potential to cause great public embarrassment for the department, and that his actions could potentially be considered criminal.
- Inform the board that you would pay for the cigarettes before walking out of the store. Let the clerk know that you will pay for Officer Smith's cigarettes because he may have forgotten to pay for them, and that you are going to speak to Officer Smith.
- Bring it to Officer Smith's attention that he did not pay for the cigarettes. If Officer Smith says he is sorry and that he just forgot to pay for the cigarettes, let him know that you paid for the cigarettes, but several citizens saw what happened and that the best course of action is to notify a supervisor.
- Inform your supervisor at once. It is likely that the supervisor will report to the convenience store and inquire further about the matter. Inform the convenience store clerk that you are waiting for a supervisor who likely will want to talk to her.

Do not be alarmed if oral board members ask follow-up questions to the answers you give. For example, the oral board might ask a follow-up question such as: "What if Officer Smith informs you, 'I know I did not pay for the cigarettes; do not worry about it. I do it all the time.' " Of course, your reply to the follow-up question should be, "I am aware that Officer Smith's actions are illegal and unethical, and I will notify a supervisor immediately." The interview board may ask another follow-up question, such as, "Would you arrest Officer Smith?" An appropriate response is that you would notify a supervisor and wait for further direction.

Question 2

You have just completed your patrol shift. It is about 11:30 pm. You are off duty and driving home when you decide to stop at your favorite local 24-hour diner and grab a bite to eat. After being seated, you order your favorite menu item. The diner is crowded and several customers greet you and engage in small talk. While waiting on your food order you notice a customer, a male in his early 30s, arguing with the server about how horrible his meal was. After a few minutes, the customer begins to yell louder, "I am not paying for this horrible food!" His rant continues and he becomes increasingly agitated. It appears that the unruly customer may also be intoxicated. You are in full uniform and, because you are a regular customer of the restaurant, most of the patrons and restaurant employees know you. The irate customer continues yelling that he is not paying for his food. The restaurant becomes quiet and several people turn and look at you as if to ask, "Are you going to do something?" How would you handle this situation?

Possible Answer to Question 2

This question presents you with an unruly and possibly intoxicated customer in a restaurant. You are a regular patron of the restaurant who stopped to grab a bite to eat after your patrol shift had ended. You are off duty but in full uniform. How would you handle the agitated customer? Here are a few possible things to consider when answering the hypothetical question:

- Call 9-1-1. Let dispatch know that you are an off-duty police officer who needs officers to respond immediately to the restaurant due to the unruly customer. Let them know that you will be keeping the individual under observation and will attempt to keep him contained.
- Visually scan the person to see if he is carrying any kind of weapon that could be used against you, other customers, or to harm himself.
- If the individual remains seated at the table, and does not appear to become more agitated, keep him under observation as long as possible, and then approach him, in order to talk to him.
- If the individual continues to be aggressive or threatens other customers or employees, you have to take prompt action before the situation escalates.
- Approach the person and identify yourself as a police officer: "I'm Officer Jones with the police department."
- As a start, attempt to de-escalate the situation with effective communication skills. You can respond with something like this: "Sir, it appears as

though you are having a rough day. I have bad days myself from time to time. Would you mind if we chat about it?" Again, the objective is to use verbalization skills to de-escalate the situation.

- Let the oral board know that because the customer is becoming more irate, you believe you have to act so the situation does not escalate further. Your objective is to keep the unruly customer talking until on-duty police officers arrive to assist in taking the person into custody. Simply talking with the individual in order to de-escalate the situation may be an effective resolution until other officers arrive.

The oral board interviewers may intensify the situation by saying suppose the unruly customer yells, "I don't want to talk with you, cop!" Then he suddenly bang his fists on the table, startling other customers. Some customers run for the door. What would you do then? An appropriate response would be as follows:

- I would continue to communicate with the unruly person while assessing any immediate threat to myself, other customers, or employees. I would have other customers move back while continuing to communicate with the unruly person. I would keep the situation contained as long as possible until on-duty police officers arrive.

Again, the oral board may intensify the situation by adding, "What if the individual lunges in an aggressive manner toward you as if he is going to strike you? What would you do then?" You reply as follows:

- Because the individual has lunged in an aggressive manner toward me, and it is clear that communicating with the individual is ineffective, I would have no choice but to attempt to restrain and arrest the person in a manner consistent with my training. I would order the person to the ground and, if he refused and continued to become aggressive toward others or me, I would use my Taser, if necessary, to restrain the individual and handcuff him using reasonable and necessary force. I would also direct an employee of the restaurant to call 9-1-1 and let them know to have the officers expedite.

While the two hypothetical questions are similar to those you may be asked during your oral interview, please remember that these are presented as examples to get you thinking about the structure of hypothetical questions. It is recommended that you prepare in advance for the oral interview board and reflect on the types of questions you could be asked. If you properly prepare, there is a good chance that you will perform well during the oral interview.

Your job is to show the oral interview board that you are:

Competent	Well balanced
Even tempered	Not a liability
A good communicator	Positive in your attitude
Prepared	Enthusiastic
A problem solver	Confident
Honest	A good investment for the police department

Understanding the Video and Essay Exams

Although the multiple-choice written exam is the most common test used by police agencies, particularly in medium-to-large-sized departments, other types of examinations are sometimes used—specifically, a video test and an essay test. These examinations basically evaluate the same ability areas tested in the typical written test, but use different formats.

The basic test-taking tips and suggestions for how to plan to take the test discussed in the previous chapter generally also apply to these alternate format examinations.

VIDEO TESTING

Video testing is not yet a common method of testing law enforcement applicants, but it is gaining in popularity for several reasons. First, it allows applicants to view streaming video instead of merely reading a scenario. This avoids issues associated with reading errors and more closely simulates a police officer's experiences on the job. This test permits applicants with *common sense* but weaker academic skills to score well, while applicants with strong academic skills but weaker common sense often do poorly.

Second, video tests can be simultaneously graded. This means that the written or knowledge-based portion of the exam may be given the day before another aspect of the exam rather than several weeks in advance. The scores from video exams are quickly available for use in calculating an applicant's total score on all of the law enforcement tests. Finally, these tests are easy to administer. They do not require a proctor to set a time limit; the program merely ends at the end of the allotted time. These tests can be set to vary the presentation of questions, making it more difficult for applicants to cheat.

Finally, video tests are easy to update on an annual or semi-annual basis. The cost of developing a test and then generating brand new paper materials every time an exam is given can be quite high. Video tests are cost-effective to develop and are flexible enough to allow them to be modified for every examinee to limit opportunities for cheating.

In a typical video test, the viewer sees a series of short videos and then answers any questions presented. The questions are usually in multiple-choice format. However, the focus of the questions is much broader than the focus of questions presented in written exams. The question may be phrased to evaluate social skills or one's ability to correctly perceive the danger involved in a situation. The questions may also be phrased to assess the same types of abilities evaluated by standard written exams, such as problem sensitivity and the ability to memorize.

Essay Exams

Essay exams are an uncommon tool for evaluating law enforcement applicants, but a few mid-size cities do use this question format. Essays are actually an effective tool for evaluating written expression, reasoning, and problem sensitivity. They also provide the law enforcement agency with an opportunity to evaluate the applicant's thinking processes and common sense. Multiple-choice questions prevent agencies from seeing how an applicant might evaluate a scenario without direction, while essay exams give an applicant wide latitude to exhibit common sense skills. Essay exams also provide law enforcement agencies a way to see how an applicant might evaluate a scenario without direction, and an insight into possible personality disorders inappropriate for a law enforcement officer. Multiple-choice questions do not facilitate such fine-tuning.

CHAPTER 8

Police Training

Your Goals for This Chapter

- Learn about state training requirements.
- Find out what subjects are taught in police training academies.

In modern policing, training of recruits has become a necessity. Police officers cannot be expected to perform the duties and responsibilities of a police officer without training.

There are two important reasons why police departments must comprehensively train police recruits. First, Title 42 of the United States Code, Section 1983, provides citizens with an avenue of redress for violating constitutional rights, as addressed in the Bill of Rights in the United States Constitution. Police officers who violate Section 1983 can be prosecuted in federal courts by the federal government. Not only is it likely that one will be terminated from employment for violating this law, police officers have also been incarcerated for violating the constitutional rights of citizens. Second, police chiefs are held accountable for the training or lack of training police officers receive. Police chiefs, police departments, and municipalities have been sued in civil courts by citizens for the harms caused by poor training of police officers, causing those departments and municipalities to pay out significant sums of tax dollars to the individuals who suffered the harm.

STATE REQUIREMENTS

Most states have mandated that police officers receive training. The hours required for police recruit training vary from state to state. Generally, states require a minimum of 12 weeks of recruit police training. To assist smaller police departments, a few states allow very small police departments to hire probationary law enforcement officers, but the states require that these probationary officers successfully pass the training provided by the police academy within the first year of being hired.

Generally, medium-sized and large cities require that police recruits receive police recruit training prior to working as police officers. In addition, it is not unusual for these departments to require more training than small departments. Generally, larger departments have training requirements ranging from 22 weeks to about 18 months. Once recruit training school has been competed police recruits then have several months of *field training*. Field training refers to working under the supervision of a senior police officer.

TRAINING SUBJECTS

Police recruit training subjects are taught at police academies. The hours for the training courses vary depending on the time frame of the training facility.

A list of commonly taught courses is as follows:

Law

United States Constitution and Bill of Rights
State Criminal Laws
Testifying in Court
State and Federal Criminal Procedures
Laws of Arrest, Search and Seizure
Juvenile Code and Procedures
Alcohol Beverage Control Laws
Traffic Code
Laws of Evidence
Civil and Criminal Liability of Police
Use of Force—Legal Aspects
Civil Process
Legal Guidelines in Interrogation

Police Patrol Procedures

Introduction to Patrol
Crowd Control/Chemical Agents
Officer Survival
Mechanics of Arrest
Criminal Justice Information System
DUI Recognition and Apprehension
Vehicle Stops
Building Searches
Crimes in Progress Calls
Hazardous Material Awareness Level
Handcuffing and Search Techniques
Occupational Protection Usage and Environment

Police Investigation Procedures

Collecting, Recording and Protecting Physical Evidence
Narcotics and Dangerous Drugs
Laboratory Services and Polygraphy
Techniques of Interviews, Admissions and Statements
Accident Investigation

Arson Investigation
Developing Informants
Bomb Calls, Threats and Investigations
Crimes against Persons
   Assault
   Robbery
   Sex Crimes
   Hostage Situations
   Death Investigations
   Hate-bias Crimes
   Physical and Sexual Abuse of Children

Crimes against Property
   Credit Card Fraud
   Checks and Frauds
   Burglary
   Theft

Human Relations

Interpersonal Communications
   Communication Process
   Cultural Awareness
   Police Professionalism

Crisis Situations
   Domestic Violence
   Crisis Intervention
   Abnormal Behavior

Police—Community Relations
   Crime Prevention
   Community and PR

Demonstrable/Proficiency Areas

Report Writing
Defensive Tactics
Firearms
Fingerprinting
Emergency Vehicle Operations
Practical Problems in Felony Stops
Practical Problems in Criminal Investigations
Moot Court
Practical Problems in Officer Survival
Practical Problems in Crisis Intervention
Physical Training

Medical/Emergency

Basic First Aid
CPR
Infectious Diseases

EXAMINATIONS

Police recruits are expected to successfully pass all course work with a minimum score of 70 percent. Most academies limit the opportunities for recruits to repeat failed exams over any of the required areas of study. Thus, the time spent at police academies is intended to be a time of intense focus and will require all recruits to prove their ability to learn the standards for carrying out the duties of policing both quickly and well.

CONDUCT AND BEHAVIOR

Police recruits are expected to conduct themselves in a highly professional manner and to avoid problems with the law and the general public. Recruits can be dismissed from the academy for illegal, unethical or inappropriate behavior. Additionally, recruits will be expected to avoid any actions that create even the appearance of impropriety. By adhering to these rigorous educational and behavioral standards, police recruits grow to understand the high expectations that the public places upon its law enforcement officers.

PART III

PRACTICE LAW ENFORCEMENT TESTS

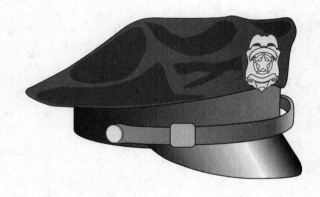

PRACTICE TEST 1

Similar to the Seattle, Washington, Law Enforcement Exam

This chapter includes samples of the pretest materials typically supplied to applicants, a sample test and an answer key to the test.

Answer Sheet

Section 1: Vocabulary

1. Ⓐ Ⓑ Ⓒ Ⓓ
2. Ⓐ Ⓑ Ⓒ Ⓓ
3. Ⓐ Ⓑ Ⓒ Ⓓ
4. Ⓐ Ⓑ Ⓒ Ⓓ
5. Ⓐ Ⓑ Ⓒ Ⓓ

6. Ⓐ Ⓑ Ⓒ Ⓓ
7. Ⓐ Ⓑ Ⓒ Ⓓ
8. Ⓐ Ⓑ Ⓒ Ⓓ
9. Ⓐ Ⓑ Ⓒ Ⓓ
10. Ⓐ Ⓑ Ⓒ Ⓓ

11. Ⓐ Ⓑ Ⓒ Ⓓ
12. Ⓐ Ⓑ Ⓒ Ⓓ
13. Ⓐ Ⓑ Ⓒ Ⓓ
14. Ⓐ Ⓑ Ⓒ Ⓓ
15. Ⓐ Ⓑ Ⓒ Ⓓ

16. Ⓐ Ⓑ Ⓒ Ⓓ
17. Ⓐ Ⓑ Ⓒ Ⓓ
18. Ⓐ Ⓑ Ⓒ Ⓓ
19. Ⓐ Ⓑ Ⓒ Ⓓ
20. Ⓐ Ⓑ Ⓒ Ⓓ

Section 2: Ability to Observe and Recall Information

1. Ⓐ Ⓑ Ⓒ Ⓓ
2. Ⓐ Ⓑ Ⓒ Ⓓ
3. Ⓐ Ⓑ Ⓒ Ⓓ
4. Ⓐ Ⓑ Ⓒ Ⓓ
5. Ⓐ Ⓑ Ⓒ Ⓓ

6. Ⓐ Ⓑ Ⓒ Ⓓ
7. Ⓐ Ⓑ Ⓒ Ⓓ
8. Ⓐ Ⓑ Ⓒ Ⓓ
9. Ⓐ Ⓑ Ⓒ Ⓓ
10. Ⓐ Ⓑ Ⓒ Ⓓ

11. Ⓐ Ⓑ Ⓒ Ⓓ
12. Ⓐ Ⓑ Ⓒ Ⓓ
13. Ⓐ Ⓑ Ⓒ Ⓓ
14. Ⓐ Ⓑ Ⓒ Ⓓ
15. Ⓐ Ⓑ Ⓒ Ⓓ

16. Ⓐ Ⓑ Ⓒ Ⓓ
17. Ⓐ Ⓑ Ⓒ Ⓓ
18. Ⓐ Ⓑ Ⓒ Ⓓ
19. Ⓐ Ⓑ Ⓒ Ⓓ
20. Ⓐ Ⓑ Ⓒ Ⓓ

Section 3: Ability to Observe Report Information

1. Ⓐ Ⓑ Ⓒ Ⓓ
2. Ⓐ Ⓑ Ⓒ Ⓓ
3. Ⓐ Ⓑ Ⓒ Ⓓ
4. Ⓐ Ⓑ Ⓒ Ⓓ
5. Ⓐ Ⓑ Ⓒ Ⓓ

6. Ⓐ Ⓑ Ⓒ Ⓓ
7. Ⓐ Ⓑ Ⓒ Ⓓ
8. Ⓐ Ⓑ Ⓒ Ⓓ
9. Ⓐ Ⓑ Ⓒ Ⓓ
10. Ⓐ Ⓑ Ⓒ Ⓓ

11. Ⓐ Ⓑ Ⓒ Ⓓ
12. Ⓐ Ⓑ Ⓒ Ⓓ
13. Ⓐ Ⓑ Ⓒ Ⓓ
14. Ⓐ Ⓑ Ⓒ Ⓓ
15. Ⓐ Ⓑ Ⓒ Ⓓ

16. Ⓐ Ⓑ Ⓒ Ⓓ
17. Ⓐ Ⓑ Ⓒ Ⓓ
18. Ⓐ Ⓑ Ⓒ Ⓓ
19. Ⓐ Ⓑ Ⓒ Ⓓ
20. Ⓐ Ⓑ Ⓒ Ⓓ

Section 4: Ability to Write Reports and Complete Forms

1. Ⓐ Ⓑ Ⓒ Ⓓ
2. Ⓐ Ⓑ Ⓒ Ⓓ
3. Ⓐ Ⓑ Ⓒ Ⓓ
4. Ⓐ Ⓑ Ⓒ Ⓓ
5. Ⓐ Ⓑ Ⓒ Ⓓ
6. Ⓐ Ⓑ Ⓒ Ⓓ
7. Ⓐ Ⓑ Ⓒ Ⓓ
8. Ⓐ Ⓑ Ⓒ Ⓓ
9. Ⓐ Ⓑ Ⓒ Ⓓ
10. Ⓐ Ⓑ Ⓒ Ⓓ
11. Ⓐ Ⓑ Ⓒ Ⓓ
12. Ⓐ Ⓑ Ⓒ Ⓓ
13. Ⓐ Ⓑ Ⓒ Ⓓ
14. Ⓐ Ⓑ Ⓒ Ⓓ
15. Ⓐ Ⓑ Ⓒ Ⓓ
16. Ⓐ Ⓑ Ⓒ Ⓓ
17. Ⓐ Ⓑ Ⓒ Ⓓ
18. Ⓐ Ⓑ Ⓒ Ⓓ
19. Ⓐ Ⓑ Ⓒ Ⓓ
20. Ⓐ Ⓑ Ⓒ Ⓓ

Section 5: Applying Learned Material

1. Ⓐ Ⓑ Ⓒ Ⓓ
2. Ⓐ Ⓑ Ⓒ Ⓓ
3. Ⓐ Ⓑ Ⓒ Ⓓ
4. Ⓐ Ⓑ Ⓒ Ⓓ
5. Ⓐ Ⓑ Ⓒ Ⓓ
6. Ⓐ Ⓑ Ⓒ Ⓓ
7. Ⓐ Ⓑ Ⓒ Ⓓ
8. Ⓐ Ⓑ Ⓒ Ⓓ
9. Ⓐ Ⓑ Ⓒ Ⓓ
10. Ⓐ Ⓑ Ⓒ Ⓓ
11. Ⓐ Ⓑ Ⓒ Ⓓ
12. Ⓐ Ⓑ Ⓒ Ⓓ
13. Ⓐ Ⓑ Ⓒ Ⓓ
14. Ⓐ Ⓑ Ⓒ Ⓓ
15. Ⓐ Ⓑ Ⓒ Ⓓ
16. Ⓐ Ⓑ Ⓒ Ⓓ
17. Ⓐ Ⓑ Ⓒ Ⓓ
18. Ⓐ Ⓑ Ⓒ Ⓓ
19. Ⓐ Ⓑ Ⓒ Ⓓ
20. Ⓐ Ⓑ Ⓒ Ⓓ

Section 6: Map Reading

1. Ⓐ Ⓑ Ⓒ Ⓓ
2. Ⓐ Ⓑ Ⓒ Ⓓ
3. Ⓐ Ⓑ Ⓒ Ⓓ
4. Ⓐ Ⓑ Ⓒ Ⓓ
5. Ⓐ Ⓑ Ⓒ Ⓓ
6. Ⓐ Ⓑ Ⓒ Ⓓ
7. Ⓐ Ⓑ Ⓒ Ⓓ
8. Ⓐ Ⓑ Ⓒ Ⓓ
9. Ⓐ Ⓑ Ⓒ Ⓓ
10. Ⓐ Ⓑ Ⓒ Ⓓ
11. Ⓐ Ⓑ Ⓒ Ⓓ
12. Ⓐ Ⓑ Ⓒ Ⓓ
13. Ⓐ Ⓑ Ⓒ Ⓓ
14. Ⓐ Ⓑ Ⓒ Ⓓ
15. Ⓐ Ⓑ Ⓒ Ⓓ
16. Ⓐ Ⓑ Ⓒ Ⓓ
17. Ⓐ Ⓑ Ⓒ Ⓓ
18. Ⓐ Ⓑ Ⓒ Ⓓ
19. Ⓐ Ⓑ Ⓒ Ⓓ
20. Ⓐ Ⓑ Ⓒ Ⓓ

Section 7: Grammar and Usage

1. Ⓐ Ⓑ Ⓒ Ⓓ
2. Ⓐ Ⓑ Ⓒ Ⓓ
3. Ⓐ Ⓑ Ⓒ Ⓓ
4. Ⓐ Ⓑ Ⓒ Ⓓ
5. Ⓐ Ⓑ Ⓒ Ⓓ
6. Ⓐ Ⓑ Ⓒ Ⓓ
7. Ⓐ Ⓑ Ⓒ Ⓓ
8. Ⓐ Ⓑ Ⓒ Ⓓ
9. Ⓐ Ⓑ Ⓒ Ⓓ
10. Ⓐ Ⓑ Ⓒ Ⓓ
11. Ⓐ Ⓑ Ⓒ Ⓓ
12. Ⓐ Ⓑ Ⓒ Ⓓ
13. Ⓐ Ⓑ Ⓒ Ⓓ
14. Ⓐ Ⓑ Ⓒ Ⓓ
15. Ⓐ Ⓑ Ⓒ Ⓓ
16. Ⓐ Ⓑ Ⓒ Ⓓ
17. Ⓐ Ⓑ Ⓒ Ⓓ
18. Ⓐ Ⓑ Ⓒ Ⓓ
19. Ⓐ Ⓑ Ⓒ Ⓓ
20. Ⓐ Ⓑ Ⓒ Ⓓ

Pretest Materials

Study the following materials prior to taking this exam. These materials will be provided to you in the pretest materials from the city. You may study these as much as you like prior to the exam, but you will not be allowed to refer to them during the exam. Learn to associate each drawing with its label so as to apply the correct information.

SECTION 1
VOCABULARY

Directions: Read and understand the following law enforcement-related terms and definitions and then be prepared to use this information on the actual exam to answer a series of questions.

VOCABULARY TERMS

ACCOMPLICE
To assist another person in the commission of a crime with knowledge that it will promote or facilitate the commission of the crime, an accomplice aids or agrees to aid such other person in planning or committing it.

CHAIN OF COMMAND
A supervisory hierarchy, the levels of personnel from the top to the bottom.

CHAIN OF CUSTODY
A formal process of tracking all persons having control over evidence from the initial point of receipt until final disposition of the case.

CODE
A body of law covering one general subject, established by the legislative authority of a governmental body such as a state or local government.

DISCRETION
An authority conferred by law on an official to act in accordance with that official's individual judgment.

HOMICIDE
A non-accidental killing of a human being including all degrees of murder and both types of manslaughter.

INCOMPETENT
Mentally incapable of assisting in one's own defense at trial or other stages of the criminal justice process.

JUSTIFICATION
Any defense to a criminal act in which the offender is able to show his act was done for the greater good, including self-defense and defense of others.

LATENT FINGERPRINT
A fingerprint made by the deposit of oils and/or perspiration, which is invisible to the naked eye.

MENS REA	The state of mind that accompanies an act which ultimately defines that, act as a crime, a mistake, or an accident.
PERPETRATOR	The chief actor in the commission of a crime.
PHYSICAL EVIDENCE	Any object that can establish that a crime has been committed or can provide a link between a crime and either a victim or perpetrator.
RECKLESS INTENT	To engage in conduct without intent to cause a specific harm but knowing such conduct creates a substantial risk of death or serious physical injury to another person.
VENUE	A geographical area that defines the boundaries of a court with jurisdiction to hear and determine a case.
WARRANT	In criminal proceedings, any of a number of judicially issued writs that direct law enforcement officers to perform a specific act.

ABILITY TO OBSERVE AND RECALL

Learn the details of the drawings provided below and the information provided with each drawing. Be sure to remember the caption for each drawing because the pictures will not be on the exam, and you will be asked to answer questions about each drawing.

Pay attention to the details of the drawing, including numbers, dates, signs, and other details.

FELONY CAR STOP

Officers had lawfully stopped the vehicle on the street for failing to signal a lane change. Upon approaching the vehicle after it was stopped, officers saw evidence of a serious crime lying in plain view on the back seat. Officers seized the evidence and arrested the two occupants of the vehicle. One of the occupants attempted to flee on foot but was quickly apprehended by officers. Upon arresting the driver of the vehicle police are able to lawfully search the vehicle.

FORCED CAR STOP

A high speed chase between a suspect in a drive-by shooting and state police down State Highway 50 ended when a law enforcement officer was able to use his car to force the suspect off the side of the road. Although the crash seriously damaged a patrol car and the suspect's car, there were no serious injuries. The single occupant of the pick-up truck was taken into custody. Traffic on Highway 50 was backed up for several hours.

OUTDOOR MARKET

ABILITY TO OBSERVE AND REPORT INFORMATION

SUSPECT No. 1

NAME:	Alice Bender
ALIAS:	Alice Garcia
SEX:	Female
RACE:	Hispanic
AGE:	19
HEIGHT:	5 ft 4 in
WEIGHT:	139 lbs
HAIR AND EYES:	Brown and Brown
COMMENTS:	Suspect in drug manufacturing ring. Fluent in Spanish and English.

SUSPECT No. 2

NAME:	Frank Norton
ALIAS:	None
SEX:	Male
RACE:	Caucasian
AGE:	24
HEIGHT:	5 ft 6 in
WEIGHT:	194 lbs
HAIR AND EYES:	Brown and Brown
COMMENTS:	Suspect in aggravated assault. He has a snake tattoo on his thigh. Speaks fluent Italian, English and Spanish.

SUSPECT No. 3

NAME:	Paige Brown
ALIAS:	Paige Smith
SEX:	Female
RACE:	Caucasian
AGE:	34
HEIGHT:	5 ft 7 in
WEIGHT:	121 lbs
HAIR AND EYES:	Brown and Brown
COMMENTS:	Suspected of non-custodial parental kidnapping of three children. She is known to be armed and dangerous.

SUSPECT No. 4

NAME:	Alexa Benchanko
ALIAS:	None
SEX:	Female
RACE:	Caucasian
AGE:	23
HEIGHT:	5 ft 5 in
WEIGHT:	119 lbs
HAIR AND EYES:	Black and Blue
COMMENTS:	Suspected of bank robbery. Speaks with a strong Eastern European accent. Butterfly tattoo across right shoulder blade and on left ankle. Pierced nose, tongue, and navel.

TURN TO THE NEXT PAGE

SECTION 4
ABILITY TO WRITE REPORTS AND COMPLETE FORMS

General Rules for Completing the STANDARD OFFENSE REPORT Form

Box 1	Date offense started	Enter the month, day, and year on which the offense occurred.
Box 2	Time offense started	Give the exact time that the offense started. Use military time (add 12 hours to all P.M. hours). The offense starts at the time the law is actually broken.
Box 3	Location of offense	Provide the street name and address of the offense. If no actual address at site, use closest approximation of address preceded by *appx.*
Box 4	Date of report	Give the exact day on which the offense was reported.
Box 5	Date offense ended	If the offense continued over more than one day, enter the month, day, and year on which the offense concluded.
Box 6	Time offense ended	Give the exact time that the offense ended. Use military time (add 12 hours to all P.M. hours). The offense ends at the time the perpetrator is either taken into custody or completely concludes the criminal acts and leaves the scene.
Box 7	Number of victims	Include the number of individuals physically threatened by the offender(s) at the site of the offense. For theft crimes write "owner."
Box 8	Victim injuries	List minor injuries to individuals that occurred at the scene, if any, such as bruises, or scratches. If victim(s) taken to hospital write "transported" followed by the hospital's name.
Box 9	Title	Write the Title number of the offense. For criminal acts write "9." For property crimes write "9A." Example: Theft is contained in Title "9A."
Box 10	Chapter/Section	Write the Chapter and Section numbers of the offense as provided by state code. For example: Theft would be cited as "9A.56.020."
Box 11	Attempt or complete	Mark the appropriate line indicating whether the crime was attempted or completed that is noted in Box 10.
Box 12	Description of offense	Write the legal description of the offense, associated with section of the statute violated.
Box 13	Hate/bias	Write either "yes" or "no" depending upon the perceived intent of the offender as required by statute.
Box 14	Exceptional clearance	Mark the appropriate line indicating reason for departing standard protocol.
Box 15	Offender suspected of using	Mark the appropriate line indicating whether any of the enhancing products were utilized in the offense. (May mark as many as 3, or "N/A" if not applicable.)
Box 16	Type of Force/Weapon	Indicate the type of weapon used including: firearm, knife, blunt object, poison, vehicle, explosive, fire, drugs, or any other recognized agent of harm. May write unknown if unsure. Do not include weapons seized as a result of a search or arrest, or are otherwise evidence of a crime, but not used to harm or force another.

General Rules for Completing the VEHICLE COLLISION REPORT Form

Box 1	Date	Enter the month, day, and year on which the collision occurred.
Box 2	Location of offense	Provide the street name and address of the collision. If no actual address at site, use closest approximation of address preceded by *appx*.
Box 3	Nearest intersection	Write the names of both intersecting streets at the closest intersection. If equal distance from two intersections write the name of the more major intersection.
Box 4	No. vehicles	Write the total number of vehicles involved in the collision.
Box 5	No. transported by ambulance	Write the total number of individuals transported by ambulance as a direct result of the collision, including those declared dead at the scene.
Box 6	Time of accident	Give the exact time that the collision occurred. Use military time (add 12 hours to all P.M. hours). If unsure proceed time with *appx*.
Box 7	No. of deceased at scene	Write the total number of individuals declared dead at the scene of the accident.
Box 8	Citations issued	Write the first and last name of any vehicle operator issued a traffic citation as a result of this accident, and then write the legal description of the infraction/offense for which a citation was issued. (If more than two vehicles were involved in the collision additional vehicle collision report forms will need to be filled out and attached with identical case numbers assigned to all vehicle collision reports utilized for the case.)
Box 9	Description of vehicle No.1	Write the make, model, color, year and any visible damage associated with vehicle No.1.
Box 10	Description of vehicle No.2	Write the make, model, color, year and any visible damage associated with vehicle No.2.
Box 11	Weather conditions	Mark the appropriate line indicating any applicable weather conditions. Under other include temperature, amount of light available and any other relevant environmental factors.
Box 12	No. of Associated criminal case	Indicate the case number of any criminal case arising out of this collision alleging felony or misdemeanor offenses in addition to traffic offenses.

APPLYING LEARNED MATERIAL

VEHICLE SEARCHES

One of the duties of law enforcement officers is traffic enforcement. Generally, when an officer sees a violation of the traffic laws the officer has probable cause to stop the vehicle. Probable cause to stop the vehicle arises out of the officer's knowledge that an infraction of the traffic laws has occurred and a belief that the infraction was caused by the driver of the vehicle seen violating the law. Probable cause requires a clear link between an illegal act and an individual. For example, when an officer sees a vehicle speeding, the officer has a clear link between the driver of the vehicle and the violation of the law.

Upon stopping a vehicle for a traffic infraction the officer must use extreme care when approaching the occupants of the vehicle. Although the majority of traffic stops result in an irritated driver leaving with a citation, there is always a possibility that a driver will react to the stop with violence. The reason for the violence could be merely that the driver is emotionally out of control. It could also be something more serious: an individual who is transporting evidence of criminal activity in his/her vehicle or an individual on the run from the law.

The Fourth Amendment to the Constitution of the United States requires that law enforcement only conduct a search after obtaining a warrant from the local magistrate. However, the United States Supreme Court has developed several exceptions to that rule. Each of these exceptions to the warrant requirement will still require that the officer establish probable cause to justify the search.

Law enforcement who merely suspect that a vehicle contains evidence of criminal activity are limited in their options for searching the vehicle. Reasonable suspicion is a lower standard of proof than probable cause. It requires more than a "gut feeling" or a "hunch." Reasonable suspicion requires that an officer be able to clearly articulate his/her reasons for being suspicious. For example, an officer could support being reasonably suspicious if he stops a vehicle transporting two teenage males at 3 A.M. through a neighborhood several miles from the address shown on the driver's license, soon after several reports of burglaries were reported in the neighborhood. Although nothing concrete links the occupants to the burglaries the officer can explain why he is suspicious of them.

Reasonable suspicion that criminal activity is afoot will only support asking the occupants of the vehicle to provide identification and a general explanation of their actions or reason for being in the location where they were stopped. This low-level questioning is known as a *stop* or a *Terry stop*. Additionally, if the officer reasonably believes that an individual presents a threat of danger, the officer may conduct a *frisk* of the individual. A frisk is a limited pat down of the exterior of an individual's clothing to feel for weapons. A frisk is not to be used as justification for a thorough search of the individual.

If a law enforcement officer has a reasonable suspicion that a vehicle contains evidence of criminal activity, but has not established probable cause to support his belief that evidence of criminal activity will be found in the vehicle, the officer may ask the driver of the vehicle for permission to search the vehicle. If another occupant of the vehicle is the owner of the vehicle, however, that is the individual who must give permission to search. Individuals are not required to give their consent to search, but law enforcement is not required to advise them of their right to refuse. If an individual refuses to consent to the search, their refusal does not create probable cause to believe that the vehicle contains evidence of criminal activity. When an individual refuses to consent to a search, law enforcement must generally release the individual and their vehicle without further delay.

Probable cause to support a search of the vehicle requires something to clearly link the vehicle to a criminal act beyond a traffic infraction. Sometimes, as an officer approaches a vehicle that the officer has stopped for a traffic infraction, the officer will see evidence of a criminal act lying out in plain view. For example, an officer may see a clear bag of a green botanical substance or an object used for self-administering illegal substances (drug paraphernalia) lying on the dashboard of the vehicle. Or, an officer may smell an odor of marijuana (plain smell). Upon seeing what appears to be evidence of criminal activity in plain view, the officer has a clear link between the occupant(s) of the vehicle and criminal activity. The officer has probable cause to believe that the vehicle contains evidence of criminal activity and may search the vehicle. While plain view is not a search, evidence left in plain view will establish the probable cause necessary to support a vehicle search. A vehicle search is one of the exceptions to the warrant clause.

Another exception to the warrant clause is the search incident to arrest. Whenever an officer has lawfully placed an individual under arrest, the officer may conduct a contemporaneous search of the individual's *wingspan*. The term *wingspan* is not defined to be the length that the arrested individual's arms can reach. The term is defined to be the individual's immediate surroundings. When an individual is taken from a car and placed under arrest, their wingspan includes the entire passenger portion of the vehicle. Most searches of vehicles arise out of this exception to the warrant clause.

A final exception to the warrant clause that is applicable to vehicle searches is a search based on exigent (emergency) circumstances. If an officer has reason to believe that an individual is in serious danger or is placing others in serious danger, the officer may act to prevent that serious harm. For example, if an officer is given reliable information that a vehicle is transporting a bomb, the officer may stop the vehicle and may take the action necessary to locate and disarm the bomb.

SECTION 6
MAPS AND SPATIAL REASONING

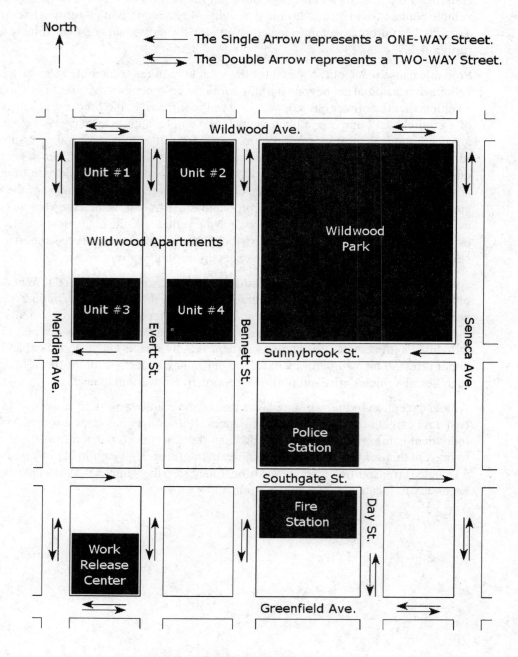

North

The Single Arrow represents a ONE-WAY Street.

The Double Arrow represents a TWO-WAY Street.

MAP OF CENTRAL CITY 1

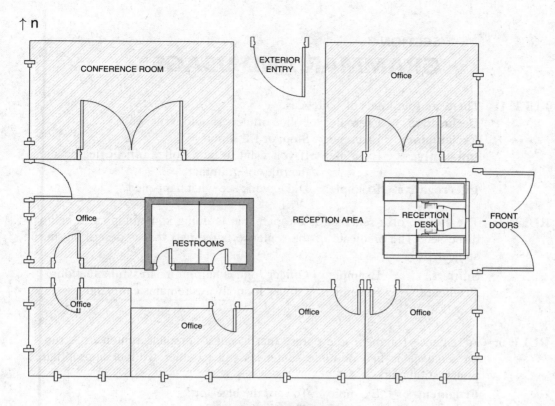

MAP OF OFFICE BUILDING 1

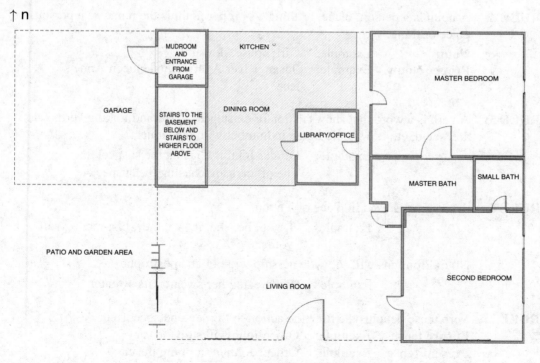

MAP OF HOME 1

SECTION 7
GRAMMAR AND USAGE

RULE 1: There are four kinds of sentences.

Declarative	Example:	Police officers should write well.
Exclamatory	Example:	Stop, or I'll shoot!
Imperative	Example:	If you want to be a police officer, learn the rules of grammar.
Interrogative	Example:	Did anyone see what happened?

RULE 2: The subject of a sentence is the part that is doing something or is being discussed. The predicate of the sentence is the part that is describing the subject.

Subject	Example:	<u>Officer John</u> is helpful in stressful situations.
Predicate	Example:	Officer John <u>always remains calm and focused</u>.

RULE 3: A sentence fragment is a phrase that is not a complete sentence. A run-on sentence is two or more sentences run together without appropriate punctuation marks.

Fragment	Example:	Toward the bus stop.
Run-on	Example:	The suspect ran, I gave chase.

RULE 4: A noun is a person, place, or thing. A proper noun is the name of a person, place or thing.

Noun	Example:	Girl, house, flower
Proper Noun	Example:	Susan, River Apartments, Queen Anne's lace

RULE 5: A verb is a word that shows action or existence. Verbs and linking verbs (is, are, seem, etc …) should agree in number with the subject.

Example:	Officer John <u>is chasing</u> the suspect.
	The officers <u>are chasing</u> the suspect.

RULE 6: A pronoun is used in place of a noun.

Examples:	I, you, he, she, it, we, they, his, me, myself, yours, etc.

Note: Pronouns will show ownership without an apostrophe

Example:	His sweater, her sweater, its sweater

RULE 7: Verb tense denotes the time the action in the sentence occurred.

Future tense	Example:	Office John <u>will stop</u> the car.
Present tense	Example:	Officer John <u>is stopping</u> the car.
Past tense	Example:	Officer John <u>stopped</u> the car.

RULE 8: An adjective is a word used to describe a noun or pronoun. It should usually answer the questions: "How many?" "What kind?" or "Which one?"

Example: Officer John is the <u>most efficient</u> law enforcement officer.

RULE 9: An apostrophe may be used to:

Show possession   Example: John's sweater
Show a contraction   Example: Does not can be contracted to doesn't

RULE 10: Each sentence should begin with a capital letter, end with an appropriate punctuation mark, and use commas to separate phrases.

Example: Officer John is investigating the possible disappearance of a girl, reported as a runaway, who is only six-years-old.

Practice Test 1

Note: This test contains 140 multiple-choice questions, divided into seven sections. In each section the questions are numbered 1–20. Mark your answers on the answer sheet provided. The following pages present samples of the pretest materials typically supplied to applicants, a sample test, and an answer key to the test.

SECTION 1
VOCABULARY

Use the information provided in the pretest materials to answer the following questions. You may not refer to any pretest materials or notes during the exam.

1. The offender claimed that he committed the assault but that he was acting in self-defense. The offender is:

   (A) Insane
   (B) Claiming a justification
   (C) Incompetent
   (D) Claiming an alibi

2. The police detective is called to the scene of a homicide but told nothing else by dispatch. Which of the following statements can the detective infer is true before reaching the scene?

   (A) The victim is dead.
   (B) The perpetrator acted with premeditation.
   (C) The perpetrator was committing a serious felony when the homicide occurred.
   (D) The perpetrator was angry at the time the homicide occurred.

3. A police officer is told to assist in gathering all physical evidence at a crime scene. He looks around the area but does not see anything that looks like evidence of a crime. Has he completed his duty?

   (A) Yes. Physical evidence must be visually identifiable.
   (B) Yes. Physical evidence is evidence associated with the victim.
   (C) No. Physical evidence is evidence associated with the perpetrator.
   (D) No. Physical evidence includes items that are not clearly visible such as latent fingerprints.

GO ON TO THE NEXT PAGE

4. The Police Manual states that all officers must report questions or concerns about other officers through the official chain of command. Officer Martin has seen his partner remove evidence from a crime scene without logging it in as required. Officer Martin should _____.

   (A) Report his concerns to his union representative.
   (B) Talk with his partner, unofficially, to try to find out what is going on.
   (C) Report his concerns to his direct supervisor.
   (D) Send an anonymous note to the Chief of Police.

5. Sergeant Martin identified Exhibit 4 as a necktie found in the bedroom of the Smith residence. When Martin testified that the evidence tag on Exhibit 4 indicated that another officer had processed the evidence, defense counsel objected based on foundation for the _____ and the State withdrew the exhibit. However, Detective Ferris later identified the evidence tag on Exhibit 4, testifying that Martin gave him the evidence and he tagged it and sent it to the State Patrol Lab thus resolving the earlier issue.

   The appropriate term to fill in the blank above is:

   (A) Latent fingerprint
   (B) Physical evidence
   (C) Chain of custody
   (D) Discretion

6. Officer Martin had authority to enforce the criminal laws of both the state and his city, as both the state and his city have enacted criminal _____.

   (A) Laws
   (B) Codes
   (C) Jurisdictions
   (D) Venues

7. State law and departmental policy states that "offender's vehicles could be impounded at the direction of law enforcement present at the scene." Both state law and departmental policy were defining the scope of _____ applicable to vehicle impoundment.

   (A) A warrant
   (B) Physical evidence
   (C) Chain of custody
   (D) Officer discretion

8. The offender is legally incompetent. This means that the offender:

   (A) Is incapable of assisting in his own defense.
   (B) Has a legal justification for his actions.
   (C) Was legally insane at the time he committed the offense.
   (D) Is unable to afford legal counsel.

GO ON TO THE NEXT PAGE

9. Professor Martinez taught a course about human sexuality at the local community college. A female student signed a complaint against Professor Martinez alleging that she distributed obscene literature to the class. Professor Martinez will likely not be charged with any offense because the law concerning obscene materials excludes "those persons or entities having scientific, educational, or similar reason for possessing such materials." This law gives Professor Martinez _____ for possessing and disseminating the information to her students.

(A) Lack of *mens rea* so she cannot be held accountable
(B) Discretion
(C) A legally recognized justification
(D) A right to distribute obscene material whenever she likes

10. Officer Martin found a latent fingerprint. This means she found a fingerprint ___.

(A) After the investigation officially concluded
(B) That is invisible to the naked eye
(C) That was left by a member of the investigative team
(D) That was unidentifiable due to significant residue and deposits

11. John wanted to try out his new sports car to see how fast it would go. After dark he went out to a stretch of paved road that was seldom used and put the gas pedal to the floorboard. After a few seconds the vehicle had exceeded the speed limit and was about to go into a blind curve. Before John could slow his car, another vehicle came around the turn and the two vehicles collided causing the driver in the other car severe injuries. Before deciding whether to charge John with a crime, the officer gathered as much information about John's actions in order to determine John's _____.

(A) Authority
(B) Discretion
(C) Competency
(D) *Mens rea.*

12. After investigation, Officer Martin determined that the facts showed that John's behavior was reckless. This means that John:

(A) Could not have known that speeding down a dark road could cause serious harm to others.
(B) Was less at fault for the accident than the other driver.
(C) Knew there was a substantial risk that speeding down a dark road could cause serious harm to others.
(D) Was a juvenile.

GO ON TO THE NEXT PAGE

13. Dominic went into a store to rob it while his brother Louis waited in the car. Louis' job was to keep the car running so that Dominic would be able to escape the scene of the robbery as fast as possible. Carl was sitting on a bench down the street with a cell phone ready to call Dominic as soon as he heard sirens in the area. Who was/were the accomplice(s)?

(A) Carl and Dominic
(B) Dominic and Louis
(C) Louis and Carl
(D) Dominic

14. Dominic went into a store to rob it while his brother Louis waited in the car. Louis' job was to keep the car running so that Dominic would be able to escape the scene of the robbery as fast as possible. Carl was sitting on a bench down the street with a cell phone ready to call Dominic as soon as he heard sirens in the area. Who was/were the perpetrator(s)?

(A) Carl and Dominic
(B) Dominic and Louis
(C) Louis
(D) Dominic

15. Officer Peterson was through investigating a homicide in Edwardsville. He needed to file his case with the appropriate court. He knows that only state courts have jurisdiction to hear homicide cases, but he doesn't like the state court judges in his area. Officer Peterson decides to file his case in the state court located in a large metropolitan area on the other side of the state, outside the geographical area of the state court for Edwardsville. Will the state court in the metropolitan area be able to accept this case?

(A) Yes, as long as a court has jurisdiction it may accept the case.
(B) Yes, a police officer has discretion to file his case in any court of competent jurisdiction.
(C) No, a court must have both jurisdiction and venue.
(D) Yes, each case has its own individual venue.

16. Officer Peterson tells his supervisor that he is acting on a warrant. From this information alone, what can the supervisor determine that Officer Peterson is doing?

(A) He is serving an arrest warrant.
(B) He is serving a bench warrant.
(C) He is serving a search warrant.
(D) The supervisor needs more information.

GO ON TO THE NEXT PAGE

17. Which of the following defenses to a crime is NOT a justification?

   (A) Self-defense
   (B) Defense of others
   (C) Insanity
   (D) Defense of property

18. Officer Smith found an empty whiskey bottle on the back floorboard of Petra's car after Petra's vehicle is involved in an accident. Officer Smith believes that Petra is under the influence of alcohol. The whiskey bottle should be considered physical evidence because _____.

   (A) it used to contain an alcoholic beverage
   (B) it can establish a link between Petra and the use of alcohol
   (C) it can establish a chain of custody between Petra and the alcohol
   (D) it can establish that Petra used discretion to drink an alcoholic beverage

19. Officer Peterson drafts and signs an arrest warrant and gets ready to serve it. His supervisor stops him and tells him the warrant is not valid. What is the primary problem with Officer Peterson's arrest warrant?

   (A) Officer Peterson, a law enforcement officer, has no authority to arrest.
   (B) Officer Peterson, a law enforcement officer, has no authority to sign an arrest warrant.
   (C) Officer Peterson, a law enforcement officer, has no authority to serve warrants.
   (D) Officer Peterson, a law enforcement officer, has no authority to request an arrest warrant.

20. Greg sees a man waving a knife at a small child in a parked car. Greg grabs a baseball bat and breaks the driver's side window of the car. Before the man in the vehicle can react Greg takes his knife away. When the police arrive the man in the vehicle asks them to charge Greg with criminal destruction of property. After hearing the facts, the police decline to arrest Greg because _____.

   (A) Greg obtained physical evidence of a crime for them.
   (B) Greg is a hero.
   (C) Greg was not the perpetrator of the more serious crime.
   (D) Greg had a lawful justification to support his actions.

STOP. THIS IS THE END OF SECTION 1.

ABILITY TO OBSERVE AND RECALL

Use the drawings provided in the pretest materials to answer the following questions. You may not refer to any pretest materials or notes during the exam.

The following questions are in reference to the drawing labeled **"FELONY CAR STOP,"** which was provided in the pretest materials.

1. How many people were under arrest?

    (A) 1
    (B) 2
    (C) 3
    (D) 4

2. How many police officers were on the scene?

    (A) 2
    (B) 4
    (C) 6
    (D) 8

3. Where was the arrest taking place?

    (A) In a parking lot
    (B) On the side of the highway
    (C) On a residential street
    (D) At the police station

4. Why was the arrest occurring?

    (A) Suspicion that the driver had committed a traffic offense.
    (B) Suspicion that the driver had attempted to evade and elude officers.
    (C) Suspicion that the driver was under the influence of intoxicants.
    (D) Suspicion that the driver and occupants were involved in a serious crime.

5. What grounds did the police use to justify the lawful search of the vehicle?

    (A) Search incident to arrest
    (B) Plain view
    (C) Traffic stop
    (D) Search of a motor vehicle

GO ON TO THE NEXT PAGE

The following questions are in reference to the drawing labeled "**FORCED CAR STOP**," which was provided in the pretest materials.

6. How many vehicles were involved in the collision?

(A) 1
(B) 2
(C) 3
(D) 4

7. What roadway did the collision occur upon?

(A) Highway 80
(B) Market Street
(C) Highway 50
(D) Memphis Avenue

8. What type of vehicle was the suspect driving?

(A) Sedan
(B) Jeep
(C) Van
(D) Pick-up

9. What information was provided on the roadway sign shown in the drawing?

(A) Highway 80 exit
(B) Market Street exit
(C) Welcome to Central City
(D) Speed limit 45

10. What criminal act was the driver suspected of committing just prior to the onset of the high-speed chase?

(A) Kidnapping
(B) Traffic offenses
(C) Drive-by shooting
(D) Assault of a law enforcement officer

11. The suspect's vehicle was eventually pinned between a patrol car and a
_____.

(A) Guard rail
(B) Second patrol car
(C) Semi truck
(D) The vehicle was not pinned

GO ON TO THE NEXT PAGE

12. How many patrol cars were visible in the drawing?

(A) 1
(B) 2
(C) 3
(D) 4

13. What number was shown on the roadside mile marker?

(A) 234
(B) 187
(C) 546
(D) 53

The following questions are in reference to the drawing labeled **"OUTDOOR MAR-KET"** which was provided in the pretest materials.

14. How many police officers are shown in the drawing?

(A) 1
(B) 2
(C) 3
(D) 4

15. What type of items are available at the outdoor market?

(A) Clothing
(B) Crafts
(C) Vegetables
(D) Paintings

16. Based on the apparel of the shoppers, what is the weather?

(A) Cold
(B) Hot
(C) Raining
(D) Snowing

17. How many people are shown being arrested?

(A) 1
(B) 2
(C) 3
(D) None

18. The type of buildings shown surrounding the outdoor market are:

(A) Generally 1 story high
(B) Generally 2–3 stories high
(C) Generally 4 or more stories high
(D) Too varied to categorize

GO ON TO THE NEXT PAGE

19. The sign on the building on the right side of the photo says:

(A) Restaurant
(B) Memphis Building
(C) Outdoor Market Square
(D) Stark Street Diner

20. The addresses shown on the buildings reveal what pattern?

(A) The buildings are numbered sequentially with odd numbers.
(B) The buildings are numbered sequentially with even numbers.
(C) The buildings are numbered sequentially with both odd and even numbers.
(D) The buildings are not numbered sequentially.

STOP. THIS IS THE END OF SECTION 2.

ABILITY TO OBSERVE AND REPORT INFORMATION

Use the information provided in the pretest materials to answer the following questions. You may not refer to any pretest materials or notes during the exam.

1. This man is wanted for:

    (A) Rape
    (B) Murder
    (C) Drug manufacturing
    (D) Aggravated assault

2. Which of the following statements is NOT true about this suspect?

    (A) He is 194 lbs.
    (B) He has a snake tattoo on his bicep.
    (C) He is 5 ft 6 in tall.
    (D) He has no known aliases.

3. What is this man's age?

    (A) 19
    (B) 24
    (C) 29
    (D) 34

4. Which of the following is TRUE about this suspect?

    (A) His last name is Norris.
    (B) His last name is North.
    (C) His last name is Norton.
    (D) His last name is Northern.

GO ON TO THE NEXT PAGE

5. Which of the following is TRUE about this suspect?

(A) He may pretend to not speak English to avoid answering questions.
(B) He may pretend not to understand an Italian interpreter by speaking Spanish.
(C) He may pretend not to understand a Spanish interpreter by speaking Italian.
(D) All of the above.

6. This woman is wanted for:

(A) Rape
(B) Murder
(C) Drug manufacturing
(D) Aggravated assault

7. Which of the following statements is NOT true about this suspect?

(A) She is 151 lbs.
(B) She has an alias.
(C) She is 5 ft 4 in tall.
(D) She is Hispanic.

8. What is this woman's age?

(A) 19
(B) 24
(C) 29
(D) 34

GO ON TO THE NEXT PAGE

9. Which of the following is TRUE about this suspect?

(A) Her first name is Alicia.
(B) Her first name is Alice.
(C) Her first name is Alexandra.
(D) Her first name is Amelia.

10. Which of the following is TRUE about this suspect?

(A) She may pretend to not speak English to avoid answering questions.
(B) She may pretend not to understand an Italian interpreter by speaking Spanish.
(C) She may pretend not to understand a Spanish interpreter by speaking Italian.
(D) All of the above.

11. This woman is wanted for:

(A) Bank robbery
(B) Murder
(C) Drug manufacturing
(D) Aggravated assault

12. Which of the following statements is NOT true about this suspect?

(A) She is 151 lbs.
(B) She has an alias.
(C) She is Hispanic.
(D) All of the above.

GO ON TO THE NEXT PAGE

13. What is this woman's age?

(A) 19
(B) 23
(C) 29
(D) 34

14. Which of the following is TRUE about this suspect?

(A) She has a butterfly tattoo on her ankle.
(B) She has a pierced lip.
(C) She has a butterfly tattoo on her wrist.
(D) She has a pierced eyebrow.

15. Which of the following is TRUE about this suspect?

(A) She may pretend to not speak English to avoid answering questions.
(B) The extent of her linguistic abilities is not known.
(C) Her strong accent implies that she speaks at least one other language.
(D) All of the above.

16. This woman is wanted for:

(A) Bank robbery
(B) Kidnapping
(C) Drug manufacturing
(D) Aggravated assault

17. Which of the following statements is NOT true about this suspect?

(A) She is 121 lbs.
(B) She has an alias.
(C) She is 5 ft 7 in tall.
(D) She is Hispanic.

GO ON TO THE NEXT PAGE

18. What is this woman's age?

    (A) 19
    (B) 24
    (C) 29
    (D) 34

19. Which of the following is TRUE about this suspect?

    (A) Her first name is Peggy.
    (B) Her first name is Patty.
    (C) Her first name is Paige.
    (D) Her first name is Piper.

20. Which of the following is TRUE about this suspect?

    (A) She is a mother.
    (B) She is known to carry weapons.
    (C) She is traveling with three children.
    (D) All of the above.

STOP. THIS IS THE END OF SECTION 3.

ABILITY TO WRITE REPORTS AND COMPLETE FORMS

Use the information provided in the pretest materials to answer the following questions. You may not refer to any pretest materials or notes during the exam.

INCIDENT

On September 29, 2017, at approximately 6 P.M. Eric Jackson walked into the Super-Mart, located at 12122 E. Seneca Street. Jackson proceeded to walk through the store, and then loaded a $179 television-video cassette recorder combo into a shopping cart, removed the security tag, and pushed the cart out the front door. Two security guards observed him leaving the store with the television-video cassette recorder at 6:15 P.M., followed him into the parking lot, and confronted him. Jackson abandoned the shopping cart beside a late model maroon Buick and started to run away, but suddenly turned back. One of the guards grabbed Jackson's arm. Jackson punched the guard in the nose, attempted to hit the second guard in the arm, and ran away. The guards were unable to catch him, but a police officer positioned his car in Jackson's path and arrested him at approximately 6:22 P.M. The crime of robbery, 9A.56.190, was complete when Jackson left the store. No weapons or intoxicating substances were indicated or found at the scene. No ambulance was called.

GO ON TO THE NEXT PAGE

DATE OFFENSE STARTED	TIME OFFENSE STARTED	LOCATION OF OFFENSE	DATE OF REPORT
1	2	3	4

DATE OFFENSE ENDED	TIME OFFENSE ENDED	NUMBER OF VICTIMS	VICTIM INJURIES
5	6	7	8

TITLE	CHAPTER/SECTION	___ ATTEMPT ___ COMPLETE	EXCEPTIONAL CLEARANCE:
9	10	11	____ DEATH OF OFFENDER ____ DEATH OF VICTIM ____ JUVENILE ____ PROBATION REVOKED ____ VICTIM REFUSAL TO PROSECUTE

DESCRIPTION OF OFFENSE	HATE/BIAS	14
12	13	**OFFENDER SUSPECTED OF USING:** _____ DRUGS/NARCOTICS _____ ALCOHOL _____ COMPUTER EQUIPMENT _____ N/A 15

TYPE OF FORCE/WEAPON

16

GO ON TO THE NEXT PAGE

1. What entry should be made in box 2?

   (A) 1800 hours
   (B) 1900 hours
   (C) 1815 hours
   (D) 1922 hours

2. What entry should be made in box 7?

   (A) 1
   (B) 2
   (C) 3
   (D) 4

3. What entry should be made in box 8?

   (A) Injury to arm
   (B) Injury to nose/face
   (C) Injury to television-video recorder
   (D) No injury noted

4. What line should be marked in box 15?

   (A) Drugs/narcotics
   (B) Alcohol
   (C) Computer equipment
   (D) N/A

5. What entry should be made in box 16?

   (A) Knife
   (B) Blunt object
   (C) Vehicle
   (D) None

GO ON TO THE NEXT PAGE

INCIDENT

On August 2, 2017, at approximately 10:13 A.M., a Central City police officer stopped Jason Goodman, age 42, for making an illegal left turn at the 1300 block of Washington Streets. The officer asked Goodman for his driver's license, vehicle registration, and insurance information. Mr. Goodman said he did not have his wallet with him, but he provided the vehicle registration for his pickup truck. He also gave his name, address, and date of birth. The officer conducted a driver's check through the local police database and learned that Goodman's out of state driver's license had been suspended. The officer also smelled an odor of alcoholic beverage coming from Goodman's vehicle. The officer arrested Goodman for driving while his license was suspended, handcuffed him, searched him, and placed him in the back of his patrol car at 10:27 A.M.

A second officer arrived. Pursuant to city police procedure, the officers conducted an inventory search before impounding Goodman's truck. One of the officers began the inventory on the driver side, seeing nothing on the driver's seat, he reached under the front seat and felt a satchel directly under the driver's seat. The Officer pulled the satchel out from under the seat, unzipped the top, main portion and saw what appeared to be a gun holster. The Officer removed this object from the backpack and found a black 9mm pistol in the holster. The pistol was unloaded, but a fully loaded magazine for the pistol was found in the satchel. Goodman was also charged under CR 9.41.050 for transporting a weapon without a license.

GO ON TO THE NEXT PAGE

DATE OFFENSE STARTED	TIME OFFENSE STARTED	LOCATION OF OFFENSE	DATE OF REPORT
1	**2**	**3**	**4**

DATE OFFENSE ENDED	TIME OFFENSE ENDED	NUMBER OF VICTIMS	VICTIM INJURIES
5	**6**	**7**	**8**

TITLE	CHAPTER/SECTION	___ ATTEMPT ___ COMPLETE	EXCEPTIONAL CLEARANCE:
9	**10**	**11**	____ DEATH OF OFFENDER ____ DEATH OF VICTIM ____ JUVENILE ____ PROBATION REVOKED ____ VICTIM REFUSAL TO PROSECUTE **14**

DESCRIPTION OF OFFENSE	HATE/BIAS	
12	**13**	**OFFENDER SUSPECTED OF USING:** _____ DRUGS/NARCOTICS _____ ALCOHOL _____ COMPUTER EQUIPMENT _____ N/A **15**

TYPE OF FORCE/WEAPON
16

GO ON TO THE NEXT PAGE

6. What line should be marked in box 14?

   (A) Juvenile
   (B) Probation revoked
   (C) Victim refused to prosecute
   (D) No line should be marked

7. What line should be marked in box 11?

   (A) Attempt
   (B) Complete
   (C) Both lines should be marked
   (D) Neither line should be marked

8. Although the officer noted many details possibly associated with offenses, Goodman was actually charged with how many offenses according to the report?

   (A) 1
   (B) 2
   (C) 3
   (D) 4

9. Which of the following is the correct response to put in box 9 associated with the offense of transporting a weapon without a license?

   (A) CR
   (B) 9.41
   (C) 9
   (D) 9.41.050

10. What entry should be made in box 6?

   (A) 10:13 hours
   (B) 10:27 hours
   (C) 10:30 A.M.
   (D) Unknown at this time

GO ON TO THE NEXT PAGE

INCIDENT

On the afternoon of October 1, 2017, at approximately 4:00 P.M., a two-vehicle accident occurred in Central City. Vehicle No.1. a green Toyota Corolla driven by Harry Dillon collided with a parked Chevrolet minivan occupied by two people. A Central City Police Department code enforcement officer (CEO) on bike patrol saw Dillon staggering toward his car parked in front of 155 James Street, approximately 200 feet west of the intersection of Central and James, just prior to the accident. The CEO noticed that although the day was clear and warm with no wind, Dillon was having trouble with his balance and co-ordination. As Dillon entered his car, the CEO called dispatch to inform the police that he believed he was witnessing an intoxicated driver getting into a vehicle. The collision occurred while the CEO was still on the radio. Dillon backed into vehicle No.2, a Chevrolet minivan parked behind the Corolla. The minivan sustained a severely damaged front end. The Toyota's back end was also seriously damaged causing the trunk to open. Two clear bags containing a white powdered substance were clearly visible in the trunk. Following on-scene testing both bags were seized as evidence, and Dillon was arrested and charged with various traffic offenses and criminal offenses. (See case No. CR 100600343.)

The driver of the Chevrolet minivan was injured and was taken to hospital via ambulance. Her two-year-old son was uninjured. Dillon was uninjured, but was transported by police vehicle for blood testing.

GO ON TO THE NEXT PAGE

DATE OF COLLISION	LOCATION OF COLLISION	NEAREST INTERSECTION	NO. VEHICLES	NO. TRANSPORTED BY AMBULANCE
1	**2**	**3**	**4**	**5**

TIME OF ACCIDENT	NO. DECEASED AT SCENE	CITATIONS ISSUED
		Name of cited party:
		_____
		Violation(s):
		_____
		Name of cited party:
		_____
		Violation(s):
		_____
6	**7**	**8**

DESCRIPTION OF VEHICLE No.1:	DESCRIPTION OF VEHICLE No.2:
MAKE YEAR	MAKE YEAR
MODEL COLOR	MODEL COLOR
DESCRIPTION OF DAMAGE	DESCRIPTION OF DAMAGE
9	**10**

WEATHER CONDITIONS: ____ RAIN ____ SNOW ____ WIND ____ FOG OTHER:	No. ASSOCIATED CRIMINAL CASE
11	**12**

GO ON TO THE NEXT PAGE

11. What entry should be made in box 2?

    (A) 155 James Street
    (B) 200 W. James Street
    (C) 200 W. Central
    (D) Unknown at this time

12. What lines/entry should be made in box 11?

    (A) Wind
    (B) Fog
    (C) Clear visibility/no wind
    (D) Warm day

13. What entry should be made in box No.10?

    (A) Damaged front end
    (B) Damaged back end
    (C) No visible damage
    (D) Undetermined amount of damage

14. What entry should be made in box 5?

    (A) 1
    (B) 2
    (C) 3
    (D) 4

15. What entry should be made in box 12?

    (A) CR 343
    (B) CR 100600343
    (C) CR 1006
    (D) CR 100600334

GO ON TO THE NEXT PAGE

INCIDENT

On the evening of May 3, 2017, at approximately 7 P.M. Stacy Moore was driving herself and her husband, Trey Moore, home after attending church on Lincoln Avenue. En route to their home, the Moores had an altercation with the driver of another vehicle, Caleb Lewis. The altercation began when Lewis started tailgating the Moores and flashing his headlights. In response, Stephanie Moore slowed down and pumped her brakes, attempting unsuccessfully to get Lewis to drive around her car, a 2001 convertible yellow Volkswagen. As they approached a stoplight, Lewis pulled alongside the Moores' car and he and the passenger in his car exchanged words with Tracy Moore. The verbal altercation then ended and Stephanie Moore proceeded to drive away. At about the 2000 block of E. Lincoln, Lewis passed their car and slammed on his brakes causing the Moore vehicle to collide with the rear of the vehicle driven by Lewis, a 1991 White Ford Explorer. Lewis then left the scene but was apprehended on May 5, 2017, in an incident detailed in case No. CR 100601253. The Moore vehicle spun out of control through the intersection of Lincoln and Jefferson, hit a telephone pole, and rolled over. It came to rest in the eastbound lanes of Lincoln Avenue where other drivers rendered aide and called for assistance. Stacy Moore was seriously injured and was transported to Mercy Hospital. Trey Moore died at the scene. Lewis was charged with Manslaughter, 9A.32.060, in the criminal case associated with this traffic incident, No. CR 100601214. Weather was not a factor in this accident.

GO ON TO THE NEXT PAGE

DATE OF COLLISION	LOCATION OF COLLISION	NEAREST INTERSECTION	NO. VEHICLES	NO. TRANSPORTED BY AMBULANCE
1	**2**	**3**	**4**	**5**

TIME OF ACCIDENT	NO. DECEASED AT SCENE	CITATIONS ISSUED
		Name of cited party: _____
		Violation(s): _____
		Name of cited party: _____
		Violation(s): _____
6	**7**	**8**

DESCRIPTION OF VEHICLE No.1:	DESCRIPTION OF VEHICLE No.2:
MAKE YEAR MODEL COLOR	MAKE YEAR MODEL COLOR
DESCRIPTION OF DAMAGE	DESCRIPTION OF DAMAGE
9	**10**

WEATHER CONDITIONS: ____ RAIN ____ SNOW ____ WIND ____ FOG OTHER:	No. ASSOCIATED CRIMINAL CASE
11	**12**

GO ON TO THE NEXT PAGE

16. What entry should be made in box 5?

    (A) 1
    (B) 2
    (C) 3
    (D) 4

17. What entry should be made in box 7?

    (A) 1
    (B) 2
    (C) 3
    (D) 4

18. According to the report, which driver was issued a traffic citation at the scene?

    (A) Stephanie Moore
    (B) No one
    (C) Caleb Lewis
    (D) Trey Moore

19. Which of the following information should be marked in box 11?

    (A) Information not provided
    (B) Snow
    (C) Other
    (D) Rain

20. What entry should be made in box 12?

    (A) No. CR 100601253
    (B) No. CR 9A.32.060
    (C) No. CR 100601214
    (D) N/A

STOP. THIS IS THE END OF SECTION 4.

APPLYING LEARNED MATERIAL

The questions below are based on the information from the VEHICLE SEARCHES article provided in the pretest materials and on information provided in the incidents presented below.

INCIDENT 1

At approximately 1600 hours, Officer Patterson was patrolling in his squad car in a quiet residential neighborhood when he noticed a small white vehicle spin out and squeal its tires while making a turn. Officer Patterson had been patrolling the neighborhood because of several reports of drag racing in the area over the last several days. Officer Patterson stopped the car for violation of the traffic code. When he approached the vehicle he noticed that the driver was a male in his late teens. Officer Patterson asked the driver for his driver's license, proof of insurance, and registration. He then asked the driver why he had spun his tires. The driver answered he "was just being dumb." As the driver was answering the question Officer Patterson could smell an odor of an alcoholic beverage emanating from the driver's breath. Officer Patterson asked the driver to step out of his vehicle in order to perform field sobriety tests. The driver refused to conduct the tests. The driver was placed under arrest for suspicion of driving under the influence of alcohol.

1. Officer Patterson's probable cause to stop the small white vehicle was _____

   (A) The vehicle was in an enforcement zone.
   (B) The officer suspected the driver was driving under the influence.
   (C) The vehicle had been seen by the officer committing a traffic infraction.
   (D) The officer knew the driver and knew he was advertising his desire to drag race.

2. When Officer Patterson approached the vehicle he knew that he should use extreme care because _____

   (A) The officer knew the driver and knew he was dangerous.
   (B) It is common knowledge that drag racers are violent.
   (C) The traffic infraction was very serious and the driver knew he would go to jail.
   (D) There is always a possibility that a driver will react to a stop with violence.

GO ON TO THE NEXT PAGE

3. After asking the driver of the vehicle for his standard documents, Officer Patterson asked the driver why he had committed the traffic infraction. What illegal act did Officer Patterson have reasonable suspicion to believe was occurring in addition to the traffic violation?

(A) Driving under the influence
(B) Drag racing
(C) Possession of a stolen vehicle
(D) Both (A) and (B)

4. Which of the following statements would NOT support Officer Patterson's reasonable suspicion to believe that criminal activity was occurring beyond the traffic infraction?

(A) Time of day
(B) Recent reports from residents about drag racing in the neighborhood
(C) The age of the driver
(D) Squealing of tires in a quiet residential neighborhood

5. When Officer Patterson stopped the vehicle should he have frisked the driver?

(A) Yes, because a driver frisk is standard procedure.
(B) Only if the officer had a reasonable belief that the driver presented a threat to his safety.
(C) Yes, because it may have yielded additional evidence about criminal activity.
(D) Only if the officer had probable cause to believe that an individual has evidence of criminal activity on his person.

6. Of the following possibilities, which answer is the MOST LIKELY reason that Officer Patterson did not ask the driver of the vehicle for consent to search his vehicle?

(A) The driver did not own the vehicle.
(B) The officer was waiting for an opportunity to arrest the driver.
(C) The officer did not have a suspicion that the vehicle contained evidence of crime.
(D) The officer was trying to catch the driver off-guard so that he would admit to additional crimes.

7. What evidence supported Officer Patterson's probable cause to arrest the driver?

(A) Poor driving.
(B) The smell of alcoholic beverage on driver's breath and test refusal.
(C) Poor driving and the smell of alcoholic beverage on driver's breath.
(D) There was no probable cause to arrest the driver.

GO ON TO THE NEXT PAGE

8. If Officer Patterson searched the vehicle, what exception to the warrant requirement supported the search?

(A) Search incident to arrest.
(B) Vehicle search.
(C) Consent search.
(D) Exigent circumstances.

9. "Exigent" means _____.

(A) Exceptional
(B) Extraordinary
(C) Emergency
(D) Extraneous evidence

10. The size of an individual's *wingspan* is _____.

(A) Six feet, the average length of an adult males reach.
(B) The actual length that an individual's arms can reach.
(C) The individual's immediate surroundings.
(D) The area that the arresting officer believes that an individual could reach into and secure a weapon.

INCIDENT 2

Officer Spencer was on patrol on a residential arterial roadway at approximately 11 P.M. when he noticed a green sports car traveling toward him. A stop sign and a streetlight were located between his vehicle and the approaching vehicle. No other vehicles were in sight. Officer Spencer watched the vehicle approach the stop sign and come to a complete stop. The vehicle remained stopped at the stop sign until Officer Spencer's car had not only reached the stop sign, but had stopped at the stop sign, waited 30 seconds, and then proceeded through the stop sign. Officer Spencer watched the vehicle in his rear view mirror for approximately 15 more seconds before he saw the vehicle cross the intersection and proceed down the roadway. Officer Spencer turned around and followed the vehicle. He noticed that it crossed the center lane on three occasions within a two-block distance. Officer Spencer activated his emergency lights to signal the driver to pull over to the side of the road. As the vehicle was pulling over Officer Spencer saw the back-up lights activate and as his window was down he was also able to hear the transmission gears grinding. Officer Spencer ascertained that the driver had put the vehicle in park as it was still moving onto the shoulder of the roadway. When Officer Spencer approached the driver's side window he detected a strong odor of an alcoholic beverage emanating from within the vehicle. He asked the female driver for her driver's license. She claimed that

GO ON TO THE NEXT PAGE

she did not have it in her possession. He saw a cell phone lying on the seat next to her with its face light on. He asked her where she had been, and she replied that she had been across town with friends. He asked her where she was going, and she replied that she was going home. He asked her where she lived and she gave him an address for a street that he had seen her drive past.

11. Officer Spencer's probable cause to stop the vehicle was _____.

   (A) The vehicle was in an enforcement zone.
   (B) He suspected the driver was driving under the influence.
   (C) The vehicle had been seen by the officer committing a traffic infraction.
   (D) The driver of the vehicle seemed to be trying to avoid Officer Spencer's notice.

12. What action did Officer Spencer have only reasonable suspicion to believe was occurring?

   (A) Driving under the influence
   (B) Drag racing
   (C) Possession of a stolen vehicle
   (D) Driving without a valid driver's license

13. Which of the following statements would NOT support Officer Spencer's reasonable suspicion to believe that criminal activity was occurring beyond the traffic infraction?

   (A) The vehicle sat for a prolonged period at an intersection where no other traffic prevented it from moving.
   (B) The vehicle was a sports car.
   (C) The vehicle crossed the center lane of the roadway more than once.
   (D) The vehicle's driver had put the vehicle in park as it was still moving onto the shoulder of the roadway causing an audible grinding of the transmission's gears.

14. If Officer Spencer had reasonable suspicion to believe that a crime beyond mere traffic infractions was occurring, what additional authority did he have?

   (A) The authority to arrest the suspect.
   (B) The authority to search the suspect.
   (C) The authority to search the suspect's vehicle.
   (D) The authority to ask the suspect who they were and what they were doing in the area.

GO ON TO THE NEXT PAGE

15. If Officer Spencer had asked the driver for consent to search the vehicle and she had refused to give consent, _____.

    (A) Her refusal would support probable cause to search.
    (B) Her refusal would be grounds for arrest.
    (C) She has the right to refuse and Officer Spencer could not take any further action.
    (D) She could be kept at the scene until she gave her consent to search.

16. After approaching the driver and evaluating the interior of the vehicle, Officer Spencer suspected that _____.

    (A) The driver of the vehicle was not comfortable driving her car.
    (B) The driver of the vehicle was not familiar with her surroundings.
    (C) The driver of the vehicle was trying to hide evidence of criminal acts.
    (D) The driver of the vehicle was talking on her cell phone while driving.

17. The evidence that least supports charging the driver of this vehicle with driving under the influence is:

    (A) The odor of alcoholic beverage.
    (B) The cell phone in view and recently used.
    (C) Crossing the center lane of the roadway.
    (D) Sitting too long at an intersection when no other cars were in the area.

18. Recognizing an odor as evidence of a criminal act is called _____.

    (A) Plain view
    (B) Plain smell
    (C) Odor identification
    (D) None of the above

19. Which of the following statements is NOT TRUE concerning "reasonable suspicion"?

    (A) Reasonable suspicion is a lower standard of proof than probable cause.
    (B) Reasonable suspicion requires that an officer be able to clearly articulate his/her reasons for being suspicious.
    (C) Reasonable suspicion requires a clear link between an individual and a crime.
    (D) Reasonable suspicion requires more than a "gut feeling" or a "hunch."

GO ON TO THE NEXT PAGE

20. Which of the following statements is NOT TRUE concerning "probable cause" to stop a vehicle involved in a traffic infraction?

(A) Probable cause requires a clear link between the illegal act and an individual.

(B) Probable cause to stop a vehicle is only necessary to justify a subsequent search.

(C) Probable cause to stop a vehicle arises out of the officer's knowledge that the infraction was caused by the driver of the vehicle seen violating the law.

(D) Probable cause to stop a vehicle arises out of the officer's knowledge that an infraction of the traffic laws has occurred.

STOP. THIS IS THE END OF SECTION 5.

MAP READING

Use the information provided in the pretest materials to answer the following questions. You may not refer to any pretest materials or notes during the exam.

TO ANSWER THE FOLLOWING QUESTIONS UTILIZE INFORMATION PROVIDED IN THE DRAWING LABELED **"MAP OF CENTRAL CITY."**

1. Police receive a call that a burglary is in progress at the Northeast corner of Everett St. and Wildwood Ave. If police are able to travel directly from the police station of the reported site of the burglary which direction will they need to go?

   (A) Northeast
   (B) Southeast
   (C) Southwest
   (D) Northwest

2. Which direction of travel is permitted on Sunnybrook Street?

   (A) Vehicles may travel both directions.
   (B) Vehicles may only travel west.
   (C) Vehicles may only travel east.
   (D) Vehicles may only travel north.

3. Which direction of travel is permitted on Everett Street?

   (A) Vehicles may travel both directions.
   (B) Vehicles may only travel west.
   (C) Vehicles may only travel east.
   (D) Vehicles may only travel north.

4. Which two streets only permit one-way travel?

   (A) Wildwood and Everett
   (B) Seneca and Sunnybrook
   (C) Southgate and Sunnybrook
   (D) Wildwood and Seneca

5. A police cruiser is headed south at the intersection of Wildwood and Everett. Which street will he turn east on to reach the police station?

   (A) Day Street
   (B) Seneca Ave
   (C) Meridian Ave
   (D) Southgate St

GO ON TO THE NEXT PAGE

---

6. Which street is the only one-way street abutting Wildwood Park?

(A) Seneca Ave
(B) Southgate St
(C) Sunnybrook St
(D) Southhampton Rd

7. Which direction must police travel from the police station to reach the Work Release Center?

(A) Southeast
(B) South
(C) Southwest
(D) Northeast

8. Police receive a report of a domestic incident on Everett Street in front of Unit No. 1 of the Wildwood Apartment Complex. If police are able to travel directly from the police station of the reported site of the incident which general direction will they need to go?

(A) Northeast
(B) North
(C) Northwest
(D) Southwest

9. Which building is the police station located nearest to?

(A) Work release center
(B) Fire station
(C) Unit No. 3 of Wildwood Apartment Complex
(D) Unit No. 4 of Wildwood Apartment Complex

10. The police station is located on the _____ corner of Bennett St and Southgate.

(A) Northeast
(B) North
(C) Northwest
(D) Southwest

TO ANSWER THE FOLLOWING QUESTIONS UTILIZE INFORMATION PROVIDED IN THE DRAWING LABELED "MAP OF OFFICE BUILDING."

Police receive a call that an armed man has entered an office building and is currently barricaded inside the conference room. Civilians are still inside the building seeking the best shelter they can find. Study this diagram so that when you arrive on the scene, you will understand the layout of the bank. You will be asked to recall the information shown here without the use of this diagram.

GO ON TO THE NEXT PAGE

11. How many offices are located in the building?

(A) 3
(B) 4
(C) 5
(D) 7

12. If all of the offices are currently occupied as well as the reception desk, what is the minimum number of civilians currently working in this building?

(A) 3
(B) 4
(C) 5
(D) 7

13. If the suspect exits through the door of the conference room, which exterior door would he be closest to?

(A) North
(B) West
(C) East
(D) South

14. If the suspect exits through the window of the conference room which side of the building will he be on?

(A) North
(B) West
(C) East
(D) South

15. In which corner of the building was the largest office located?

(A) Northwest
(B) Northeast
(C) Southwest
(D) Southeast

16. Judging by the thickness of the walls, which room will provide the greatest safety to the civilians inside?

(A) Conference room
(B) Manager's office
(C) Restrooms
(D) Reception area

GO ON TO THE NEXT PAGE

17. If it seems advisable to evacuate the building, through which door will you recommend that civilians exit the building?

(A) North
(B) West
(C) East
(D) South

TO ANSWER THE FOLLOWING QUESTIONS UTILIZE INFORMATION PROVIDED IN THE DRAWING LABELED **"MAP OF HOUSE."**

Police receive a call that a distraught man has barricaded himself inside his home and is holding his wife and infant daughter hostage. You do not know where inside the building the wife and baby are being located. Study this diagram so that when you arrive on the scene, you will understand the layout of the house. You will be asked to recall the information shown here without the use of this diagram.

18. How many levels are in this home?

(A) 1
(B) 2
(C) 3
(D) 4

19. In addition to the sliding glass door that leads to the patio, how many exterior doors to this home are you aware of?

(A) 1
(B) 2
(C) 3
(D) 4

20. How many enclosed rooms (rooms that can be closed off from other areas of the house) are located on the main floor?

(A) 2
(B) 4
(C) 6
(D) 8

STOP. THIS IS THE END OF SECTION 6.

GRAMMAR AND USAGE

Use the information provided in the pretest materials to answer the following questions. You may not refer to any pretest materials or notes during the exam.

---

1. Which of the following is grammatically CORRECT?

   (A) Stop right now.
   (B) Stop right now!
   (C) Stop right now?
   (D) Stop, right now!

2. Which of the following is grammatically CORRECT?

   (A) Officer Pete are running.
   (B) Officer Pete be running.
   (C) Officer Pete is running.
   (D) Officer Pete were running.

3. Which of the following is grammatically INCORRECT?

   (A) Officer John ran to the bus stop.
   (B) Officer John, grasping his radio, ran to the bus stop.
   (C) Officer John grasping his radio at the bus stop.
   (D) Officer John, grasping his radio and weapon belt, ran to the bus stop as fast as he had ever run in his life.

4. Which of the following is CORRECT?

   (A) It's cold outside.
   (B) Its cold outside.
   (C) Iss cold outside.
   (D) Its' cold outside

5. Which of the following is NOT a noun?

   (A) John
   (B) San Francisco
   (C) Rock
   (D) Run

6. Which of the following is a VERB?

   (A) John
   (B) San Francisco
   (C) Rock
   (D) Run

GO ON TO THE NEXT PAGE

7. Which of the following is CORRECT?

   (A) I approached the passenger, Thad Rose, he had had a few beers also.
   (B) I approached the passenger, Thad Rose, he had had a few beers, also.
   (C) I approached the passenger Thad Rose he had had a few beers also.
   (D) I approached the passenger, Thad Rose. He had had a few beers also.

8. Which is NOT a sentence fragment?

   (A) Running to catch the suspect.
   (B) Every time I looked at the suspect.
   (C) When I searched the suspect.
   (D) I completed the arrest of the suspect.

9. Which sentence is CORRECT?

   (A) John is a criminal.
   (B) John is a criminal
   (C) john is a criminal.
   (D) john is a criminal

10. Which sentence uses verb tense correctly?

   (A) Officer John stopped the vehicle and walks toward the occupant.
   (B) Officer John stopped the vehicle and walked toward the occupant.
   (C) Officer John stops the vehicle and walked toward the occupant.
   (D) Officer John was stopping the vehicle and walks toward the occupant.

11. Which of the following uses a pronoun in place of the subject?

   (A) He ran away from Officer John.
   (B) Paul ran away from Officer John.
   (C) The dog ran away from Officer John.
   (D) The little boy ran away from Officer John.

12. Which of the following sentences is CORRECT?

   (A) I will do the paperwork yesterday.
   (B) I did the paperwork later today.
   (C) I did the paperwork yesterday.
   (D) I did the paperwork tomorrow.

GO ON TO THE NEXT PAGE

13. Which of the following sentences is CORRECT?

   (A) We had reports of drag racers from past days.
   (B) We had received reports of drag racers in the past few days.
   (C) We had received reports of drag racers in the past days.
   (D) We had reports of drag racers in past few days.

14. Which of the following is an exclamatory sentence?

   (A) Pull your car over to the side of the road!
   (B) Will you please pull your car over to the side of the road?
   (C) After you pass this next vehicle, pull your car over to the side of the road.
   (D) Pull your car over to the side of the road.

15. Which sentence is CORRECT?

   (A) That sweater is hers.
   (B) That sweater is her's.
   (C) That sweater is hers'.
   (D) That sweater is her's'.

16. Which sentence is CORRECT?

   (A) I then took Mr. Young to the county jail, after further testing, Mr. Young tested above the legal limit for breath alcohol level.
   (B) I then took Mr. Young, to the county jail, after further testing, Mr. Young tested, above the legal limit, for breath alcohol level.
   (C) I then took Mr. Young to the county jail. After further testing, Mr. Young tested above the legal limit for breath alcohol level.
   (D) I then took Mr. Young to the county jail after further testing. Mr. Young tested above the legal limit for breath alcohol level.

17. Which sentence is CORRECT?

   (A) This house is there's.
   (B) This house is their's.
   (C) This is house is theirs.
   (D) This is house is theres.

18. Which sentence is CORRECT?

   (A) Is this your sweater?
   (B) Is this you're sweater?
   (C) Is this youre sweater?
   (D) Is this your' sweater?

GO ON TO THE NEXT PAGE

19. Read the following sentence and identify the subject.
Officer John is careful to use correct grammar when writing police reports.

(A) Officer John
(B) grammar
(C) police reports
(D) writing

20. Read the following sentence and identify the verb.
Officer John is careful to use correct grammar when writing police reports.

(A) Is
(B) Use
(C) Writing
(D) Reports

STOP. THIS IS THE END OF PRACTICE TEST 1.

Answer Key

Section 1: Vocabulary	Section 2: Ability to Observe and Recall	Section 3: Ability to Observe and Report Information
1. B	1. B	1. D
2. A	2. B	2. B
3. D	3. C	3. B
4. C	4. D	4. C
5. C	5. B	5. D
6. B	6. B	6. C
7. D	7. C	7. A
8. A	8. D	8. A
9. C	9. B	9. B
10. B	10. C	10. A
11. D	11. A	11. A
12. C	12. B	12. D
13. C	13. D	13. B
14. D	14. C	14. A
15. C	15. C	15. D
16. D	16. A	16. B
17. C	17. D	17. D
18. B	18. C	18. D
19. B	19. B	19. C
20. D	20. A	20. D

Section 4: Ability to Write Reports and Complete Forms

1. C
2. B
3. B
4. D
5. D
6. D
7. B
8. A
9. D
10. B
11. A
12. C
13. A
14. A
15. B
16. B
17. A
18. B
19. A
20. C

Section 5: Applying Learned Material

1. C
2. D
3. D
4. A
5. B
6. C
7. B
8. A
9. C
10. C
11. C
12. A
13. B
14. D
15. C
16. D
17. B
18. B
19. C
20. B

Section 6: Map Reading

1. D
2. B
3. A
4. C
5. D
6. C
7. C
8. C
9. B
10. D
11. D
12. D
13. B
14. B
15. B
16. C
17. C
18. C
19. C
20. C

Section 7: Grammar And Usage

1. D
2. C
3. C
4. A
5. D
6. D
7. D
8. D
9. A
10. B
11. A
12. C
13. B
14. A
15. A
16. C
17. C
18. A
19. A
20. A

PRACTICE TEST 2

**Similar to the State of Massachusetts and
San Antonio, Texas, Law Enforcement Exams**

Answer Sheet

Section 1: Memorization

1. Ⓐ Ⓑ Ⓒ Ⓓ
2. Ⓐ Ⓑ Ⓒ Ⓓ
3. Ⓐ Ⓑ Ⓒ Ⓓ
4. Ⓐ Ⓑ Ⓒ Ⓓ
5. Ⓐ Ⓑ Ⓒ Ⓓ
6. Ⓐ Ⓑ Ⓒ Ⓓ
7. Ⓐ Ⓑ Ⓒ Ⓓ
8. Ⓐ Ⓑ Ⓒ Ⓓ
9. Ⓐ Ⓑ Ⓒ Ⓓ
10. Ⓐ Ⓑ Ⓒ Ⓓ

Section 2: Visualization

11. Ⓐ Ⓑ Ⓒ Ⓓ
12. Ⓐ Ⓑ Ⓒ Ⓓ
13. Ⓐ Ⓑ Ⓒ Ⓓ
14. Ⓐ Ⓑ Ⓒ Ⓓ
15. Ⓐ Ⓑ Ⓒ Ⓓ
16. Ⓐ Ⓑ Ⓒ Ⓓ
17. Ⓐ Ⓑ Ⓒ Ⓓ
18. Ⓐ Ⓑ Ⓒ Ⓓ
19. Ⓐ Ⓑ Ⓒ Ⓓ
20. Ⓐ Ⓑ Ⓒ Ⓓ
21. Ⓐ Ⓑ Ⓒ Ⓓ
22. Ⓐ Ⓑ Ⓒ Ⓓ
23. Ⓐ Ⓑ Ⓒ Ⓓ
24. Ⓐ Ⓑ Ⓒ Ⓓ

Section 3: Spatial Orientation

25. Ⓐ Ⓑ Ⓒ Ⓓ
26. Ⓐ Ⓑ Ⓒ Ⓓ
27. Ⓐ Ⓑ Ⓒ Ⓓ
28. Ⓐ Ⓑ Ⓒ Ⓓ
29. Ⓐ Ⓑ Ⓒ Ⓓ
30. Ⓐ Ⓑ Ⓒ Ⓓ
31. Ⓐ Ⓑ Ⓒ Ⓓ
32. Ⓐ Ⓑ Ⓒ Ⓓ
33. Ⓐ Ⓑ Ⓒ Ⓓ
34. Ⓐ Ⓑ Ⓒ Ⓓ
35. Ⓐ Ⓑ Ⓒ Ⓓ
36. Ⓐ Ⓑ Ⓒ Ⓓ

Section 4: Verbal Expression

37. Ⓐ Ⓑ Ⓒ Ⓓ
38. Ⓐ Ⓑ Ⓒ Ⓓ
39. Ⓐ Ⓑ Ⓒ Ⓓ
40. Ⓐ Ⓑ Ⓒ Ⓓ
41. Ⓐ Ⓑ Ⓒ Ⓓ
42. Ⓐ Ⓑ Ⓒ Ⓓ
43. Ⓐ Ⓑ Ⓒ Ⓓ
44. Ⓐ Ⓑ Ⓒ Ⓓ
45. Ⓐ Ⓑ Ⓒ Ⓓ
46. Ⓐ Ⓑ Ⓒ Ⓓ

Section 5: Verbal Comprehension

47. Ⓐ Ⓑ Ⓒ Ⓓ
48. Ⓐ Ⓑ Ⓒ Ⓓ
49. Ⓐ Ⓑ Ⓒ Ⓓ
50. Ⓐ Ⓑ Ⓒ Ⓓ
51. Ⓐ Ⓑ Ⓒ Ⓓ

52. Ⓐ Ⓑ Ⓒ Ⓓ
53. Ⓐ Ⓑ Ⓒ Ⓓ
54. Ⓐ Ⓑ Ⓒ Ⓓ
55. Ⓐ Ⓑ Ⓒ Ⓓ
56. Ⓐ Ⓑ Ⓒ Ⓓ

57. Ⓐ Ⓑ Ⓒ Ⓓ
58. Ⓐ Ⓑ Ⓒ Ⓓ

Section 6: Problem Sensitivity

59. Ⓐ Ⓑ Ⓒ Ⓓ
60. Ⓐ Ⓑ Ⓒ Ⓓ
61. Ⓐ Ⓑ Ⓒ Ⓓ
62. Ⓐ Ⓑ Ⓒ Ⓓ
63. Ⓐ Ⓑ Ⓒ Ⓓ

64. Ⓐ Ⓑ Ⓒ Ⓓ
65. Ⓐ Ⓑ Ⓒ Ⓓ
66. Ⓐ Ⓑ Ⓒ Ⓓ

Section 7: Deductive Reasoning

67. Ⓐ Ⓑ Ⓒ Ⓓ
68. Ⓐ Ⓑ Ⓒ Ⓓ
69. Ⓐ Ⓑ Ⓒ Ⓓ
70. Ⓐ Ⓑ Ⓒ Ⓓ
71. Ⓐ Ⓑ Ⓒ Ⓓ

72. Ⓐ Ⓑ Ⓒ Ⓓ
73. Ⓐ Ⓑ Ⓒ Ⓓ
74. Ⓐ Ⓑ Ⓒ Ⓓ

Section 8: Inductive Reasoning

75. Ⓐ Ⓑ Ⓒ Ⓓ
76. Ⓐ Ⓑ Ⓒ Ⓓ
77. Ⓐ Ⓑ Ⓒ Ⓓ
78. Ⓐ Ⓑ Ⓒ Ⓓ
79. Ⓐ Ⓑ Ⓒ Ⓓ

80. Ⓐ Ⓑ Ⓒ Ⓓ
81. Ⓐ Ⓑ Ⓒ Ⓓ
82. Ⓐ Ⓑ Ⓒ Ⓓ
83. Ⓐ Ⓑ Ⓒ Ⓓ
84. Ⓐ Ⓑ Ⓒ Ⓓ

Section 9: Information Ordering

85. Ⓐ Ⓑ Ⓒ Ⓓ
86. Ⓐ Ⓑ Ⓒ Ⓓ
87. Ⓐ Ⓑ Ⓒ Ⓓ
88. Ⓐ Ⓑ Ⓒ Ⓓ
89. Ⓐ Ⓑ Ⓒ Ⓓ

90. Ⓐ Ⓑ Ⓒ Ⓓ
91. Ⓐ Ⓑ Ⓒ Ⓓ
92. Ⓐ Ⓑ Ⓒ Ⓓ

Practice Test 2

Note: This test has 92 multiple-choice questions. Mark your answers on the answer sheet provided.

SECTION 1
Memorization

Begin by looking at the drawing of the neighborhood scene on the next two pages. You may look at the drawing for five minutes. At the end of the five-minute period, turn the page so that you can no longer see the drawing. Then you will be asked to answer 10 questions about the scene.

GO ON TO THE NEXT PAGE

GO ON TO THE NEXT PAGE

GO ON TO THE NEXT PAGE

1. How many motor vehicles were parked in front of houses in the scene?

   (A) 3
   (B) 5
   (C) 7
   (D) 9

2. How many total law enforcement and emergency vehicles were visible in the scene?

   (A) 0
   (B) 2
   (C) 4
   (D) 6

3. How many individuals were under arrest in the scene?

   (A) 0
   (B) 1
   (C) 2
   (D) 3

4. What type of vehicles appeared to be involved in a collision?

   (A) SUV and van
   (B) Van and pickup
   (C) Pick-up and sedan
   (D) Sedan and SUV

5. What was the lowest house number visible in the scene?

   (A) 2202
   (B) 2302
   (C) 2321
   (D) 2324

6. Based upon the clues provided in the scene, what was the name of the street?

   (A) Merritt Street
   (B) Montgomery Street
   (C) Park Street
   (D) Tree Avenue

7. How many total law enforcement personnel were visible in the scene?

   (A) 3
   (B) 5
   (C) 7
   (D) 9

GO ON TO THE NEXT PAGE

8. The house numbers were all numbered _____.

   (A) Odd
   (B) Even
   (C) Both odd and even, but non-consecutive
   (D) Consecutively

9. How many trees were visible in the scene?

   (A) 0
   (B) 1
   (C) 3
   (D) 5

10. How many law enforcement officers had their guns drawn?

    (A) 0
    (B) 1
    (C) 2
    (D) 3

STOP. THIS IS THE END OF SECTION 1.

Visualization

The first face shown, and identified as "suspect," was drawn based upon descriptions provided by witnesses of crimes. It is believed that the suspect has made an effort to change his/her appearance. Select the lettered face, shown beside the suspect's face, that most closely resembles the suspect.

11.

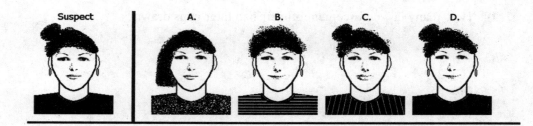

12.

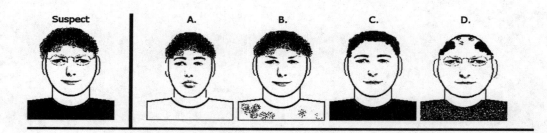

GO ON TO THE NEXT PAGE

13.

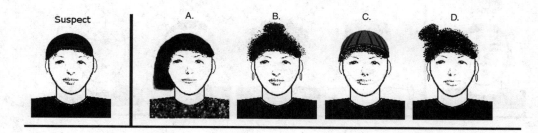

14.

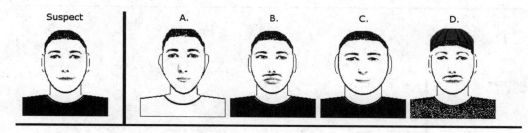

15.

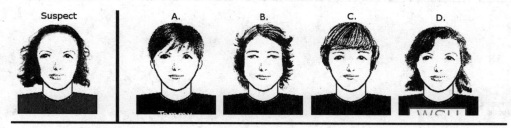

GO ON TO THE NEXT PAGE

16.

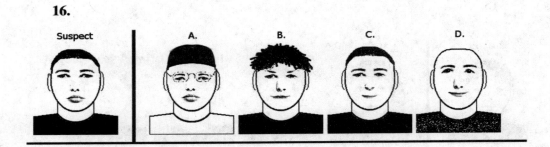

Select which of the four lettered vehicles most closely resembles the suspect's vehicle.

17.

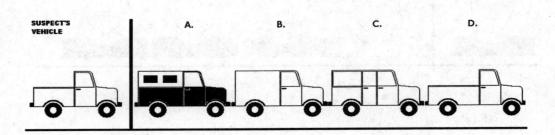

18.

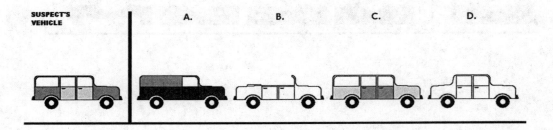

GO ON TO THE NEXT PAGE

19.

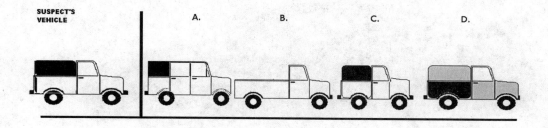

20.

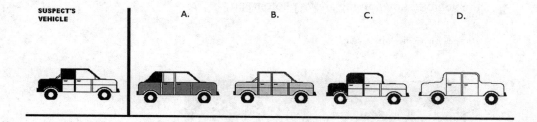

21.

Which one of the following photographs* best matches the tire rims of the vehicle shown in the above photograph?

*Images from WheelShack.com.

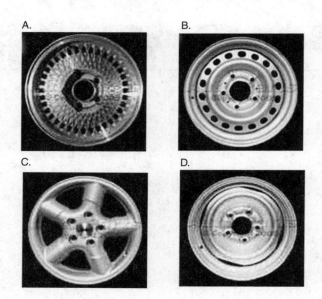

A.

B.

C.

D.

GO ON TO THE NEXT PAGE

22.

Which one of the following photographs* best matches the tire rims of the vehicle shown in the above photograph?

*Images from WheelShack.com

A.

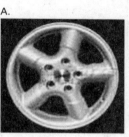

B.

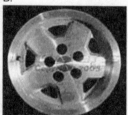

C.

D.

GO ON TO THE NEXT PAGE

23. Police Officer Johnson follows a perpetrator to a street with the following set of buildings. As he watches the buildings from across the street, Officer Johnson sees the perpetrator run into the fourth building from the right. Officer Johnson notes the shape of the building and runs to the back to try to stop the perpetrator from running out of the back of the building.

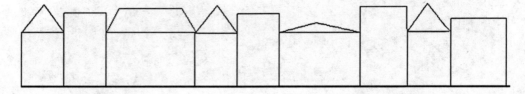

When Officer Johnson reaches the alley behind this set of buildings he is too close to count which building he should enter but is able to determine the shapes of the buildings as he passes them. Which building should Officer Johnson watch for the perpetrator?

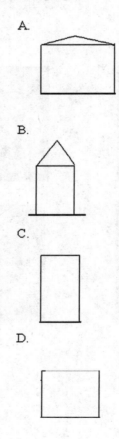

A.

B.

C.

D.

GO ON TO THE NEXT PAGE

24. Police Officer Johnson is on a beat patrol and passes the following set of buildings:

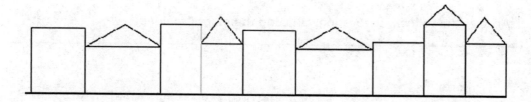

When Police Officer Johnson walks to the back of this set of buildings, which of the following will best match the buildings as seen from the back?

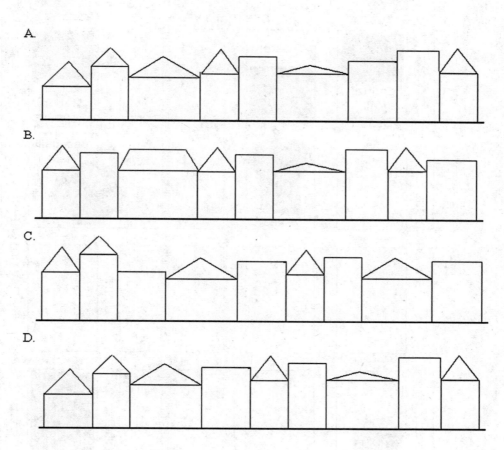

A.

B.

C.

D.

STOP. THIS IS THE END OF SECTION 2.

SPATIAL ORIENTATION

Answer the following questions utilizing the maps provided.

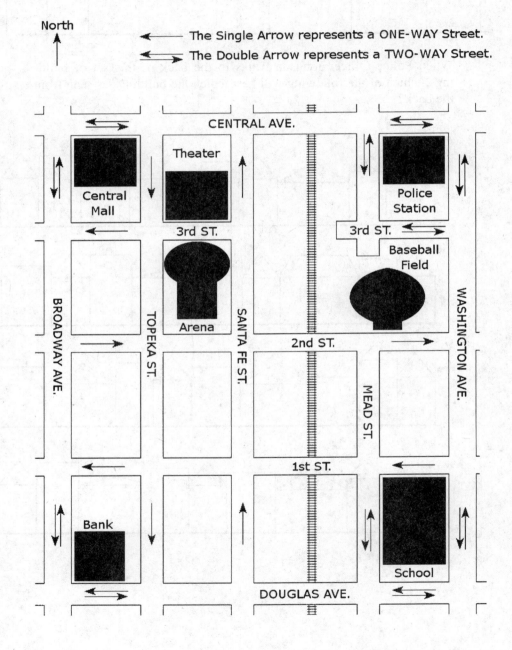

North

⟵ The Single Arrow represents a ONE-WAY Street.

⟷ The Double Arrow represents a TWO-WAY Street.

GO ON TO THE NEXT PAGE

25. You are on patrol at the intersection of Central and Broadway. You are in the middle of a turn to travel south on Broadway when you receive a call to respond to a traffic accident. You continue south two blocks, then east three blocks, and then south one block. When you stop you are at the intersection of:

(A) 2nd and Mead
(B) Mead and Douglas Ave
(C) 1st and Mead
(D) 1st and Santa Fe

26. You are sitting at the intersection of Central and Santa Fe. You are dispatched to 1st and Santa Fe. Which is the most direct route to reach your destination without breaking any traffic laws?

(A) Travel three blocks south on Santa Fe to 1st St.
(B) Travel one block west to Topeka, south four blocks to Douglas Ave, east one block to Santa Fe, and then north one block north to 1st St.
(C) Travel east two blocks to Washington Ave, south four blocks to Douglas Ave, west two blocks to Santa Fe, and then north one block to 1st St.
(D) Travel one block west to Topeka, south three blocks to 1st St., east one block to Santa Fe.

27. You are dispatched from the police station to the Arena, which has parking lot entrances on its southeast and southwest corners. If you are starting from Central and Washington, which is the most direct route to your destination without breaking any traffic laws?

(A) Travel two blocks west on Central, and two blocks south on Santa Fe, and enter the Arena from the southeast corner.
(B) Travel three blocks south on Washington, two blocks west on 1st street, one block north on Santa Fe, and enter the Arena from the southeast corner.
(C) Travel two blocks south on Washington, two blocks west on 2nd St, and enter the Arena from the southeast corner.
(D) Travel three blocks west on Central, two blocks south on Topeka, and enter the Arena from the southwest corner.

28. You are on patrol at the intersection of 3rd St. and Washington. You are continuing to travel south on Washington when you receive a call to respond to a battery. You continue to travel south two blocks, west two blocks, north two blocks, and then west two blocks. When you stop you are at the intersection of:

(A) 3rd and Topeka
(B) 2nd and Broadway
(C) 3rd and Broadway
(D) 3rd and Santa Fe

GO ON TO THE NEXT PAGE

29. You are on patrol, heading south through the intersection at Central and Broadway, when you see a vehicle matching the description provided in a recent drive-by shooting. You follow the vehicle while waiting for dispatch to respond to your request for information about the vehicle registration. You head south for two blocks, east for three blocks, south for two blocks, east for one block, then north for four blocks, then west for three blocks. You finally receive the information you need and you decide to pull the vehicle over. Where should you tell dispatch to send back-up?

(A) 3rd and Topeka
(B) 2nd and Santa Fe
(C) Central and Topeka
(D) Central and Washington

GO ON TO THE NEXT PAGE

TURN TO THE NEXT PAGE

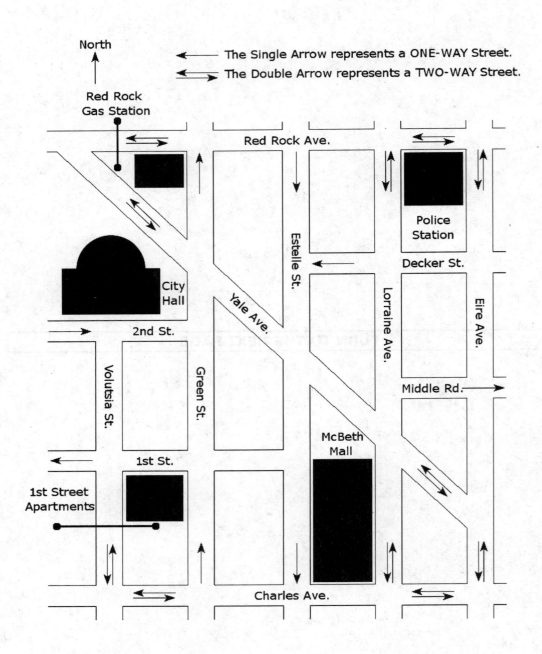

30. You are on patrol at the intersection of Charles and Eire Avenues. You are in the middle of a turn to travel west on Charles Ave. when you receive a call to respond to a traffic accident. You continue west four blocks, then north one block. When you stop you are at the intersection of:

(A) Redrock and Lorraine
(B) Redrock and Yale
(C) 1st and Volutia
(D) 1st and Charles

31. You are dispatched from the police station to City Hall, which has an entrance at 2nd and Green. If you are starting at Redrock and Eire, which is the most direct route to your destination without breaking any traffic laws?

(A) Travel one block south to Decker, two blocks west to Estelle, one block south to Yale, one block NW on Yale, south one block to 2nd and Green.
(B) Travel west three blocks to Green St, then south two blocks to 2nd and Green.
(C) Travel four blocks south on Eire, three blocks west on Charles St, and two blocks north to 2nd and Green.
(D) Travel three blocks south on Eire, three blocks northwest on Yale, and one block south to 2nd and Green.

32. You are on sitting at a stationary patrol at the corner of Redrock and Yale Avenues. You receive a call to respond to a domestic situation. You start your car and travel southeast two blocks, south one block, and then west two blocks. When you stop you are at the intersection of:

(A) Redrock and Lorraine
(B) Redrock and Yale
(C) 1st and Volutia
(D) 1st and Charles

33. You are on routine traffic patrol, heading north through the intersection at Charles and Volutsia, when you see a vehicle commit a traffic infraction. You activate your lights but the vehicle fails to stop. Then, the vehicle speeds up in an attempt to evade and elude. You carefully follow the vehicle after receiving permission. You travel two blocks north, then one block east, then a short block north, then three blocks southeast, then two blocks north, and two blocks west where the vehicle collides with a street light. Where should you notify dispatch to send assistance?

(A) Red Rock and Yale
(B) Red Rock and Lorraine
(C) Decker and Lorraine
(D) Decker and Estelle

GO ON TO THE NEXT PAGE

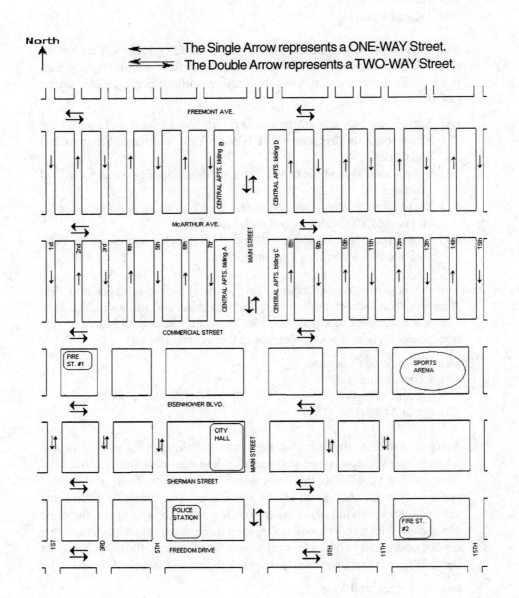

The Single Arrow represents a ONE-WAY Street.
The Double Arrow represents a TWO-WAY Street.

34. Officer Maxwell lives on the NW corner of 5th and McArthur. His address is 197 South 5th Street. He knows the address of the police station is 501 South 5th Street. He is called out to assist at an emergency at 297 South 5th Street. What is the closest intersection to the scene of the emergency?

(A) 5th and Commercial
(B) 5th and Eisenhower
(C) 5th and McArthur
(D) 5th and Fremont

35. You are on routine traffic patrol, heading north through the intersection at 9th and Freedom Drive, when you see a vehicle commit a traffic infraction. You activate your lights but the vehicle fails to stop. Then, the vehicle speeds up in an attempt to evade and elude. You carefully follow the vehicle after receiving permission. You note that you travel two blocks north, then one block east, then three blocks north, then two blocks west where the vehicle attempts to hide by pulling into a driveway and turning off its lights. Where should you notify dispatch to send assistance?

(A) 11th and Freemont
(B) 10th and Freemont
(C) 11th and McArthur Ave
(D) 10th and McArthur Ave

36. You are on patrol at the intersection of 1st and Freedom Avenue. You are proceeding east on Freedom when you receive a call to respond to a traffic accident. You continue east three blocks, then north four blocks, then west six blocks and north one block. When you stop you are at the intersection of:

(A) 3rd and Freemont
(B) 12th and Freemont
(C) 13th and Freemont
(D) 2nd and Freemont.

STOP. THIS IS THE END OF SECTION 3.

Verbal Expression

Answer the following questions. Some questions will require you to select the sentence that most accurately represents the facts, and other questions will require you to put the sentences into sequential order.

---

37. A police officer was the first to arrive at the scene of a possible neighborhood disturbance. He observes a large man, standing on top of a car, and hitting it with a sledgehammer. The neighbors are standing around watching, but no one is interfering in the destruction of the vehicle. When the officer's supervisor arrives at the scene he asks the officer for a brief report. The officer could report the information most correctly by stating:

(A) "The big guy on the car seems to be scaring the rest of these folks. They are too afraid to do anything to stop him."
(B) "The big guy on the car is out of control. We are going to need back-up."
(C) "The big guy is hitting the car with a sledge hammer, and the rest of these folks are just watching."
(D) "The big guy is tearing up someone's car and he needs to be stopped."

38. A police officer is dispatched to respond to a report of a foul odor coming from a house. When the officer arrives he is met by a neighbor who has a key to the house from which the odor is emanating. The neighbor explains he only uses the key when the homeowner is on vacation, but he hasn't seen the man in a few weeks. The officer takes the key, opens the door, and is almost overwhelmed by the strong smell in the house. Upon investigation he finds a man seated in a chair in the living room with an apparent gunshot wound to the head. When the officer's supervisor arrives at the scene he asks the officer for a brief report. The officer could report the information most correctly by stating:

(A) "We got us a homicide."
(B) "An adult male was found dead in the house. It looks like he has a gunshot wound in his head."
(C) "This guy has been dead in there for so long it had to have been a suicide."
(D) "An adult male was found dead in the house. It looks like he committed suicide."

GO ON TO THE NEXT PAGE

39. A police officer is dispatched to respond to a report of a child with a gunshot wound to the abdomen. The officer interviews the father, Mark, and learns these facts. When Mark was cleaning his gun the telephone rang. He left the gun on the table while he went to the adjoining room to answer the phone. Just a few moments later he heard a gunshot and Newton, his son, screamed. When the officer's supervisor arrives at the scene he asks the officer for a brief report. The officer could report the information most correctly by stating:

(A) "This guy shot his kid and he won't admit it."
(B) "This idiot left a loaded gun where a kid could reach it and then walked away."
(C) "The father reported that he was cleaning his gun. He put the gun down to answer the phone, and then heard a gunshot and his son scream."
(D) "The father reported that when he was cleaning his gun the phone rang. He put the gun down for just a second while he went to answer the phone. Just a couple seconds after he set down the gun, his son grabbed it and shot himself."

40. A police officer is dispatched to respond to a report of a vehicle accident. When he arrives he speaks to the driver. The driver said he saw someone on the freeway overpass and then a large rock hit his windshield. The rock shattered his windshield and caused him to lose control of his car. His car is totalled and his family is being transported to the hospital for minor injuries. When the officer's supervisor arrives at the scene he asks the officer for a brief report. The officer could report the information most correctly by stating:

(A) "The driver of the vehicle lost control of his vehicle and totalled it."
(B) "The driver of the vehicle claims that someone threw a rock off the overpass and hit his windshield. He lost control of his car, totalled the vehicle, and his family has suffered minor injuries."
(C) "The driver of the vehicle told me that a rock hit his windshield and shattered it. He thought he saw someone on the overpass just before his windshield was hit. After his windshield was hit he lost control of his car, totalled the vehicle, and his family has suffered minor injuries."
(D) "This guy is already looking for a way to make some money off this accident. Either someone else threw a rock at his car and caused this wreck, or a rock fell off the overpass and the state is going to be liable."

GO ON TO THE NEXT PAGE

41. A police officer is dispatched to respond to a report of a home invasion. When he arrives at the scene he speaks to the homeowner, Darren. Darren tells the officer that he awakened in the night when he heard a noise. He quietly went past the children's rooms and checked that they were okay. Then he went down the stairs, grabbing a gun from the hall closet. He saw a person in his home that he did not recognize, who appeared to be loaded down by carrying Darren's television out the door. Darren shot at the intruder but claims he missed. He also admits that he shot at the intruder's vehicle, a large dark-colored van. When the officer's supervisor arrives at the scene he asks the officer for a brief report. The officer could report the information most correctly by stating:

(A) "We are looking for a possible gunshot victim. I will notify the hospitals to be on the lookout."

(B) "The homeowner stated that he shot twice: once at the intruder and once at the intruder's van. He claims he missed both times."

(C) "The homeowner stated that he shot at both the intruder and the intruder's van. He claims he missed the intruder when he shot at him. We should be on alert for a large dark colored van in this area with possible bullet holes."

(D) "The homeowner claims he shot at an intruder, but he never mentioned where his wife was then, or is now. I think we are looking at a possible murder."

42. Officer Patterson is preparing an incident report. The report will include the following statements. These statements are not listed in the correct order. Put the sentences into the most logical order.

1. *Mrs. Adams explained that she then saw Abe carry the teapot out to the driveway where he handed it to Ben.*

2. *Mrs. Adams stated that on Thursday evening she saw Abe pick up the silver teapot with her name engraved on it, which she received for her 45th birthday.*

3. *Mrs. Adams concluded her statement by stating that she is very angry about the loss of her teapot because she had told Abe numerous times to never touch it.*

4. *Officer Patterson responded when Mrs. Adams called for a police officer to come to her home to take her statement.*

5. *Mrs. Adams began by stating that her son, Abe, and his friend, Ben, were at her house Thursday evening.*

(A) 1, 2, 3, 4, 5
(B) 1, 3, 5, 2, 4
(C) 4, 5, 2, 1, 3
(D) 4, 5, 3, 2, 1

GO ON TO THE NEXT PAGE

43. Officer Jones is preparing an incident report. The report will include the following statements. These statements are not listed in the correct order. Put the sentences into the most logical order.

1. "Honest Clem" Stephens, a used car dealer, called for police assistance.
2. The couple asked to drive the minivan for a few hours to see how it handled on the highway versus city driving. Because it was a common request "Honest Clem" agreed.
3. A week has passed and the couple has not returned the minivan.
4. Honest Clem told Officer Jones that a nice young couple came in looking for a new car.
5. Honest Clem took the young couple to test drive several different models before they decided on a minivan that they liked.

(A) 1, 2, 3, 4, 5
(B) 1, 4, 5, 2, 3
(C) 4, 3, 2, 1, 5
(D) 4, 5, 3, 2, 1

44. Officer Matthews is preparing an incident report. The report will include the following statements. These statements are not listed in the correct order. Put the sentences into the most logical order.

1. Sam claimed that a new company policy required farmers to give the company title to the cattle being shipped so that the company would have legal right to sell the cattle.
2. Farmer Happy, trusting the company, helped Sam load the cattle, and signed the forms giving Sam title to the cattle in exchange for a verbal agreement that the company would pay Farmer Happy 90 percent of the amount of money that the cattle sold for at market.
3. Farmer Happy contracted with The Transport and Sell Company, a company he had used before to haul his cattle to market and sell them, to pick up 15 head of cattle for transport to market.
4. On the appointed day a semi-truck pulled up in his yard to pick up his cattle, driven by a new driver named Sam.
5. Two hours after Sam left a semi-truck from the company, driven by the driver Happy usually dealt with, showed up claiming to be from the same company, and that driver also claimed he had never heard of Sam.

(A) 1, 2, 3, 4, 5
(B) 3, 4, 1, 2, 5
(C) 4, 3, 2, 1, 5
(D) 3, 5, 4, 2, 1

GO ON TO THE NEXT PAGE

45. Officer Hussein is preparing an incident report. The report will include the following statements. These statements are not listed in the correct order. Put the sentences into the most logical order.

1. *Officer Hussein also found a white male who appeared to be in his late teens in the Johnson's kitchen, going through the drawers and holding an empty pillowcase.*
2. *Upon arriving on the scene Officer Hussein found that a large window has been broken.*
3. *Mr. Johnson and his wife are hiding upstairs in the bedroom closet and are calling from a cellular telephone.*
4. *Mr. Johnson called police at 2:00 A.M., to request immediate assistance at his home.*
5. *Mr. Johnson thinks that he hears a prowler in his kitchen.*

(A) 4, 5, 3, 2, 1
(B) 3, 4, 1, 2, 5
(C) 4, 3, 2, 1, 5
(D) 3, 5, 4, 2, 1

46. Officer Readrow is preparing an incident report. The report will include the following statements. These statements are not listed in the correct order. Put the sentences into the most logical order.

1. *The City has contacted the police to report a theft of utility services.*
2. *Upon contacting the City, the officer is informed that Krystal Smith is the occupant of the home where the utility services are being used without permission.*
3. *Krystal agrees to talk to you. She tells you that she can't afford to purchase all of her utilities.*
4. *After about twenty minutes, Krystal finally admits that she has figured out how to hook up her water without notifying the city.*
5. *Before talking with Krystal, you conduct further investigation. You learn that Krystal Smith is 19-years-old, works at T-Quik, and has lived on her own for two years.*

(A) 1, 2, 5, 3, 4
(B) 3, 4, 1, 2, 5
(C) 1, 2, 4, 5, 3
(D) 1, 2, 4, 3, 5

STOP. THIS IS THE END OF SECTION 4.

VERBAL COMPREHENSION

Read each scenario presented and complete the questions.

SCENARIO NO. 1

Typically, officers must have probable cause to believe that an individual is involved in criminal activity before interfering in that person's right to be free from governmental restraint. However, in limited circumstances an officer may have legal authority to make an *investigatory stop*. An investigatory stop is an action by law enforcement to interfere with an individual's right to liberty. This interference must be based upon an officer's reasonable suspicion that criminal activity is occurring and must be limited to that amount of time necessary to clarify the suspicious behavior.

When making a stop based on reasonable suspicion an officer need only be able to clearly state articulable facts to support his belief that criminal activity is occurring before he interferes in an individual's right to liberty. Articulable facts are more than a mere hunch. An officer should be ready to clearly list several facts that formed the basis for his belief that criminal activity was occurring.

While executing an investigatory stop, officers must act quickly to either confirm or dispel their suspicions. Courts will always inquire into the length of the detention. If the length of the stop is unreasonable, any evidence obtained from the stop will be suppressed at trial.

Why is the period of detention important? Remember, a *stop* is an investigatory tool available to law enforcement for actions based on less than probable cause. If a stop lasts too long, it may turn into a *de facto* arrest. An arrest is only lawful when supported by probable cause to believe that criminal activity is occurring: a standard somewhat higher than reasonable suspicion. Without probable cause to support the stop, the stop becomes an unlawful arrest.

47. According to this article, the length of an investigatory stop is important because:

    (A) A long stop will cause a court to inquire.
    (B) If a stop lasts too long, it may turn into a *de facto* arrest.
    (C) An investigatory stop interferes with an individual's right to liberty.
    (D) An investigatory stop is a search.

48. A *stop* is _____.

    (A) An interference with a citizen's liberty.
    (B) An illegal act by law enforcement.
    (C) A search for actions based on less than probable cause.
    (D) A traffic enforcement tool.

GO ON TO THE NEXT PAGE

49. Generally, before law enforcement arrests an individual, police must have _____ to believe that a crime is occurring/has occurred and that the individual participated in the crime.

(A) Reasonable suspicion
(B) Probable cause
(C) Beyond a reasonable doubt
(D) Articulable facts.

SCENARIO NO. 2

Officer Jones sees a vehicle he does not recognize parked on the street in a residential district that he regularly patrols. When Officer Jones checks the time he sees that it is 2:05 A.M. Officer Jones notices that an individual is sitting in the vehicle. The occupant appears to be alone. None of the homes in the area have any lights on, and it appears that everyone in the neighborhood is asleep. When Officer Jones slowly drives past the vehicle the occupant quickly lies down in the seat. Officer Jones drives around the block and re-approaches the vehicle from behind. The occupant is now sitting up again and appears to be watching Jones' patrol car in his rear view window. As Officer Jones parks his vehicle behind the occupied vehicle, the occupant jumps out of his car and starts to run toward an area between two houses. Officer Jones runs after the individual, and shouts at him to "stop!" Although the individual did not respond to Officer Jones, Jones was able to catch him as he attempted to climb over a fence into a backyard.

50. According to the preceding passage, Officer Jones drove past the suspicious vehicle _____ times without stopping before finally stopping to contact the occupant.

(A) 1
(B) 2
(C) 3
(D) 4

51. According to the preceding passage, Officer Jones was suspicious about the vehicle for all of the following reasons EXCEPT which?

(A) Officer Jones sees an occupied vehicle he does not recognize parked on the street in a residential district that he regularly patrols at 2:05 A.M.
(B) Officer Jones notices that the individual is sitting alone in the vehicle.
(C) When Officer Jones slowly drives past the vehicle the occupant quickly lies down in the seat.
(D) As Officer Jones parks his vehicle behind the occupied vehicle, the occupant jumps out of his car and starts to run toward an area between two houses.

GO ON TO THE NEXT PAGE

52. According to the preceding passage, Officer Jones discovered that _____.

(A) The individual was a teenager who was afraid to go in the house because he had missed curfew.

(B) The individual was a registered sex offender who just needed some alone time.

(C) The individual lived at the house where the car was parked, and was in the car searching for his wallet because he had discovered it was not in his pant's pocket when he was getting undressed. He had been wrongfully arrested three years earlier and still feared police.

(D) He did not have any information about the occupant of the vehicle or his reason for being in the vehicle in the middle of the night.

SCENARIO NO. 3

Officer Leventhal responds to a report of a battery. Upon arriving at the scene Officer Leventhal speaks with Adam who was involved in the incident. Adam tells Officer Leventhal that he decided to go for a run on the City Park jogging path. He had been mugged the previous month so he was a little nervous. About half way through his run he noticed that someone was following him. He became concerned, but did not leave the jogging path feeling that it was the safest place to be. Soon he could tell by the sound of the pursuer's footsteps that he was getting closer. Adam reported he was very scared, but determined not to be a victim again. He turned around and punched his pursuer in the face.

53. According to the preceding passage, the only statement that accurately reflects the information known by Officer Leventhal is:

(A) Adam was a victim of a mugging.

(B) Adam hit another runner in the face.

(C) Adam had a right to use self-defense to protect himself against his pursuer.

(D) Adam became very frightened when he believed he was being pursued and hit his pursuer in the face.

54. According to the preceding passage, Adam was nervous to go running because:

(A) He had been attacked in the park a few weeks earlier.

(B) He had been mugged the previous month.

(C) He had been mugged downtown the previous month.

(D) He had been mugged while jogging the previous month.

GO ON TO THE NEXT PAGE

55. According to the preceding passage, the only fact that police have about Adam's pursuer was that he:

(A) Raced to catch up with Adam
(B) Was a faster runner than Adam
(C) Was a mugger
(D) Would not have harmed Adam.

SCENARIO NO. 4

Officers Pam and Jornak are called to a report of a homicide at a small sports bar. Barbara, a regular patron of the bar, points out the bartender's body to the officers. She said that no one had been paying attention to what was going on in the bar until they heard someone scream because everyone was watching a good game on television. She only left her table to get beers from the bar. She didn't realize anyone was throwing a knife.

Beth, the waitress is also still on the scene. She says that the bartender was killed by Tom Stern, who she points to at a nearby table. Beth tells you that everyone in the bar was yelling at Tom to stop throwing knives because he was going to hurt someone. Tom spent about two hours throwing Bowie knives at the dartboard without incident. Then, he sent a knife flying away from the dartboard. It landed in the bartender's heart and killed him instantly.

When Officer Jornak talks to Tom he explains that he was at the bar that night playing a game he invented which he calls "Scarier Darts." The game is very like darts but uses Bowie knives in place of darts. Most nights Tom can get someone else in the bar to play with him, but that evening no one else was interested in playing. However, everyone watched him play and cheered him on. So, he played until he missed the dartboard and the knife hit the bartender.

56. According to the previous passage, which of the following statements most accurately reflects information given to the officers at the scene?

(A) Tom left the scene.
(B) Tom owed the bar a lot of money for damages from throwing knives.
(C) Tom had played his knife game in the bar before.
(D) Tom and the bartender did not get along.

GO ON TO THE NEXT PAGE

57. You believe it is critical to know whether Tom had been disrupting the rest of the bar patrons by throwing a knife at the dartboard for two hours. Which of the statements was most believable?

(A) Barbara's statement, because she didn't work for the bar, had no way of knowing either Tom or the bartender, and wasn't emotionally involved in what happened there.

(B) Beth's statement, because Barbara's statement is so unbelievable.

(C) Beth's statement, because she admits to being aware of what was happening in the bar and her statement is similar to Tom's statement.

(D) Tom's statement, because he has no interest in the outcome of the investigation.

58. Which of the following most accurately reflects what happened based upon the statements provided?

(A) Tom Stern threw a knife and it struck the bartender and killed him.

(B) Tom Stern was dating Barbara, and he was mad at the bartender for asking Barbara out.

(C) Tom Stern accidentally killed the bartender.

(D) Tom Stern was throwing the knife to irritate the waitress.

STOP. THIS IS THE END OF SECTION 5.

PROBLEM SENSITIVITY

Read the information that is provided and then answer questions 59–60.

The Department of Police and Fire have the following standard procedure for first responders arriving at the scene of a fire.

1. *Note the time of your arrival. Note the color of the flames in order to assess the intensity of the fire. Also, note the color and odor of the smoke. Keep your patrol vehicle back from the burning structure to avoid explosion.*
2. *Note the people at the scene, including those near or leaving the scene of the fire. Note any unusual behavior of people at the scene. Evacuate the area or nearby homes if the situation warrants.*
3. *Note any covered windows or doors. Note whether the covering is shades, blankets, newspapers, or any other method an arsonist might use to delay the discovery of the fire. Do not knock out any windows as the addition of air to the fire could cause it to accelerate.*
4. *Note whether any obstacles have been placed to hinder access to the building, such as a dumpster or pile of trash placed in front of a door. If doors or windows are already open and away from the area on fire, law enforcement may approach that window/door and call out for possible victims trapped inside.*
5. *Law enforcement should avoid entering a burning structure, but should note the Fire Department's method of entry into the building. Note whether any doors were locked or left open. Note whether any doors looked forced open prior to the fire.*

59. Officer May is the first responder to a building fire. He notices that he arrived at 9:10 P.M. He notes that the flames coming from the building are yellow-orange in color and that a gasoline odor exists. He then notes that no one is around the scene and that trash cans loaded with rocks have been placed in front of the two doors. Given this information what should Officer May do next?

   (A) Back away and take no further action.
   (B) Begin a preliminary determination about possible victims without entering the building.
   (C) Continue to take notes about the status of the building.
   (D) Enter the safest area of the building and look for possible victims.

GO ON TO THE NEXT PAGE

---

60. Which of the following actions would be the most potentially dangerous mistake Officer May could make?

    (A) Knock out all of the windows in preparation for the Fire Department's arrival.

    (B) Leave the scene to go in search of a fire extinguisher.

    (C) Park his patrol vehicle next to the back door to prevent any bystanders from entering the burning structure.

    (D) Begin evacuation procedures.

Read the information that is provided below and then answer questions 61–64.

Contact between police and members of the public range from friendly interactions to investigative encounters. The requirements for authorized police contact with a private person vary according to the degree of intrusiveness involved.

1. *Consensual contact. No justification is necessary. The officer should exert no authority in the situation and the citizen should understand that they are free to leave and not required to respond. Refusal to give consent to search or to answer questions does not create reasonable suspicion or probable cause.*

2. *Dog sniff. No justification is necessary. A sniff must be reasonably conducted and the person's freedom of movement or control of his or her property must not be interfered with.*

3. *Investigative Stop. Reasonable suspicion. An officer who has specific facts supporting a suspicion that a person is committing, has committed, or is about to commit a crime may stop and detain a person briefly, generally less than ten minutes. The officer may ask for identification, inquire about the person's suspicious behavior. Once the purpose of the detention is carried out the detainee must be released, unless clear evidence of criminal conduct is discovered.*

4. *Protective frisk. Reasonable suspicion. An officer may frisk a person if the officer has specific facts supporting a suspicion that the person is armed and a danger to the officer or others. The justification for a frisk may arise in any encounter with a private person.*

5. *Arrest. Probable cause. An officer has probable cause to arrest if facts and circumstances known to the officer at the time of the arrest justify a reasonable belief that the person has committed or is committing a crime.*

GO ON TO THE NEXT PAGE

61. Officer Lee notices that an unknown male has stopped his vehicle next to another vehicle to talk to a second unknown male. Officer Lee is aware that area residents have been complaining about drug trafficking in the area. Officer Lee does not see any evidence of drugs or money, but he is approximately 200 feet away from the two men. Officer Lee approaches the two men and asks them to pull their vehicles to the side of the road. He then asks to see identification for each driver. When he sees that the addresses listed on both the licenses are for homes just down the street he returns the licenses and tells both men to have a nice day. What type of police/citizen interaction has occurred?

(A) Consensual contact
(B) Investigative stop
(C) Arrest
(D) No interaction

62. Officer Jones conducts a routine traffic stop. The driver of the vehicle is acting very nervous and her hands are shaking. Officer Jones is suspicious of her behavior and asks for permission to search the vehicle. The driver refuses to give her consent. Based on this information, what may Officer Jones do next?

(A) Nothing.
(B) Require the driver to wait 25 minutes for the arrival of a drug-sniffing dog.
(C) Remove the driver from her vehicle and frisk her for weapons.
(D) Arrest the driver on suspicion of drug trafficking.

63. Officer Leon is walking through the mall when he sees two girls racing out of a store clutching their shopping bags to their chests. He sees the store manager yelling at the girls to come back. The correct level of police/citizen interaction at this point is:

(A) Consensual contact
(B) Investigative stop
(C) Arrest
(D) No interaction

64. Officer Lopez approaches an individual he knows is wanted on an active warrant for attempted murder. The correct level of police/citizen interaction at this point is:

(A) Consensual contact
(B) Investigative stop
(C) Arrest
(D) No interaction

GO ON TO THE NEXT PAGE

65. Police Officer Chow interviews four witnesses to a murder, which occurred outside of a carwash. Each of the witnesses was present at the time of the shooting. They described the perpetrator as follows:

Witness No. 1. She had short brown hair, a tattoo on her neck, and baggy shirt jeans. She was barefoot.

Witness No. 2. He was short with brown hair, a loose fitting button up shirt hanging open over a white t-shirt. He had baggy blue jeans on, and raggedy old tennis shoes.

Witness No. 3. She was average height but dressed like a boy. She had brown hair and really tanned skin. She had on a short-sleeved button up shirt over a white t-shirt, and baggy blue jeans. She had a tattoo on her neck, which was clearly visible because her hair was so short.

Witness No. 4. She was average height and was wearing baggy clothes and old tennis shoes. Her hair was pulled up into a bun so a big bruise was visible on her neck.

Based on the descriptions provided, which of the four witness statements is most likely to be correct?

(A) Witness No. 1
(B) Witness No. 2
(C) Witness No. 3
(D) Witness No. 4

GO ON TO THE NEXT PAGE

66. Police Officer Klough interviews four witnesses to a carjacking, which occurred on a busy street adjacent to a shopping mall in the late afternoon. The subject vehicle and the vehicles driven by the three other witnesses were waiting for a traffic light to turn green, when the driver of the subject vehicle was approached by the perpetrator and forced out of his vehicle. The victim and the three witnesses described the perpetrator as follows:

Witness No. 1. He was really big: about 6 ft 2 in and 250 lbs. Also, he had light brown skin. Maybe he was Hispanic.

Witness No. 2. He was average size: probably 5 ft 11 in and 160 lbs. He seemed to have dark Caucasian coloring, but it was hard to tell if he was really tanned, or maybe Hispanic. He was a young guy. He had long straight black hair cut long on the top and really short on the sides. He was wearing a black t-shirt and black jeans, and he seemed in really good shape.

Witness No. 3. He was average height and weight, in his early twenties, had dark brown hair cut short on the sides. He was dressed all in black, but was carrying an army green backpack.

Witness No. 4. He was average height, not quite 6'. He looked to be between 20 and 25-years-old. He weighed about 150–160 lbs, and he had a very athletic build. He had straight black hair under a green bandana, and was dressed in a black t-shirt and black slacks.

Based on the above information, Officer Klough should recognize that there is a problem with the description given by:

(A) Witness No. 1
(B) Witness No. 2
(C) Witness No. 3
(D) Witness No. 4

STOP. THIS IS THE END OF SECTION 6.

DEDUCTIVE REASONING

Answer questions 67–71 using the information provided below and in the questions.

Assault: A person commits the offense of assault if the person:

(1) Intentionally, knowingly, or recklessly causes bodily injury to a human being, including the person's spouse;

(2) Intentionally or knowingly threatens a human being with imminent bodily injury, including the person's spouse; or

(3) Intentionally or knowingly causes physical contact with a human being when the person knows or should reasonably believe that the other will regard the contact as offensive or provocative.

Aggravated Assault: A person commits aggravated assault if the person commits an assault as defined above and the person:

(1) Causes serious bodily injury to a human being, including the person's spouse; or

(2) Uses or exhibits a deadly weapon during the commission of an assault.

John sees his wife talking to Bill, a man who plays softball with John. He becomes enraged and approaches the two, while pulling up his sleeves. His wife notes that John's face is dark red and his expression is very angry. When John reaches his wife and Bill, he gets two inches from her face and says in a threatening voice, "I am going to kill you." Then John turns to Bill and thumps Bill on the chest with his finger twice and says, "Stay away from my wife."

67. Which of the following crimes has John committed against his wife?

   (A) Assault type (2)
   (B) Assault type (3)
   (C) Aggravated assault type (1)
   (D) No assault type crime

68. Which of the following crimes has John committed against Bill?

   (A) Assault type (1)
   (B) Assault type (3)
   (C) Aggravated assault type (1)
   (D) No assault type crime

GO ON TO THE NEXT PAGE

Ben is being driven crazy by his neighbor's barking dog. He grabs his shotgun and walks to the fence that separates their property. He points the gun at the dog and tells his neighbor he is going to kill it. The neighbor steps between Ben and the dog and says, "Put your gun down, Ben." Ben says, "I'll shoot you if I have to. Get out of the way!" Ben's wife, seeing this exchange, races out and yells, "Ben put down the gun!" Ben tells her, "Shut up! I can't take all this noise anymore."

69. What crime has Ben committed against his neighbor?

   (A) Assault type (2)
   (B) Aggravated assault type (1)
   (C) Aggravated assault type (2)
   (D) No assault type crime

70. What crime has Ben committed against his neighbor's dog?

   (A) Assault type (2)
   (B) Aggravated assault type (1)
   (C) Aggravated assault type (2)
   (D) No assault type crime

71. What crime has Ben committed against his wife?

   (A) Assault type (2)
   (B) Assault type (3)
   (C) Aggravated assault type (2)
   (D) No assault type crime

GO ON TO THE NEXT PAGE

Answer question 72 based on the following information.

Criminal Mischief: A person commits the offense of criminal mischief if, without the effective consent of the owner:

(1) He intentionally or knowingly damages or destroys the property of another;

(2) He intentionally or knowingly tampers with the property of the owner and causes either financial loss or substantial inconvenience to the owner or a third person; or

(3) He intentionally or knowingly marks upon the property of another, including inscriptions, slogans, drawings, or paintings, on the tangible property of the owner.

72. Which of the following scenarios best represents an example of "criminal mischief"?

(A) Mylo sneaks onto his neighbor's property without permission to use it as a short cut to his best friend's house.

(B) Mylo takes the pool furniture from his neighbor's back yard and sells it to get money to buy drugs.

(C) Mylo is tired of hearing the neighbor's dog barking. He has complained to the neighbor, but because the animal is a valuable stud dog, the neighbors don't want to cause it additional stress by muzzling it. Late at night, Mylo sneaks into his neighbors' back yard and releases the dog from its kennel. The dog runs off and is never seen again.

(D) Mylo loves to annoy his neighbors, so he parks his car on the street in front of their house and turns his music up as loud as it will go.

Answer question 73 based on the following information.

Theft: A person commits the offense of theft if he unlawfully appropriates the property of another with intent to permanently deprive the owner of the use of the property.

73. Which of the following scenarios best represents an example of "theft"?

(A) Tara takes her neighbor's lawn chairs without asking to use during her dinner party.

(B) Tara takes her neighbor's child because she wants one of her own.

(C) Tara finds a $100 bill lying on the sidewalk near her house. She picks it up and keeps it.

(D) Tara finds her neighbor's poodle that has wandered into Tara's backyard. She brings the poodle into her house and keeps it.

GO ON TO THE NEXT PAGE

Answer question 74 based on the following information.

Mayhem: A person commits the offense of mayhem if he acts with intent to cause harm or disfigure, cuts out or maims the tongue, puts out or destroys an eye, cuts or tears off an ear, cuts, slits or mutilates the nose or lip, or cuts off or disables a limb or member, of another person.

74. Which of the following scenarios best represents an example of *mayhem*?

(A) Clevon is driving too fast and hits a pedestrian. The pedestrian loses his eye.

(B) Clevon is playing with a knife, seeing how fast he can move it between his fingers, when suddenly he slices off his little finger.

(C) Clevon hates Maury. He waits until Maury is alone and then jumps him from behind and beats Maury's face until Maury is unconscious. Maury suffers a split lip, broken nose, two black eyes and a concussion.

(D) Clevon is pitching for his college baseball team, when the pitcher from the other team steps up to the plate. Clevon throws a fastball and it hits the other player in the face, destroying his eye.

STOP. THIS IS THE END OF SECTION 7.

INDUCTIVE REASONING

Read the information provided and then answer the questions.

Police Office Ludwig received three reports of home break-ins that all occurred in the same neighborhood during the week of June 15–21. Each report included a description of a suspect(s).

Report No. 1 (June 16): Two white males in their late teens. One was 5 ft 10 in, 150 lbs, with strawberry blond hair cut short. The other was 6 ft, 200 lbs, and wearing a ball cap which covered his hair. They both wore jeans, tennis shoes, and t-shirts.

Report No. 2 (June 18): One Hispanic male in his early twenties. He was 5 ft 11 in, 165 lbs, long dark hair held back in a short ponytail. He was wearing dark work pants and a white tank top. He appeared to have a tattoo on his right forearm.

Report No. 3 (June 19): One white male, about 18-years-old. He was tall and heavyset with very short dark brown hair. He wore jeans and a t-shirt.

On June 22nd another report of a home break-in was received. In this case, however, the four young men living in the house surprised the suspect, tackled him to the ground, and held him there while they waited for the police to arrive. Police found items from the young men's home in the suspect's car. The description of the suspect in this break-in is:

Report No. 4 (June 22): One white male, about 18-years-old, 5 ft 11 in, 160 lbs, with short blondish hair, and no visible tattoos.

75. Based on the description of the suspects in the first three reports, the suspect in Report No. 4 should also be considered a suspect in:

    (A) Report No. 1, but not Report Nos. 2 or 3
    (B) Report No. 2, but not Report Nos. 1 or 3
    (C) Report Nos. 1 and 3, but not Report No. 2
    (D) Report No. 3, but not Report Nos. 1 or 2

Police Officer Betts meets with store managers from the Westridge Shopping Mall. They are frustrated with the high number of shoplifting cases that have occurred in the last few weeks. They seem to think that the cases are related, so Officer Betts goes back to the station and pulls the reports of the six most recent occurrences.

GO ON TO THE NEXT PAGE

Report No. 1 (December 5, 5:15 P.M.): One black female, approximately 16, 5 ft 5 in, 130 lbs, with short black hair and pierced ears.

Report No. 2 (December 5, 5:17 P.M.): One white female, approximately 16, 5 ft 4 in, 115 lbs, short blond hair, very bad complexion. She had on too much makeup, and several rings.

Report No. 3 (December 7, 5:45 P.M.): One white female, approximately 17, 5 ft 7 in, 145 lbs, brown hair worn in a long ponytail. Her left ear was pierced multiple times.

Report No. 4 (December 7, 6:15 P.M.): One Asian female, approximately 20, 5 ft 3 in, 115 lbs, long black hair. She wore a lot of makeup.

Report No. 5 (December 7, 7:30 P.M.): One white female, approximately 17, 5 ft 5 in, very slender, hair under a cap, poor complexion.

Report No. 6 (December 8, 10:30 A.M.): One black female, approximately 40, 5 ft 3 in, 165 lbs, with hair in long braids. She had a tattoo around her wrist.

76. After reading the reports, Officer Betts has reason to believe:

(A) None of the recent incidents are related.

(B) Report Nos. 1 and 6 are related, but none of the other cases are related.

(C) Report Nos. 2 and 5 are related, but none of the other cases are related.

(D) Report Nos. 2, 3 and 5 are related, but none of the other cases are related.

Police Officer Mayfair is assigned to the local high school as the school resource officer. School administration has spoken to him about targeting bullying on campus, so he has begun by reviewing reports of incidents that have unidentified suspects.

Report No. 1: Female Freshman student reported being threatened by unidentified white male student, approximately 5 ft 9 in, 150 lbs, dirty brown hair, and a poor complexion.

Report No. 2: Male Freshman student reported being held down by three student athletes wearing letter jackets, while a fourth student went through the freshman's backpack. Two of the suspects were Hispanic, one was white and one was black. They were all described as average build.

GO ON TO THE NEXT PAGE

Report No. 3: Male Freshman student reported being shoved into a locker by two unknown older students, while other students stood around and laughed. One of the suspects was white and the other was black. Both were described as "bigger" than the victim.

Report No. 4: Male Junior student reported having his backpack taken from him in the library, and dumped out on the floor of the main hallway. The suspect in this case is believed to be a white male student, also in the Junior class. The suspect is described at 5 ft 11 in, 160 lbs, dark brown hair, well-dressed.

A few days after reviewing these reports, Officer Mayfair interrupts a situation involving a freshman student being held by one senior student while another senior student goes through the freshman's locker and dumps his belongings onto the floor. Both of the senior students are Hispanic, well-dressed in jeans, dress shirts, and letterman jackets. One is approximately 6ft, 180 lbs, while the other is slightly shorter and slimmer.

77. After reading the reports, Officer Mayfair has reason to believe:

    (A) None of the incidents are related.
    (B) Report No. 2 is related to Officer Mayfair's new case, but none of the other cases are related.
    (C) Report Nos. 2 and 3 are related to Officer Mayfair's new case, but none of the other cases are related.
    (D) Report Nos. 2, 3 and 4 are related to Officer Mayfair's new case, but the other case is not related.

Officer Tao has been assigned to a special task force targeting crime that occurs within a one-mile area. The task force has determined that most carjacking takes place between 8 P.M. and 10 P.M. on Friday, Saturday, and Sunday evenings. Muggings are most likely to occur between 10 P.M. and 1 A.M. in the commercial district, while thefts are most likely to occur between 1 A.M. and 4 A.M. in the Sunset Apartment Complex. Parking lots are the favorite places to commit a carjacking, and most carjackers use a handgun to carry out their crime, while unlighted side streets are the scenes for most muggings. Thefts are usually occurring from unlocked cars parked in front of the owner's apartment.

78. Officer Tao would be most likely to reduce the number of carjackings by patrolling:

    (A) 8 P.M. to 10 P.M. in the commercial district
    (B) 10 P.M. to 1 A.M. around the mall parking lots
    (C) 1 A.M. to 4 A.M. in the commercial district
    (D) 8 P.M. to 10 P.M. around the mall parking lots

GO ON TO THE NEXT PAGE

79. Officer Tao would be most likely to reduce muggings by patrolling:

(A) 8 P.M. to 10 P.M. in the commercial district
(B) 10 P.M. to 1 A.M. around the mall parking lots
(C) 10 P.M. to 1 A.M. in commercial district
(D) 1 A.M. to 4 A.M. in areas with unlighted side streets

80. Officer Tao would be most likely to reduce thefts by patrolling:

(A) 1 A.M. to 4 A.M. at the apartment complex
(B) 1 A.M. to 4 A.M. in the commercial district
(C) 10 P.M. to 1 A.M. at the apartment complex
(D) 8 P.M. to 10 P.M. in areas with unlighted side streets

Officer Menendez patrols beat 4, an area that is very diverse. After several months Officer Menendez comes to the conclusion that rape, car theft, assault, and property crimes all occur regularly within his area of patrol.

The majority of rapes occur between the hours of 3 A.M. and 5 A.M., while the most car thefts occur between 11 P.M. and 1 A.M. Assaults are most likely to occur between 7 P.M. and 11 P.M. and property crimes seem to primarily occur between 8 A.M. and 5 P.M.

Assaults are most likely to occur on unlighted side streets around Apple Street, the area where most of the bars are located. Rapes are most likely to occur on Martin and Fillmore Streets, the area where the two largest college dorms are built. Car thefts are most likely to occur around Randall Avenue, as the tenants of the apartment buildings in that area tend to park there. Property crimes are most likely to occur in the Sunrise Housing Addition.

In addition, Officer Menendez recognizes that property crimes are most likely to occur Monday through Friday, while rapes and assaults are more likely Friday through Monday. Car theft seems to regularly occur Tuesday through Thursday, when fewer people are at the bars.

81. Officer Menendez would be most likely to reduce the number of property crimes by patrolling:

(A) 3 A.M. to 5 A.M. in the area around the Sunrise Housing Addition, on Tuesday through Thursday.
(B) 11 P.M. to 1 A.M. in the area around the Sunrise Housing Addition, on Monday through Friday.
(C) 8 A.M. to 5 P.M. in the area around the Sunrise Housing Addition, on Monday through Friday.
(D) 7 P.M. to 11 P.M. in the area around the Randall Avenue Apartment Complex, on Friday through Monday.

GO ON TO THE NEXT PAGE

82. Officer Menendez would be most likely to reduce the number of assaults by patrolling:

(A) 7 P.M. to 11 P.M. in the area around the Randall Avenue Apartment Complex, on Friday through Monday.

(B) 11 P.M. to 1 A.M. in the area around the Sunrise Housing Addition, on Monday through Friday.

(C) 8 A.M. to 5 P.M. in the area around the Randall Avenue Apartment Complex, on Friday through Monday.

(D) 7 P.M. to 11 P.M. in the area around Apple Street, on Friday through Monday.

83. Officer Menendez would be most likely to reduce the number of rapes by patrolling:

(A) 3 A.M. to 5 A.M. in the area around the Sunrise Housing Addition, on Tuesday through Thursday.

(B) 3 A.M. to 5 A.M. in the area around Martin and Fillmore Streets, on Friday through Monday.

(C) 11 P.M. to 1 A.M. in the area around the Sunrise Housing Addition, on Monday through Friday.

(D) 11 P.M. to 1 A.M. in the area around Martin and Fillmore Streets, on Friday through Monday.

84. Officer Menendez would be most likely to reduce the number of car thefts by patrolling:

(A) 11 P.M. to 1 A.M. in the area around the Sunrise Housing Addition, on Tuesday through Thursday.

(B) 11 P.M. to 1 A.M. in the area around the Randall Avenue Housing Addition, on Monday through Friday.

(C) 11 P.M. to 1 A.M. in the area around the Sunrise Housing Addition, on Tuesday through Thursday.

(D) 7 P.M. to 11 P.M. in the area around the Randall Avenue Apartment Complex, on Friday through Monday.

STOP. THIS IS THE END OF SECTION 8.

SECTION 9
Information Ordering

When responding to a robbery-in-progress call:

1. *Proceed to the scene rapidly using lights and sirens, but use extreme caution traveling busy roadways. To avoid causing the suspect to flee or take hostages, it is best when approaching the scene by vehicle to turn off sirens, but leave light bar activated.*
2. *Assume the robber is at the scene and armed and dangerous, unless otherwise advised by a reputable source such as dispatch or another officer at the scene. Do not approach the structure being robbed, in order to minimize the suspect's reasons for using a weapon or causing harm to anyone at the scene.*
3. *The first officer at the scene should maintain contact with dispatch until a supervisor arrives at the scene. Provide dispatch with all pertinent information including people at or near the scene, vehicles at the scene, entrances and exits to the building, and anything that appears to be suspicious or dangerous in nature.*
4. *Second officer at the scene will be directed to take specific action by a supervisor through dispatch until a supervisor arrives at the scene. Until receiving other instructions, the second officer on the scene should identify and monitor any other possible entrances or exits to the building. If circumstances permit, the second or subsequent officers may look for and immobilize the suspect's vehicle if possible or may begin traffic control if necessary.*
5. *Every effort should be made to avoid a hostage situation, including calling for SWAT back up, bringing in a negotiator, and refusing to allow the suspect to leave the scene.*
6. *Make an immediate arrest at the scene if possible.*

85. Officer Tatum has been called to the scene or a robbery in progress at a funeral home located on a deserted roadway. As he parks his car back from the entrance to the funeral home, he notices that he is the second officer to arrive at the scene, and that the only other vehicles are located in a small parking lot near his vehicle. He notifies dispatch of his position. Dispatch acknowledges his transmission. What action should Officer Tatum take next?

    (A) Wait in his car until he receives further instructions.
    (B) Walk over to the first officer on the scene and ask for further instructions.
    (C) Walk around the parking lot writing down license tag numbers.
    (D) Determine the location of any other entrances or exits to the building.

GO ON TO THE NEXT PAGE

---

86. Officer Ottaki is the first officer to arrive at the scene of a possible robbery in progress. He has already turned off the siren on his patrol vehicle, so he gets out of his vehicle and starts to look around. What should Officer Ottaki do next?

(A) Contact dispatch with information about the scene.
(B) Look in the front windows to determine if the robbers are visible.
(C) Walk around the building to identify additional entrances and exits.
(D) Begin placing barricades in the street to prevent traffic from driving through the area.

When arriving at the scene of a possible assault or battery, a law enforcement officer should:

1. *Visually determine the level and type of harm suffered by the victim: emotional, minor physical, or serious physical harm. Request medical assistance if needed.*
2. *All individuals at the scene of an assault involving weapons should be frisked to insure officer safety. Do not allow anyone to leave the scene until you have identified them and taken a statement.*
3. *Seek a description of the suspect, including name and address if known. Determine if the perpetrator is still at the scene.*
4. *If the alleged perpetrator is present and probable cause exists to support an arrest, then the suspect should be arrested and Mirandized. If the alleged perpetrator is present and reasonable suspicion exists to support a short detention, the individual should be temporally detained to determine his/her identification and reason for being in the area. Do not ask a suspect to provide details about the incident until they have been Mirandized, even if they are not yet under arrest. If the short detention results in additional evidence being discovered that supports an arrest, then the individual should be arrested and Mirandized. If the short detention does not provide additional evidence the individual should be released.*
5. *Ask the victim to provide a preliminary verbal explanation of the incident. Determine if a weapon was used in the incident and the location of any such weapon.*
6. *Take down the names of any witnesses, and their statements.*
7. *Have photographs taken of injuries suffered by the victim, as well as any additional physical evidence available at the scene such as broken windows, damaged walls, etc.*

87. Officer Green arrives at the scene of a possible domestic dispute. He is approached by a female who is hysterical and three small children who are all crying loudly. He notices a male walking toward a car parked in the driveway. What should Officer Green do first?

(A) Stop the man from leaving in the car.
(B) Ask the female, "What happened?"
(C) Ask the female to identify the suspect.
(D) Ask the male, "What happened?"

GO ON TO THE NEXT PAGE

88. Officer Lopez arrives at the scene of an alleged bar fight. He approaches a group of people who appear to be standing in a huddle in the parking lot, and asks them, "What is going on?" A woman steps forward and shows the officer her arm which has teeth marks on it from an obvious bite by a human. What should Officer Green do next?

(A) Photograph the bite wound.
(B) Take down the names of each of the people standing in the huddle.
(C) Look for the suspect.
(D) Get a description of the suspect from the victim.

89. Officer O'Malley has been working the scene of an alleged assault that occurred at a bridal shop. He knows that the alleged victim claims the alleged perpetrator waived a knife at her to get her to give up a bridal gown that was on sale, but as yet his only evidence is the victim's statement. He approaches the alleged perpetrator. According to the departmental policy what should he do next?

(A) Warn her not to do it again and send her home.
(B) Frisk her for weapons.
(C) Ask her to give a statement.
(D) Detain her and then Mirandize her.

Upon arrival at the scene of a building with an activated burglar alarm, the officer should:

1. *Note any open doors or windows, and note whether the rooftop would be a possible point of exit. Maintain radio connection to dispatch.*
2. *Note any people visible in the area, and any suspicious behavior. But, do not disregard individuals acting in a nonsuspicious manner.*
3. *When all evidence suggests that the burglar(s) are still at the scene, a determination should be made as to whether civilians are in danger. If the burglars are visible dispatch should be provided with a physical description. If no civilians appear to be in danger the officer should plan a strategy to block any escape, including disabling an apparent getaway vehicle. If civilians are in danger, the officer should call for all necessary back up to arrive immediately.*
4. *Wait for back up before entering any structure unless a civilian is clearly in danger and you have a real opportunity to assist without unnecessary danger to yourself or others at the scene. It is preferable for the burglar to exit the building and leave rather than the officer entering an occupied building and create a hostage situation.*
5. *While waiting for backup place yourself in a position that provides you the greatest possible view of the interior and exterior of the building, and any possible points of entrance or exit.*

GO ON TO THE NEXT PAGE

90. Officer Lutz arrives at the scene of a building with an activated burglar alarm. She can clearly see through the front windows of the building that two individuals are removing money from a damaged cash register. What should Officer Lutz do next?

(A) Fire her service weapon through the front of the building at the suspects.
(B) Plan a strategy for blocking an escape.
(C) Enter the structure with her service revolver drawn.
(D) Approach the front of the building and call out to the suspects to surrender.

91. Officer Plant arrives at the scene of a building with an activated burglar alarm. She cannot see inside the building, but she notices that a side door leading from an alley is open. All other doors and windows appear locked, and the roof does not have a visible means of escape. What should she do next?

(A) Enter the building with her service revolver drawn.
(B) Close and block the exterior door to prevent escape until back up arrives.
(C) Disable the suspect's vehicle.
(D) Seek a position that permits the best possible view of the entire scene.

92. Officer Nixon arrives at the scene of a burglary of a convenience store. He can clearly see through the front window that the clerk of the store has a gun to her head, and she is trying to open a cash register. Customers of the store are gathered at the rear of the store and the suspect occasionally appears to shout something at them. What should Officer Nixon do next?

(A) Enter the building with his service revolver drawn.
(B) Block any exit by the suspect.
(C) Contact dispatch with a description of the suspect and the situation, and wait for backup.
(D) Develop a plan for rescuing the civilians inside the building.

STOP. THIS IS THE END OF PRACTICE TEST 2.

Answer Key

Section 1: Memorization

1. B
2. B
3. C
4. C
5. C
6. C
7. B
8. A
9. C
10. B

Section 2: Visualization

11. A—notice the shape of the mouths
12. B—notice the shape of the mouths
13. B—notice the shape of the noses
14. D—notice the shape of the mouths
15. D—notice the shape of the mouths
16. D—notice the shape of the noses and mouths
    A—notice the shape of the mouths
17. A—the only short bed pick-up
18. C—the only other SUV
19. D—the only other midsize pick-up
20. B—the only other short bed, extended cab pick-up
21. B
22. C
23. A
24. C

Section 3: Spatial Orientation

25. C
26. B
27. D
28. C
29. C
30. C
31. C
32. C
33. D
34. A
35. B
36. D

Section 4: Verbal Expression

37. C
38. B
39. C
40. C
41. C
42. C
43. B
44. B
45. A
46. A

Section 5: Verbal Comprehension

47. B
48. A
49. B
50. A
51. B
52. D
53. D
54. B
55. B
56. C
57. C
58. A

Section 6: Problem Sensitivity

59. B
60. C
61. B
62. A
63. B
64. C
65. C
66. A

Section 7: Deductive Reasoning

67. A
68. B
69. C
70. D
71. D
72. C
73. D
74. C

Section 8: Inductive Reasoning

75. A
76. C
77. C
78. D
79. C
80. A
81. C
82. D
83. B
84. B

Section 9: Information Ordering

85. D
86. A
87. A
88. D
89. B
90. B
91. B
92. C

PRACTICE TEST 3
Similar to the New York City Law Enforcement Exam

Answer Sheet

Section 1: Memorization

1. (A) (B) (C) (D)
2. (A) (B) (C) (D)
3. (A) (B) (C) (D)
4. (A) (B) (C) (D)
5. (A) (B) (C) (D)

6. (A) (B) (C) (D)
7. (A) (B) (C) (D)
8. (A) (B) (C) (D)
9. (A) (B) (C) (D)
10. (A) (B) (C) (D)

Section 2: Spatial Orientation, Visualization, Written Expression, Problem Sensitivity, Deductive Reasoning, Inductive Reasoning, and Information Ordering

11. (A) (B) (C) (D)
12. (A) (B) (C) (D)
13. (A) (B) (C) (D)
14. (A) (B) (C) (D)
15. (A) (B) (C) (D)

16. (A) (B) (C) (D)
17. (A) (B) (C) (D)
18. (A) (B) (C) (D)
19. (A) (B) (C) (D)
20. (A) (B) (C) (D)

21. (A) (B) (C) (D)
22. (A) (B) (C) (D)
23. (A) (B) (C) (D)
24. (A) (B) (C) (D)
25. (A) (B) (C) (D)

26. (A) (B) (C) (D)
27. (A) (B) (C) (D)
28. (A) (B) (C) (D)
29. (A) (B) (C) (D)
30. (A) (B) (C) (D)

31. (A) (B) (C) (D)
32. (A) (B) (C) (D)
33. (A) (B) (C) (D)
34. (A) (B) (C) (D)
35. (A) (B) (C) (D)

36. (A) (B) (C) (D)
37. (A) (B) (C) (D)
38. (A) (B) (C) (D)
39. (A) (B) (C) (D)
40. (A) (B) (C) (D)

41. (A) (B) (C) (D)
42. (A) (B) (C) (D)
43. (A) (B) (C) (D)
44. (A) (B) (C) (D)
45. (A) (B) (C) (D)

46. (A) (B) (C) (D)
47. (A) (B) (C) (D)
48. (A) (B) (C) (D)
49. (A) (B) (C) (D)
50. (A) (B) (C) (D)

51. (A) (B) (C) (D)
52. (A) (B) (C) (D)
53. (A) (B) (C) (D)
54. (A) (B) (C) (D)
55. (A) (B) (C) (D)

56. (A) (B) (C) (D)
57. (A) (B) (C) (D)
58. (A) (B) (C) (D)
59. (A) (B) (C) (D)
60. (A) (B) (C) (D)

61. Ⓐ Ⓑ Ⓒ Ⓓ   74. Ⓐ Ⓑ Ⓒ Ⓓ
62. Ⓐ Ⓑ Ⓒ Ⓓ   75. Ⓐ Ⓑ Ⓒ Ⓓ
63. Ⓐ Ⓑ Ⓒ Ⓓ   76. Ⓐ Ⓑ Ⓒ Ⓓ
64. Ⓐ Ⓑ Ⓒ Ⓓ   77. Ⓐ Ⓑ Ⓒ Ⓓ
65. Ⓐ Ⓑ Ⓒ Ⓓ   78. Ⓐ Ⓑ Ⓒ Ⓓ

66. Ⓐ Ⓑ Ⓒ Ⓓ   79. Ⓐ Ⓑ Ⓒ Ⓓ
67. Ⓐ Ⓑ Ⓒ Ⓓ   80. Ⓐ Ⓑ Ⓒ Ⓓ
68. Ⓐ Ⓑ Ⓒ Ⓓ   81. Ⓐ Ⓑ Ⓒ Ⓓ
69. Ⓐ Ⓑ Ⓒ Ⓓ   82. Ⓐ Ⓑ Ⓒ Ⓓ
70. Ⓐ Ⓑ Ⓒ Ⓓ   83. Ⓐ Ⓑ Ⓒ Ⓓ

71. Ⓐ Ⓑ Ⓒ Ⓓ   84. Ⓐ Ⓑ Ⓒ Ⓓ
72. Ⓐ Ⓑ Ⓒ Ⓓ   85. Ⓐ Ⓑ Ⓒ Ⓓ
73. Ⓐ Ⓑ Ⓒ Ⓓ   86. Ⓐ Ⓑ Ⓒ Ⓓ

Practice Test 3

Note: This test has 86 multiple-choice questions, grouped into two sections. The first section (questions 1–10) tests memorization skills. The second section (questions 11–86) tests a variety of other topics. Mark your answer choices on the answer sheet provided.

SECTION 1
MEMORIZATION

This section of the test seeks to determine your ability to memorize and retain new information encountered as a routine part of a task or job. On the next two pages you will see a drawing of a typical scene. You may inspect the scene for five minutes, but you may not take notes or write on anything. At the conclusion of the inspection period, you will begin a five-minute *hold* period. During this time you will be expected to think about what you saw in the drawing. **During the hold period, do not look at the drawing.** (You may wish to cover it with another sheet of paper, or as an alternative, turn back to this page.) On the actual exam, you will not be allowed to look back at the drawing during either the hold period or while answering the exam questions.

At the conclusion of the hold period, turn to the page following the drawing. (Make sure you do not look at the drawing itself.) You will see a series of multiple-choice questions regarding the details presented in the drawing. You may begin answering the questions immediately.

GO ON TO THE NEXT PAGE

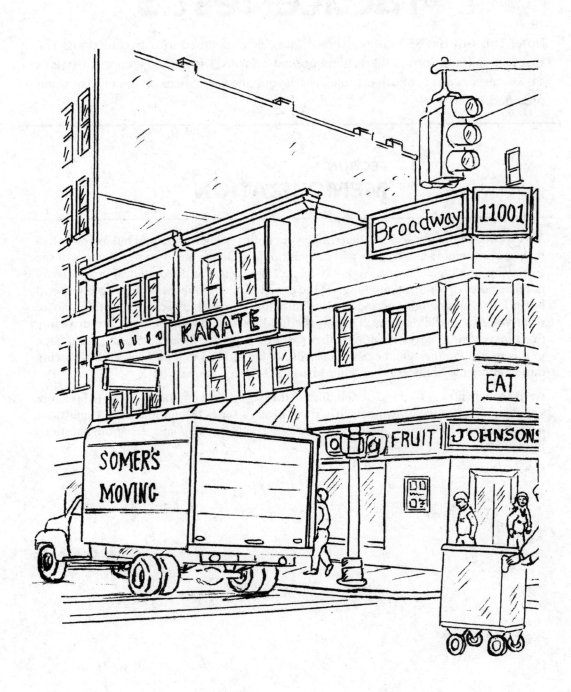

GO ON TO THE NEXT PAGE

GO ON TO THE NEXT PAGE

1. What type of business is the primary focus in the drawing?

   (A) Clothing store
   (B) Restaurant
   (C) Moving and transportation business
   (D) Gym

2. What was the name of the business which is the primary focus in the drawing?

   (A) Murphy's
   (B) Eat
   (C) Johnson's
   (D) Somer's

3. Based on the clothing and signs shown in the drawing, what time of year is depicted in the drawing?

   (A) Spring
   (B) Summer
   (C) Fall
   (D) Winter

4. What object was the man in the front, center portion of the drawing holding onto?

   (A) Wheelchair
   (B) Stroller
   (C) Shopping cart
   (D) Rolling bin

5. What type of workout studio was shown in the drawing?

   (A) Karate
   (B) Dance
   (C) Tai Kwan Do
   (D) Yoga

6. What was the address of the workout studio?

   (A) 1200 Main
   (B) 10011 Broadway
   (C) 10011 Main
   (D) 1200 Broadway

7. What was the price of the sandwich shown in the drawing?

   (A) 99 cents
   (B) $1.99
   (C) $2.99
   (D) $3.99

GO ON TO THE NEXT PAGE

8. What was the name of the company that owned the large van shown in the drawing?

(A) Murphy's
(B) Clark's
(C) Johnson's
(D) Somer's

9. How many vehicles are shown parked along Main Street?

(A) 1
(B) 2
(C) 3
(D) 4

10. How many people are shown crossing the street outside of a marked crosswalk?

(A) 1
(B) 2
(C) 3
(D) 4

> **YOU HAVE COMPLETED THE MEMORY PORTION OF THIS EXAMINATION.**
> **COMPLETE QUESTIONS 11–86. BE SURE TO READ EACH QUESTION CAREFULLY.**

Spatial Orientation, Visualization, Written Expression, Problem Sensitivity, Deductive Reasoning, Inductive Reasoning, and Information Ordering

11. A hotel manager was a witness to a carjacking that occurred in front of the hotel where he was working. He tells you that he was looking north out of his office window and watching traffic when he saw the carjacking occur. He watched the suspect head right down the road until he turned right at the intersection.

    According to the information supplied by the witness, which direction was the suspect driving when he was last seen?

    (A) North
    (B) South
    (C) East
    (D) West

12. A mother came to the station to report a missing child. She told you that her daughter was playing in the front yard, while she (the mother) watched her through the front window. The street in front of the house is an east-west road, and the house is located on the north side of the road. She looked up and noticed her child was no longer in the front yard. Although she didn't see the little girl, she did look left down the street and saw a large white van making a left turn. She was able to get a partial tag number for the van.

    According to the information supplied by the mother, which direction was the white van driving when last seen?

    (A) North
    (B) South
    (C) East
    (D) West

GO ON TO THE NEXT PAGE

13. A robbery victim, still standing at the spot where he was robbed, reports that his wallet was stolen by a masked man. When asked which direction the man went after taking the wallet, the victim states that he saw the man running east until he turned right into an alley. You note that the crime occurred on the south side of the street.

According to the information supplied by the victim, which direction was the suspect running when he was last seen?

(A) North
(B) South
(C) East
(D) West

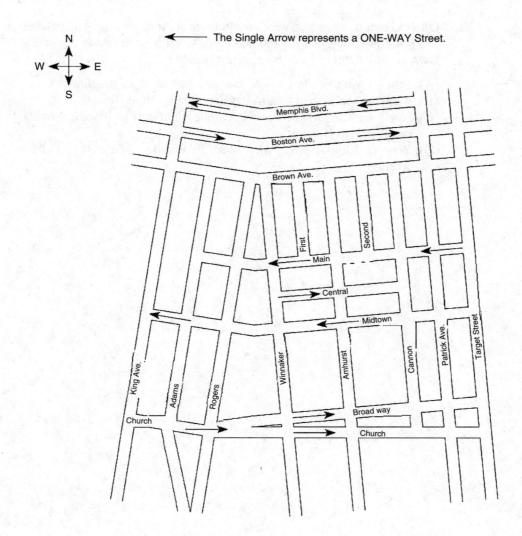

14. Officer Maxwell is at the intersection of Church and King Ave, heading north on King. He is called to a traffic accident at Cannon and Main. Without breaking any traffic laws, what is Officer Maxwell's shortest route?

(A) North to Brown Avenue, then east to Patrick Avenue, then south to Main, then west to Cannon.

(B) East on Church, then continuing east on Broadway to Cannon, then north on Cannon to Main.

(C) North on King to Midtown, then east on Midtown to Cannon, then north to Main.

(D) East on Church to Adams, North on Adams to Main, then east on Main to Cannon.

15. Officer Faxton is heading west on Midtown at Amhurst. He is dispatched to a possible robbery at Boston and Patrick. Without breaking any traffic laws, what is Officer Faxton's shortest route?

(A) East on Midtown to Patrick Avenue, then north to Boston.

(B) North to Main, then east to Patrick, then north to Boston.

(C) North on Amhurst to Brown Avenue, then east to Patrick Avenue, then north to Boston.

(D) West to King Avenue, then north to Boston, then east to Patrick Avenue.

GO ON TO THE NEXT PAGE

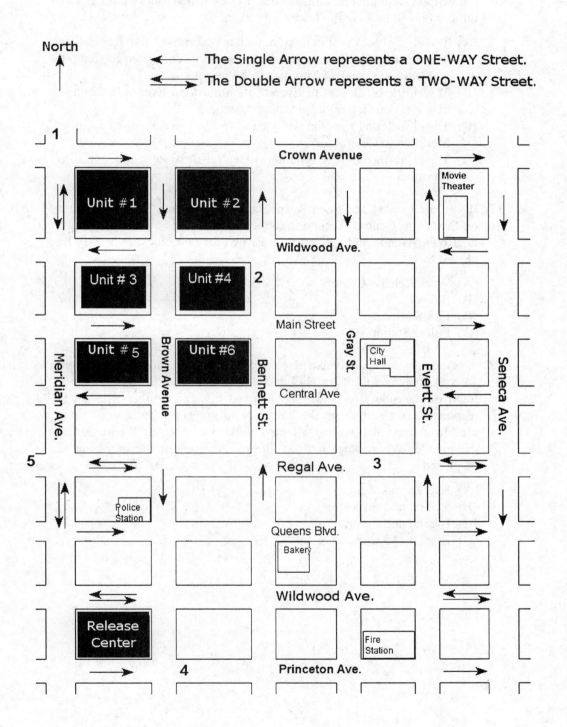

North

← The Single Arrow represents a ONE-WAY Street.
⇄ The Double Arrow represents a TWO-WAY Street.

1

Crown Avenue

Movie Theater

Unit #1   Unit #2

Wildwood Ave.

Unit #3   Unit #4   2

Main Street

Gray St.

City Hall

Unit #5   Unit #6

Meridian Ave.   Brown Avenue   Bennett St.   Central Ave

Everett St.   Seneca Ave.

5   Regal Ave.   3

Police Station

Queens Blvd.

Bakery

Wildwood Ave.

Release Center

Fire Station

4   Princeton Ave.

GO ON TO THE NEXT PAGE

16. Officer Powell is called to the scene of an emergency at Central and Meridian. He is currently traveling east on Princeton Avenue at about Gray Street. Without breaking any traffic laws, which route would require Officer Powell to drive the fewest city blocks?

(A) Travel one block east to Everett, then north on Everett to Regal, then west on Regal to Brown Avenue, then north on Brown to Central, and west one block to Meridian Avenue.

(B) Travel one block east to Everett, then north on Everett to Central, then west on Central to Meridian Avenue.

(C) Travel west on Princeton Avenue to Meridian Avenue, then north on Meridian to Central.

(D) Travel north on Gray Avenue to Central then west on Central to Meridian.

17. If you are located at Crown Avenue and Seneca, and then travel south on Seneca to Central Avenue, and then travel west on Central Avenue to Brown Avenue and the south on Brown for two blocks, you will be closest to:

(A) Work Release Center
(B) Bakery
(C) Fire Station
(D) Police Station

18. A parade is scheduled to take place on Saturday morning from 10 A.M. to 11 A.M., between the City Hall and the Fire Station on Everett Street. Each of the side streets will be blocked off, but Officer Braxton is responsible for setting up the barricade to prevent unauthorized vehicles from traveling on the affected portion of Everett Street during the parade. Where does it make the most sense for the barricade to be placed?

(A) Everett and Main
(B) Everett and Princeton
(C) Everett and Central
(D) Everett and Crown

GO ON TO THE NEXT PAGE

19. While investigating a robbery Officer Lenin receives the following description of the suspect. The eyewitnesses described him as a "big white guy" wearing blue casual dress-type pants, a blue striped shirt, and brown work boots. The witnesses also told the police that defendant was "very large, about 6 ft 2 in," and 250–275 lbs, with chestnut brown hair, clean shaven, rotten teeth, and bad breath and dark hair. Which one of the pieces of information provided by the eyewitnesses should Officer Lenin consider the most helpful in identifying the suspect?

(A) Chestnut brown hair
(B) Wearing a striped shirt
(C) Clean shaven
(D) Rotten teeth

20. A victim of an assault gave the following description of her assailant. She described him as dark or olive skinned, possibly Hispanic or Middle-Eastern, at least 30, average height and weight, with black hair and a mustache. She noticed he had homemade tattoos on his hands, between the first finger and thumb, which were blackish green in color, and that he was wearing old jeans and a dark hooded sweatshirt. Which of the pieces of information provided by the victim should law enforcement consider the most helpful in identifying the suspect?

(A) Wearing old jeans and a dark hooded sweatshirt
(B) Black hair and a mustache
(C) Possibly Hispanic or Middle-Eastern
(D) Blackish green homemade tattoos on his hands

21. An eyewitness to a hit-and-run automobile accident stated that he got a brief glance at the driver of the vehicle. He described him as an older teenager, white, clean-shaven, with a shaved head, and a lot of piercings in his left ear. The earlobe had a very large pierced hole in it, but nothing was suspended from the lobe. He was wearing a large, orange winter coat, but was sitting low enough in the seat that only his shoulders could be clearly seen. Which of the pieces of information provided by the witness should law enforcement consider the most helpful in identifying the suspect?

(A) Facial Hair
(B) Race
(C) Clothing
(D) Hair color/length

GO ON TO THE NEXT PAGE

22. Officers respond to the report of an assault involving a man and woman outside a convenience store. The woman is unconscious and must be transported to the hospital. Several witnesses to the incident give varying descriptions of the perpetrator. Which one of the following is most likely to be correct?

(A) A bald black male of average height and weight and wearing glasses.
(B) A black male, approximately 5 ft 9 in tall, wearing dark clothing, black leather gloves, very little hair on his head, a few days' beard growth on his face, and glasses.
(C) A black male, approximately 5 ft 10 in tall, wearing dark clothing, black leather gloves, and a wig.
(D) A black male, approximately 5 ft 11 in tall, wearing dark clothing, black leather gloves, having a shaved head and a little facial hair.

23. Officers respond to the report of a carjacking. Several witnesses to the incident gave varying descriptions of the perpetrator. Which one of the following is most likely to be correct?

(A) A white man approximately 5 ft 10 in tall, with shoulder-length gray hair, wearing blue jeans and a blue shirt.
(B) A white man approximately 5 ft 11 in tall, with shoulder-length dark hair with a lot of gray, wearing blue jeans and a blue sweatshirt.
(C) A white man approximately 5 ft 10 in tall, with shoulder-length dark hair with a lot of gray, wearing blue jeans and a blue shirt.
(D) A white man approximately 5 ft 9 in inches tall, with shoulder-length dark hair with a lot of gray, wearing blue coveralls.

24. Officers respond to the report of armed robbery of a convenience store. Several witnesses to the incident give varying descriptions of the perpetrator. Which one of the following is most likely to be correct?

(A) A Hispanic male in his twenties.
(B) A Hispanic male with short, black hair and weighing about 225 lbs.
(C) A Hispanic male with short hair, 5 ft 9 in inches tall, weighing about 200 lbs, and wearing a blue sweatshirt.
(D) An Italian male in his mid-twenties, 5 ft 8 in or 5 ft 10 in tall, and wearing a dark sweatshirt and blue running pants with three white stripes.

GO ON TO THE NEXT PAGE

Answer questions 25 and 26 using the following information.

Officer Leevon is assigned to the Baraga Housing Development on East 22nd and Sunset Avenue. Leevon familiarizes himself with the crime statistics of the six buildings in the development for the month of July. All the robberies took place at 14 East 22nd Street. All the assaults took place at 9 Sunset Avenue. Mailboxes were broken into only at 11 Sunset Avenue. All the rapes took place at 16 East 22nd Street. All the assaults happened between 9 P.M. and 11 P.M. Robberies occurred between 11 P.M. and 2 A.M. The mailboxes were broken into between 3:30 A.M. and 4:30 A.M. Rapes occurred early in the early morning when women were leaving clubs to head home for the evening, about 2 A.M. to 3 A.M.

When Leevon is working a 9 P.M. to 5 A.M. shift, he must divide his time among the four buildings to prevent these crimes.

25. To reduce the number of assaults he should patrol:

   (A) From 2 A.M. to 3 A.M. at 14 East 22nd Street
   (B) From 3:30 A.M. to 4:30 A.M. 11 Sunset Avenue
   (C) From 9 P.M. to 11 P.M. 9 Sunset Avenue
   (D) From 11 P.M. to 2 A.M. at 14 East 22nd Street

26. To reduce the number of robberies he should patrol:

   (A) From 9 P.M. to 11 P.M. 16 East 22nd Street
   (B) From 11 P.M. to 2 A.M. at 14 East 22nd Street
   (C) From 2 A.M. to 3 A.M. 16 East 22nd Street
   (D) From 3:30 A.M. to 4:30 A.M. at 14 East 22nd Street

Answer question 27 based on the information given in the question

27. Lieutenant Bett, assigned to police investigations, is asked to review crime statistics for a commercial section of Levitt Street to determine the most effective assignment of officers to reduce crime aimed at the local businesses. Lt. Bett determines that convenience stores that close at 11 P.M. and reopen at 5:30 A.M. average one armed robbery for every three months, while such establishments open 24 hours a day average two armed robberies per month. Gas stations that close at 11 P.M. and reopen at 5:30 P.M. average six gas run-offs per day, while gas stations that are open 24 hours average 14 gas run-offs per day.

GO ON TO THE NEXT PAGE

Based only upon the crime statistics provided, how should Lt. Bett advise police administration as to the most effective assignment of law enforcement to combat crime on Levitt Street?

(A) More officers should be assigned to patrol Levitt Street between 8 A.M. and 5 P.M.
(B) More officers should be assigned to patrol Levitt Street between 5 P.M. and 11 P.M.
(C) More officers should be assigned to patrol Levitt Street between 11 P.M. and 5:30 A.M.
(D) More officers should be assigned to patrol Levitt Street between 5:30 A.M. and 8 A.M.

Answer questions 28 and 29 using the following information.

A special law enforcement team aimed at reducing crimes against the elderly was told to focus their efforts on a neighborhood with a very high population of retired persons. Crime statistics over a three-month period showed that the majority of crimes against the elderly in this neighborhood were financial exploitation, assault, and theft committed by family members, acquaintances, and caretakers. Financial exploitation was most often committed by females between the ages of 15 and 30. Assault was most often committed by females aged 45–55. Theft was most often committed by males.

28. The team is advised by a local bank that checks bearing the name Mrs. Leahy, who is an 85-year-old woman living in the team's target area, have been cashed throughout the city over the previous seven days, totaling almost $7,000 in purchases. The signature on the checks does not match the signature on file with the bank for the account. Only four people have had access to the woman's checks. Which one is most likely the perpetrator of the offense?

(A) Mrs. Leahy's cleaning woman, Alice, age 42.
(B) Mrs. Leahy's daughter who lives with her, age 55.
(C) Mrs. Leahy's granddaughter, age 22.
(D) Mrs. Leahy's grandson, age 17.

29. Upon investigation of a local pawnshop, the team discovers it has a large number of goods available for sale that match reports of items stolen from Mr. Rahi, a 69-year-old retired landscaper. Only four people have had unlimited access to Mr. Rahi's property over the three-month period during which the reported thefts have occurred. Which one is most likely the perpetrator of the offense?

(A) Mr. Rahi's cleaning woman, Alice, age 42
(B) Mr. Rahi's daughter who lives with him, age 55
(C) Mr. Rahi's granddaughter, age 22
(D) Mr. Rahi's grandson, age 17

GO ON TO THE NEXT PAGE

Answer the following questions based on the information provided in the question.

30. A police officer may have to arrest an individual to protect another individual from continued physical violence when evidence exists to show that one person has already caused harm to the other, or is attempting to cause harm to the other.

   Which of the following situations is most likely going to result in police making an arrest?

   (A) Mr. Beeson screaming at his wife in a restaurant.
   (B) Mr. Kylin pulling the car over and ordering his wife to get out.
   (C) Mr. Silvers ripping a necklace off his wife's neck, and throwing her out of the house.
   (D) Mr. Cagen throwing his wife's belongings out on the lawn and locking her out of the house.

31. For which of the following should a police officer close a roadway?

   (A) A blizzard
   (B) The road has numerous potholes
   (C) The road was recently repaved
   (D) A wet roadway

32. In which of the following situations should an officer assist in resolving an argument?

   (A) When a mother and her teenage daughter are arguing about whether the mother will purchase the daughter a new outfit.
   (B) When an employee and his boss are arguing about which one will purchase a replacement tool broken by the employee.
   (C) When a shop manager is insisting that a man open his bag before he leaves the store.
   (D) When two young men are debating which of their sports teams will win the championship.

33. Some situations require a police officer to contact another governmental agency to resolve a situation. Which of the following situations should be referred to another agency?

   (A) A dog that is perpetually barking.
   (B) A husband who has struck his wife in public.
   (C) A woman who has shot the neighbor's dog.
   (D) A teenager who has threatened another teenager.

GO ON TO THE NEXT PAGE

34. In a few limited circumstances a police officer may need to enter a home without permission from the occupant. What is one situation that may require such an entry?

(A) When a child appears to be chronically absent from school.
(B) When a bicycle that is reported stolen is found.
(C) When a dog is found with the address on its collar.
(D) When an older person has not been seen outside the home for several days.

35. Some situations require a police officer to contact another governmental agency to resolve a situation. Which of the following situations should be referred to another agency?

(A) A 16-year-old who has shoplifted from a convenience store.
(B) A 20-year-old who has been found transporting alcoholic beverages.
(C) A 12-year-old who appears to be malnourished and never has money for lunch.
(D) An 18-year-old found drag racing.

36. Lieutenant Davies must submit his weekly report of traffic citations issued by his unit. Six officers issued 50 tickets each, 4 officers issued 30 tickets each, and 2 officers issued 15 tickets each. How many total tickets were issued by Lt. Davies unit?

(A) 300
(B) 5
(C) 450
(D) 95

37. Paula Moskoweitz has reported to the police that some expensive sweaters have been stolen from her store. She states that her early morning inventory showed that she had 31 sweaters prior to opening the store for the day. During the day, receipts showed 6 sweaters were sold, 14 sweaters were transferred to another store, and 2 sweaters were returned to the manufacturer due to defects. At the end of the day, Paula's inventory only shows that 7 sweaters are in the store. How many sweaters is Paula alleging were stolen?

(A) 2
(B) 9
(C) 7
(D) 5

GO ON TO THE NEXT PAGE

38. The precinct has hired 30 officers to be equally spread across 5 police units. How many new officers will each unit gain?

(A) 35
(B) 25
(C) 6
(D) 150

39. Four items stolen in a recent burglary were valued at $2,432.00. A pawnshop was found to be in possession of three of the items reported stolen in that burglary. Item A is valued at $421, item B is valued at $704, and item C is valued at $963. What is the value of the item that has not yet been recovered?

(A) $1307
(B) $1469
(C) $2088
(D) $344

40. A clothing company reports the theft of several products. Three sweaters valued at $12.00 each, five pairs of jeans valued at $20.00 each, and seven blouses valued at $15.00 each were taken. What is the total value of all of the items stolen?

(A) $241
(B) $47
(C) $35
(D) $235

41. Officer Johnson has 56 boxes of home safety brochures to distribute among 8 different police precincts. How many boxes of brochures will each precinct receive?

(A) 5
(B) 6
(C) 7
(D) 8

GO ON TO THE NEXT PAGE

42. The members of the traffic control unit issued the following citations during a recent seven-day period.

> Officer Maxim issued 46 citations
> Officer Mendosa issued 57 citations
> Officer Carosa issued 32 citations
> Officer Hussein issued 27 citations

How many total citations were issued by the traffic control unit for this time period?

(A) 164
(B) 162
(C) 167
(D) 174

43. During a training session on ethics, recruits are given the following list of unethical behaviors.

While on duty, law enforcement officers shall not:
1. Accept free food or coffee from a business
2. Spend excessive amounts of time at a single business
3. Accept gifts or gratuities, including money
4. Drink alcohol or use any type of illegal substance
5. Target individuals based upon race, ethnicity, or culture.

Based upon the list of ethical violations provided, what would be the primary purpose of these requirements?

(A) Prevent illegal behavior
(B) Prevent the perception that officers only care about personal gain
(C) Prevent the perception that officers are ethnically biased
(D) Prevent the appearance of impropriety

Answer question 44 based upon the following information.

In a law class conducted at the Academy the recruits were given the following definitions for Assault.

Class A Assault includes when a person acts:

1. With intent to cause serious physical injury to another person, he causes such injury to such person or to a third person by means of a deadly weapon or a dangerous instrument; or
2. With intent to disfigure another person seriously and permanently, or to destroy, amputate or disable permanently a member or organ of his body, he causes such injury to such person or to a third person.

GO ON TO THE NEXT PAGE

Class B Assault includes when a person acts:

1. *With intent to cause serious physical injury to another person, he causes such injury to such person or to a third person; or*
2. *With intent to cause physical injury to another person, he causes such injury to such person or to a third person by means of a deadly weapon or a dangerous instrument.*

44. After reviewing the laws shown above, it would be most correct for a recruit to conclude that:

(A) Class A Assault is a more serious crime than Class B Assault.
(B) Class B Assault is a more serious crime than Class A Assault.
(C) Neither class of Assault crimes is more serious than the other.
(D) Class B Assaults involve use of weapons and Class A assaults do not.

45. Recruit officers have been given the statements from four eyewitnesses. Which of the statements is most likely to be correct?

1. *"An Hispanic female, about 5 ft 2 in, 115 lbs, with reddish-brown wavy waist length hair, and wearing a pair of red shorts and a white t-shirt, was running away from the victim. She was sprinting in very high-heeled shoes, and she was carrying a large black briefcase."*
2. *"An Asian female, about 5 ft 2 in, 100 lbs, with dark brown long hair, and wearing a pair of red shorts and a white t-shirt, was running away from the victim. She was wearing medium-heeled shoes, and she was carrying a large black briefcase."*
3. *"An Hispanic female, about 5 ft 1in, 115 lbs, with brown straight long hair, and wearing a pair of red pants and a white t-shirt, was running away from the victim. She was running, and she was carrying a large black suitcase."*
4. *"An Indian female, about 5 ft, 115 lbs, with reddish-brown wavy hair, and wearing a pair of red shorts and a white t-shirt, was running away from the victim. She was wearing very high-heeled shoes, and she was carrying a large black backpack."*

(A) 1
(B) 2
(C) 3
(D) 4

46. Four witnesses to a hit and run accident identified the suspect's vehicle as a white minivan. However, the four possible license plate numbers are different. Which one of the following is most likely to be correct?

(A) 121CJX
(B) 121CLR
(C) 121OLR
(D) 111CLR

GO ON TO THE NEXT PAGE

Answer questions 47–49 based upon the following information.

The fine for exceeding the maximum speed limit is calculated as follows:

1–10 miles per hour (mph) over the limit, $30

11–20 mph over the limit, $30 plus $6 per mph over 10 mph over the limit

21–30 mph over the limit, $90 plus $9 per mph over 20 mph over the limit

31 and more mph over the limit, $180 plus $15 per mph over 30 mph over the limit

Court costs are additional to the fine and included as part of every citation.

47. Officer Maxwell has issued a speeding citation for 45 mph in a 30 mph zone. If mandatory court costs are $50, which of the following equations will provide an accurate amount of the total cost of the citation?

(A) $30 + 50$
(B) $30 + (6 \times 15) + 50$
(C) $15(45 - 31) + 30 + 50$
(D) $30 + [6(15 - 10)] + 50$

48. Officer Maxwell has issued a speeding citation for 62 mph in a 55 mph-zone. If mandatory court costs are $50, which of the following equations will provide an accurate amount of the total cost of the citation?

(A) $30 + 50$
(B) $30 + (6 \times 7) + 50$
(C) $15(62 - 55) + 30 + 50$
(D) $15(62) + 30 + 50$

49. Officer Maxwell has issued a speeding citation for 85 mph in a 40 mph zone. If mandatory court costs are $50, which of the following equations will provide an accurate amount of the total cost of the citation?

(A) $180 + 50$
(B) $180 + (15 \times 15) + 50$
(C) $15(45 - 30) + 30 + 50$
(D) $180 + (15(85 - 30)) + 50$

GO ON TO THE NEXT PAGE

Answer questions 50 and 51 based upon the following information.

Disobeying traffic control device	$60
Violating pedestrian control signal	$40
Violating flashing traffic signals	$50
Violating lane-control signal	$30
Driving on left side of roadway	$55
Failure to keep right to pass oncoming vehicle	$70
Improper passing; increasing speed when passed	$25
Improper passing on right	$45

50. Officer Delmario has stopped Delvona Driver for running a red light. Which of the following fines should he note on the face of the citation issued to Delvona?

(A) $50.00
(B) $55.00
(C) $60.00
(D) $30.00

51. Officer Ngo has stopped Owen Operator for aggressively working to prevent other drivers from passing him. Although Operator never violated the posted speed limit he did vary his speed from 45 mph to 65 mph depending on how close other vehicles came to passing his vehicle. Which of the following fines should he note on the face of the citation issued to Owen?

(A) $55.00
(B) $70.00
(C) $25.00
(D) $45.00

GO ON TO THE NEXT PAGE

Answer questions 52–55 based upon the following information.

The first face shown, and identified as "suspect," was drawn based upon descriptions provided by witnesses of crimes. It is believed that the suspect has made an effort to change his/her appearance. Select which of the lettered faces, shown beside the suspect's face, most closely resembles the suspect.

52.

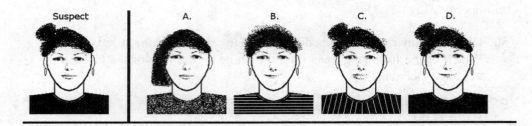

53.

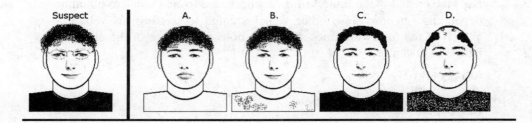

GO ON TO THE NEXT PAGE

54.

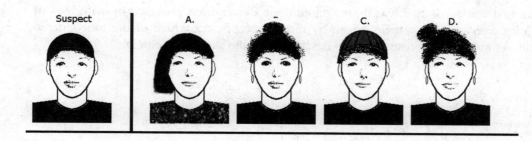

55.

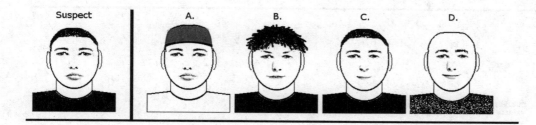

GO ON TO THE NEXT PAGE

Answer questions 56–57 based upon the following information.

The first vehicle shown was drawn based upon descriptions provided by witnesses of crimes who saw the vehicle driven by the suspect. Select which of the four lettered vehicles most closely resembles the description of the suspect's vehicle.

56.

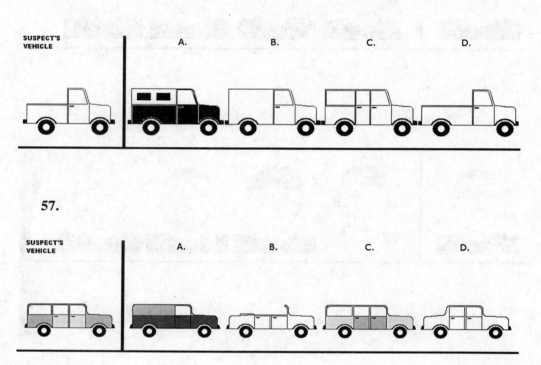

58. Which one of the following photographs* best matches the tire rims the vehicle shown in the above photograph?

*Images from WheelShack.com

A.

B.

C.

D.

59. Which one of the following photographs best matches the tire rims the vehicle shown in the above photograph?

*Images from WheelShack.com

A.

B.

C.

D.

GO ON TO THE NEXT PAGE

Answer questions 60–64 based upon the following information.

Police recruits were told the following rules for requesting search warrants based upon information gained from confidential informants (CI).

1. Community member standard. The CI must either be well known in the community to be a person upon whom police may reasonably rely to provide only credible information, and circumstances and evidence known to law enforcement support the information provided; or
2. Known informant standard. The CI must have provided information in the past that proved to be reliable, and circumstances and evidence known to law enforcement support the information provided.

As part of a training exercise the recruits were given the following *scenario.*

In December 2017, the police received a tip from a previously unknown person that a man named "Pete" was selling cocaine at 15502 Parklane Avenue, No. 234 in Atlantic City. The address was on the ground floor of a two-story apartment building that is located in the Parklane Apartment Complex. The informant described Pete as white, about 25, 5 ft 9 in tall, and 235 lbs. After the police showed the informant pictures of Chris Moore, Jarvis Petry, and William Moore, the informant identified Pete as William. A criminal background check revealed that both Chris and William Moore had previous convictions for drug offenses and Petry had a conviction for weapons trafficking.

The informant agreed to help police perform a controlled buy at 15502 Parklane Avenue, No. 234. The informant claimed to live in apartment No. 233, next door to Pete and directly across from the stairwell leading upstairs. This information was never verified. The layout of the buildings within the apartment complex prevented police from gaining a direct view of the entrance to apartment No. 234, but they knew based upon having accessed the other buildings within the complex that the ground floor of building No. 200 contained apartments numbered 230, 231, 232, 233, and 234. The hallway to access the front doors of these apartments was offset from the heavy wooden entry door to the building. As a result, police did not see the informant physically enter the residence. They could observe only the general area of the apartment building. Later, the informant met the police at the predetermined location where he told the officers that while inside apartment No. 234, he handed money to Pete in exchange for cocaine. A field test confirmed that the substance was indeed cocaine.

The police applied for a warrant to search 15502 Parklane Avenue, No. 234. Police Detective Roberts submitted a sworn affidavit in support of the warrant. The affidavit described the informant as having proven reliable and that he provided information in the past that resulted in the arrest of numerous suspects. It further described the informant's identification of William Moore and Moore's criminal history. The affidavit detailed the controlled drug purchase conducted with the assistance of the informant at 15502 Parklane Avenue, No. 234, including the fact that police were unable to establish surveillance directly on the entrance to that apartment. The affidavit recited that police

GO ON TO THE NEXT PAGE

had received numerous complaints from residents about constant drug activity in the 15000 block of Parklane Avenue. It also stated that it is difficult for police to gain entry to Parklane Apartment Complex without being noticed.

60. Should the police detective have requested a search warrant to search the apartment?

(A) Yes. The CI met the community member standard.
(B) Yes. The CI met the known informant standard.
(C) No. The CI did not meet either standard.
(D) No. The police had no supporting evidence to support the CI's allegations.

61. What was the real name of the person accused of selling drugs?

(A) Pete Moore
(B) William Moore
(C) Chris Moore
(D) Jarvis Petry

62. Based upon the information provided, how many apartments are most likely located within building No. 200?

(A) 5
(B) 9
(C) 10
(D) 15

63. Which apartment was located directly across from the stairwell?

(A) No. 231
(B) No. 232
(C) No. 233
(D) No. 234D

64. How did police establish that the CI entered Pete's apartment?

(A) The police saw the CI leave the apartment.
(B) Police watched the CI enter the apartment.
(C) The CI told police he entered the apartment.
(D) The police used video surveillance to see the CI enter the apartment.

GO ON TO THE NEXT PAGE

65. Rape—The crime of rape is committed when:

1. *A male, being 18 years of age or older, engages in sexual intercourse with a woman of any age who does not consent; or*
2. *A male, being 18 years of age or older, engages in sexual intercourse with a female 14 years of age or younger; or*
3. *A male, being 20 years of age or older, engages in sexual intercourse with a female 16 years of age or younger.*

Vernon, age 19, participates in acts of sexual intercourse with the following people in the following situations. Which of the following situations is NOT an example of rape?

(A) An unconsenting female who is 13-years-old?
(B) A consenting female who is 14-years-old?
(C) A frightened, unconsenting, 18-year-old female?
(D) A consenting female who is 15-years-old?

66. Indecent liberties is defined as:

1. *Any lewd fondling or touching of a child 14 or more years of age but less than 16 years of age, done by an offender age 18 or older, with the intent to arouse or to satisfy the sexual desires of either the child or the offender, or both; or*
2. *Soliciting a child 14 or more years of age but less than 16 years of age to engage in any lewd fondling or touching of the person of another with the intent to arouse or satisfy the sexual desires of the child, the offender or another.*

Walter, age 20, lewdly fondled and/or touched the following people. His intent was to arouse or satisfy his own sexual desires or the desires of the female. Which of the following situations is the best example of the crime of indecent liberties?

(A) A consenting female who is 13-years-old?
(B) A consenting female who is 16-years-old?
(C) An unconsenting female who is 18-years-old?
(D) A frightened female who is 81-years-old?

GO ON TO THE NEXT PAGE

67. A person is guilty of unlawful imprisonment in the first degree when he restrains another person under circumstances that expose the latter to a risk of serious physical injury.

   According to the definition provided, which of the following is the best example of unlawful imprisonment?

   (A) Peron, age 30, is angry at Quanita, age 30, for breaking up with him. He goes to her home and forces her to leave with him in his truck. Peron takes her to a remote location, tells her if he can't have her, no one will, and then drives away, leaving Quanita stranded.
   (B) Bill walked up Tracy as she sat in her vehicle and said, "Get out of your car or I will hurt you." Tracy, feeling intense fear that she was about to be victimized, got out of the car. Bill drove away in Tracy's car.
   (C) Charlie walks into the bank, puts a gun against Dan's head, and demands money. After receiving the money, he runs out of the bank.
   (D) At the mall one day, Mary sees a toddler screaming for his mommy to pick him up. A woman keeps telling the child to hush and says that she is not going to hold him. The child, in need of a nap and some lunch, sits down between racks of pants and begins to cry for mommy to hold him. Mary scoops the child up, comforts him, and leaves the mall with him asleep on her shoulder.

68. A person is guilty of coercion when he compels or induces a person to engage in conduct which the latter has a legal right to abstain from engaging in, or to abstain from engaging in conduct in which he has a legal right to engage, by means of instilling in him a fear that, if the demand is not complied with, the actor or another will:

   1. *Cause physical injury to a person; or*
   2. *Cause damage to property; or*
   3. *Engage in other conduct constituting a crime; or*
   4. *Accuse some person of a crime, cause criminal charges to be instituted against him, testify wrongfully; or*
   5. *Expose a secret or publicize an asserted fact, whether true or false, tending to subject some person to hatred, contempt or ridicule; or*
   6. *Perform any other act which would not in itself materially benefit the actor but which is calculated to harm another person materially with respect to his health, safety, business, calling, career, financial condition, reputation or personal relationships.*

GO ON TO THE NEXT PAGE

According to the definition provided, which of the following is the best example of coercion?

(A) Racine drives past Serita's house. Racine is angry at Serita for stealing her boyfriend so she fires shots at the garage of the house.

(B) Evan, angry at Felicity for refusing to date him, shot her in the foot.

(C) Mohammad did not want Nero dating his sister, Olivia. When Mohammad saw Nero and Olivia together he ran up to them and shook his fist in Nero's face, shouting, "I am warning you! Don't see my sister again!" Nero then told Olivia they could never date again.

(D) Mrs. Stemple states that she was in her living room watching television when her son came into the room, took her purse off her lap, and started to leave. She asked him what he was doing and started to get off the couch. He turned around and screamed at her to leave him alone.

69. Officer Russo obtained the following information when responding to the scene of a traffic accident.

Date/Time of Accident:	January 17, 2017; 7:15 A.M.
Place of Accident:	Intersection of Parkhill Court and Fairway Avenue
Name of Driver No. 1:	Pamela Bruner
Type of vehicle:	2001 Chevrolet
Injuries:	None
Vehicle Damage:	Low impact collision – dented back bumper on left side of vehicle, and broken left tail light.
Citation issued:	Inattentive driving
Name of Driver No. 2:	Steven Chang
Type of vehicle:	2005 Ford
Injuries:	None
Vehicle Damage:	Low impact collision – dented front bumper on left side of vehicle, and broken headlight.
Citation issued:	Following too close
Facts:	Driver No. 1 began to enter intersection, then attempted to stop and backup slightly. Driver No. 2 did not stop his vehicle's forward motion when Driver No. 1 stopped moving forward.

GO ON TO THE NEXT PAGE

Which of the following statements most provides the clearest, most accurate, and most complete report of the incident?

(A) Bruner is a bad driver. The accident would never have happened if she had just kept going forward.

(B) On January 17, 2017, at approximately 7:15 A.M., two vehicles were involved in a low-speed collision at the intersection of Parkhill Court and Fairway Avenue.

(C) On January 17, 2017, at approximately 7:15 A.M., a 2001 Chevrolet, driven by Pamela Bruner, and a 2005 Ford, driven by Steven Chang, were involved in a low-speed collision at the intersection of Parkhill Court and Fairway Avenue. Both vehicles suffered minor damage to their bumpers and lights.

(D) On January 17, 2017, at approximately 7:15 A.M., Pamela Bruner hit Steven Chang's car. Bruner was driving a white Chevrolet and Chang was driving a 2005 black Ford. Chang looked to be less than 18 years of age, while Bruner was at least 56-years-old.

70. Officer Guerro obtained the following information when responding to the scene of a shooting.

Date/Time of Incident:	March 2, 2017; 11:10 P.M.
Place of Accident:	Chestnut Avenue Apartment Complex, Blding No. 23
Name of Suspect:	Terrell Lopez
Address:	4746 Clifton Avenue
Age/Race/Gender:	22/White/Male
Identifying marks:	Tattoo on upper right arm
Name of Victim:	Ummi Ozokki
Address:	7970 Chestnut Avenue, Apartment No. 2307
Age/Race/Gender:	19/Black/Female
Identifying marks:	Birthmark on right side of neck
Injuries:	Bullet wound to the right foot
Incident report:	Victim identified suspect as perpetrator of injury. Suspect is the father of her one-year-old daughter. Victim transported by ambulance to Coventry Hospital. Suspect transported for booking.

GO ON TO THE NEXT PAGE

Which of the following statements provides the clearest, most accurate, and most complete report of the incident?

(A) On March 2, 2017, at approximately 11:10 P.M. Ummi Ozokki went over to Terrell Lopez's house to ask him about their daughter. He couldn't get her to leave so he shot her. Lopez was arrested on suspicion of domestic violence. Ozokki was transported by ambulance for treatment of her injuries.

(B) On March 2, 2017, at 11:10 P.M. at the Chestnut Avenue Apartments Ummi Ozokki was shot in the foot by Terrell Lopez, who is also the father of Ozokki's one-year-old daughter. Lopez was arrested and taken to jail, and Ozokki went to the hospital.

(C) On March 2, 2017, at approximately 11:15 P.M. Officer Guerro arrived at the Chestnut Avenue Apartment Complex in response to a report of a shooting. Upon preliminary investigation a suspect, Terrell Lopez age 22, was identified by the victim, Ummi Ozokki, age 19, as both the father of her one-year-old daughter and the perpetrator of her injury. Ozokki appeared to have a bullet wound to her right foot inflicted within the previous few minutes. Lopez was arrested on suspicion of domestic violence. Ozokki was transported by ambulance for treatment of her injuries.

(D) On March 2, 2017, at approximately 11:15 P.M. Terrell Lopez, age 22, went to the home of Ummi Ozokki, age 19, at the Chestnut Avenue Apartment Complex, No. 2307, to visit his daughter. While there Lopez shot Ozokki in the foot. Lopez was arrested on suspicion of domestic violence. Ozokki was transported by ambulance for treatment of her injuries.

71. Lieutenant Jantzen is reviewing the reports of three different officers, submitted about the same incident.

Officer Adair's report is as follows: Randy was babysitting some little kids so he took them to get his hair cut but left them in the car when it was 90 degrees and the kids blacked out.

Officer Banyon's report is as follows: Randolf Adams who is 17 left three young kids in his car while it was parked at the mall during the time it takes to get his hair cut when it was 90 degrees and all the children are unconscious.

Officer Cluny's report is as follows: Randolf Adams, age 17, left three small children in a parked car, unsupervised, for approximately 40 minutes. The temperature outside the vehicle was 90 degrees. When Adams returned to the car the children were unconscious.

GO ON TO THE NEXT PAGE

Which of the reports is grammatically correct?

(A) Officer Adair's report
(B) Officer Banyon's report
(C) Officer Cluny's report
(D) None of the reports are grammatically correct

72. Officer Lozoya was drafting an incident report. She drafted the following sentence in two different ways, but cannot tell which sentence would be best for inclusion in her report.

1. *All motor vehicles on Broad Street were stopped so drivers' licenses could be checked as well as vehicle operation was checked.*
2. *Vehicles on Broad Street were temporarily stopped by law enforcement as part of a vehicle safety inspection aimed at verifying that all drivers were properly licensed and that their vehicles were in basic working order.*

Which sentence is clearest and most grammatically correct?

(A) Sentence No. 1
(B) Sentence No. 2
(C) Both sentences are clear and grammatically correct
(D) Neither sentence is clear or grammatically correct

73. Officer Tuel is responsible for the Driver Awareness Program. As part of her responsibilities she must create an instruction sheet to provide to program participants.

1. *Please come to the class for six hours rested, alert, and ready to participate fully without your spouse or children to achieve full credit in the program.*
2. *Please come to the class without your spouse or children rested, alert, and ready to participate fully in the program for six hours to achieve full credit.*
3. *To achieve full credit in the program, please come to the class rested, alert, and ready to participate fully for six hours, without your spouse and children.*

Which of the sentences is both grammatically correct and is most clear in explaining the program?

(A) Sentence No. 1
(B) Sentence No. 2
(C) Sentence No. 3
(D) None of the sentences are clear or grammatically correct?

GO ON TO THE NEXT PAGE

74. Officer Twomey obtained the following information when responding to the scene of a possible carjacking.

Date/Time of Incident:	April 14, 2017; 4:20 P.M.
Place of Accident:	Intersection of Garfield and Jackson

Name of Suspect:	Henry Unruh
Address:	7453 Washington Court
Age/Race/Gender:	34/Black/Male
Identifying marks:	Mole on forehead

Name of Victim:	Betty Trujillo
Address:	876 Lincoln Avenue
Age/Race/Gender:	56/Hispanic/Female
Identifying marks:	None
Injuries:	Bruise markings on upper left arm

Incident report:	Victim identified suspect as perpetrator of injury. Suspect approached victim at intersection and forced victim out of vehicle. Victim transported by ambulance to Coventry Hospital. Suspect apprehended at 500 block of Polk.

Which of the following statements provides the clearest, most accurate, and most complete report of the incident?

(A) A car was taken on April 14, 2017, at approximately 4:20 P.M., by Henry Unruh, who hit Betty Trujillo in the arm to get her out of her vehicle at the intersection of Garfield and Jackson.

(B) On April 14, 2017, at approximately 4:20 P.M., Henry Unruh, physically forced Betty Trujillo from her vehicle at the intersection of Garfield and Jackson.

(C) Betty Trujillo was driving her car to the grocery store late yesterday afternoon when Henry Unruh came up to her and made her get out for the car by hitting her in the arm.

(D) Betty Trujillo saw Henry Unruh take a car right in front of her so he hit her.

GO ON TO THE NEXT PAGE

75. Officer Vickery obtained the following information when responding to the scene of a purse snatching.

Date/Time of Incident:	September 12, 2017; 6:40 P.M.
Place of Accident:	5100 N. Adams

Name of Suspect:	Albert Vaughan
Address:	6655 Washington Court
Age/Race/Gender:	17/White/Male
Identifying marks:	Magenta hair, pierced tongue, nose, navel, and both ears

Name of Victim:	Ngau Vo
Address:	153 Lincoln Avenue
Age/Race/Gender:	21/Asian/Female
Identifying marks:	None
Injuries:	None

Incident report:	Victim identified suspect as perpetrator of crime. Suspect approached victim from behind and pulled her purse out of her lap as victim sat on a bench waiting for a bus. Passerby tackled perpetrator and held him until police arrived. Purse recovered.

Which of the following statements provides the clearest, most accurate, and most complete report of the incident?

(A) Ngau Vo was not paying attention and let Albert Vaughan steal her purse, but a quick thinking person who was just walking by, grabbed Vaughan as he ran by and pushed him down and sat on him until the police came.

(B) On April 14, 2017 at approximately 4:20 P.M. Ngau Vo saw Albert Vaughan snatch her purse off her lap.

(C) On April 14, 2017 at approximately 4:20 P.M. Ngau Vo's purse was stolen off her lap when she was not paying attention. An unidentified individual retrieved the purse.

(D) On April 14, 2017 at approximately 4:20 P.M. Albert Vaughan took Ngau Vo's purse off of her lap as Vo sat on a bench waiting for a bus. An unidentified passerby retrieved Vo's purse by tackling Vaughan and holding him until police arrived.

GO ON TO THE NEXT PAGE

76. Officer Harrah obtained the following information when responding to the scene of a larceny.

Date/Time of Incident:	August 2, 2017; 8:15 A.M.
Place of Accident:	3232 Truman

Name of Suspect:	Sara Goldy
Address:	14444 Washington Court
Age/Race/Gender:	44/White/Female
Identifying marks:	None

Name of Victim:	ARC Delivery, Co
Address:	9999 Lincoln Avenue
Age/Race/Gender:	N/A
Identifying marks:	N/A
Injuries:	N/A

Incident report: Victim mistakenly delivered a package to suspect. The address on the package was 1444 Washington Ct. Suspect opened the package, which contained several pieces of jewelry valued at $4300 in total. Suspect attempted to pawn the jewelry on the same day the package was delivered to her home.

Which of the following statements provides the clearest, most accurate, and most complete report of the incident?

(A) Sara Goldy attempted to pawn several pieces of jewelry she did not own.
(B) Sara Goldy got lucky when she was given $4300 of jewelry.
(C) Sara Goldy received a package from ARC Delivery, Co addressed to a person other than herself. Without permission she opened the package and discovered it contained approximately $4300 of jewelry. She then attempted to pawn the items.
(D) August 2, 2017 at 8:15 A.M. ARC Delivery, Co delivered a package to Sara Goldy, 14444 Washington Court, instead of to the address on the package, 1444 Washington Court. Without permission Goldy opened the package and discovered it contained approximately $4300 of jewelry. She then attempted to pawn the items.

GO ON TO THE NEXT PAGE

Answer questions 77 and 78 based upon the following information.

After making an arrest, prisoners should be transported to the appropriate detention facility for booking. The steps of the booking procedure are:

1. The arresting officer should empty the arrestee's pockets, remove shoes and socks, and perform a pat down to check for concealed items. Shoes and socks should be returned.
2. All items obtained from arrestee must be listed on a personal property form.
3. All items that appear to be evidence of criminal activity may be seized and processed through applicable evidence procedures. An evidence receipt for each such item must be placed with the arrestee's other personal property.
4. Papers containing information relevant to a criminal investigation must be processed pursuant to applicable evidence procedures. Prior to photocopying any such item, a request shall be submitted to the forensic lab, and approved by such lab, to protect any evidence located on the original paper(s).
5. All items not seized as evidence should be secured in property bag and labeled with arrestee's name. Both the officer and arrestee must sign the personal property form acknowledging that all of arrestee's items have been secured.

77. Officer Goode has completed searching Bob Herrin for personal property after arresting him for driving under the influence. In Herrin's sock he found a small packet of a white powdered substance. What step should Officer Goode take next?

(A) Charge Herrin with possession of drugs
(B) Seize the packet and process it as evidence
(C) Secure the packet in a property bag
(D) Sign the personal property form acknowledging Herrin's property

78. Officer Highland has arrested Andrea Holt on suspicion of prostitution. He has completed searching Holt and has discovered several checks written to her in the amount of $20.00. He logs the checks onto her personal property form. What is the next step that Officer Highland should take with respect to the checks?

(A) Photocopy the checks
(B) Secure the checks in a property bag
(C) Seize the checks and fill out evidence receipts
(D) Cash the checks and put the money into Holt's property bag

GO ON TO THE NEXT PAGE

TURN TO THE NEXT PAGE

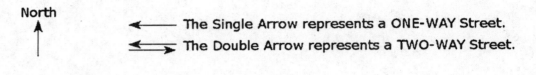

North

The Single Arrow represents a ONE-WAY Street.

The Double Arrow represents a TWO-WAY Street.

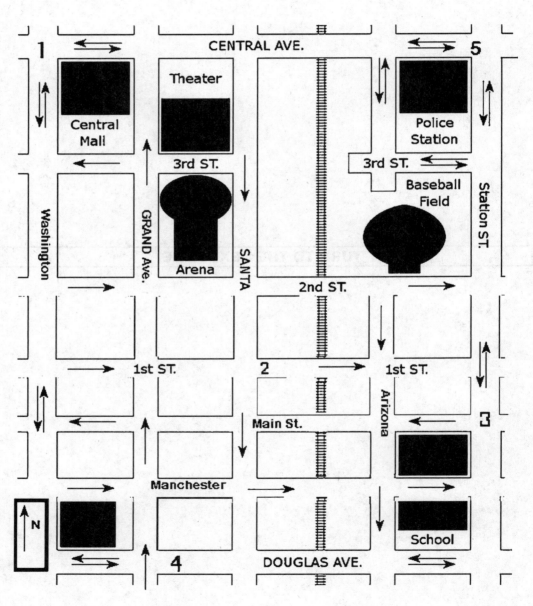

1   CENTRAL AVE.   5

Theater

Central
Mall

3rd ST.

Police
Station

Arena

Baseball
Field

2nd ST.

1st ST.   2   1st ST.   3

Main St.

Manchester

School

N   4   DOUGLAS AVE.

Washington

GRAND Ave.

SANTA

Station ST.

Arizona

GO ON TO THE NEXT PAGE

79. If you are located at Washington and Manchester and travel east to the northeast corner of the school you will be closest to point:

(A) 1
(B) 2
(C) 3
(D) 4

80. If you are located at Arizona and Douglas, then travel one block east, then travel two blocks north, then travel two blocks west, you will be closest to point:

(A) 1
(B) 2
(C) 3
(D) 4

81. Officer Jarvis is traveling south on Santa Road at about 2nd Street. He has noticed that a train is blocking both Central and 2nd Streets, although the 1st Street railroad crossing is clear. Officer Jarvis receives an emergency dispatch to the intersection of Central and Washington. Without breaking any traffic laws, the most direct route for Officer Jarvis is:

(A) Travel south to Main Street, then west on Main to Washington, then north to Central
(B) Travel west on 2nd Street to Washington, then north on Washington to Central
(C) Travel west on 1st Street to Washington, then north on Washington to Central
(D) Travel north on Santa to 3rd Street, then west on 3rd Street to Grand Avenue, then north on Grand to Central, then west on Central to Washington

82. You are located at Central and Washington. You travel two blocks south, then two blocks east, then four blocks south. You are closest to point:

(A) 2
(B) 3
(C) 4
(D) 5

GO ON TO THE NEXT PAGE

83. Police Officer Johnson is on a beat patrol and passes the following set of buildings:

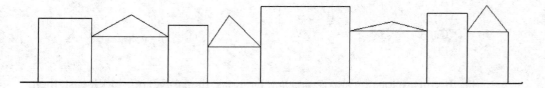

When Police Officer Johnson walks to the back of this set of buildings, which of the following will best match the buildings as seen from the back?

A.

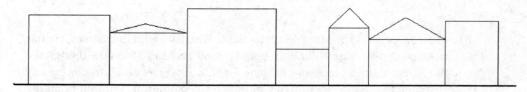

B.

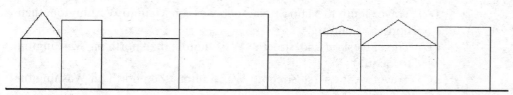

C.

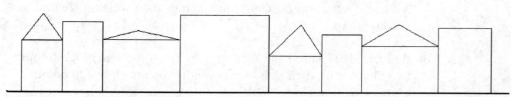

D.

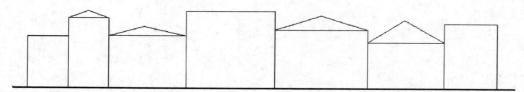

GO ON TO THE NEXT PAGE

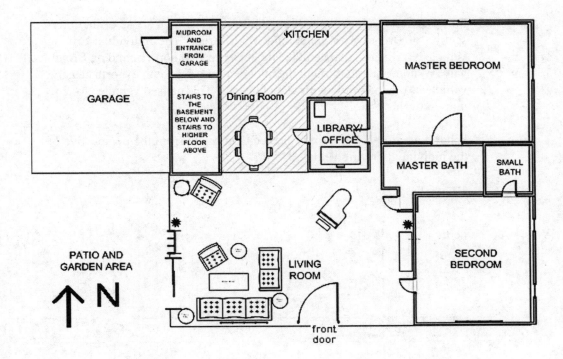

84. Officer Jackson entered the Smith home through the front door, and stopped to look around from a position in front of the grand piano bench. His back is toward the second bedroom. If he looks to his right, what will he see?

(A) The long couch
(B) The patio area
(C) The dining room table
(D) The front door

GO ON TO THE NEXT PAGE

85. Police Officer Pulaski was dispatched to an accident scene at the intersection of Broadway Avenue and Main Street. The individual driving vehicle No. 1 states that vehicle No. 3 was headed north bound on Broadway Avenue, and ran through the intersection from south to north causing vehicle No. 1 to collide with vehicle No. 3. This caused vehicle No. 2 to rear end vehicle No. 1.

What diagram best describes the accident scene from the perspective of the individual driving vehicle No. 1?

A.   B.

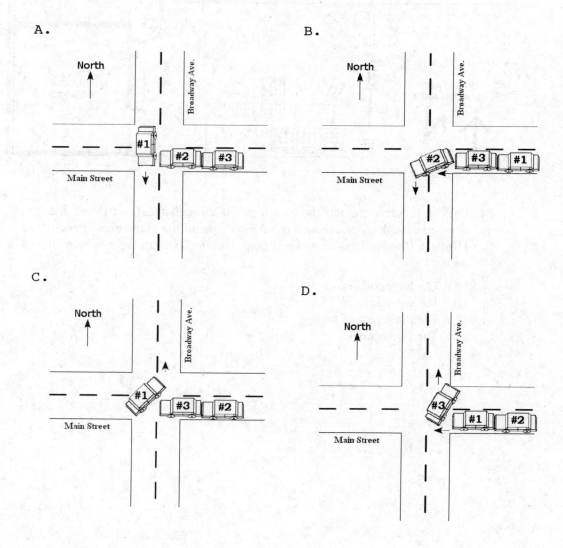

C.   D.

GO ON TO THE NEXT PAGE

86. Police Officer Choudhary was dispatched to an accident scene at the intersection of Broadway Avenue and Plum Street. The individual driving vehicle No. 3 states that while headed west bound on Plum Street, vehicle No. 1 ran through the intersection from north to south causing vehicle No. 3 to collide with vehicle No. 1. This caused vehicle No. 2 to rear end vehicle No. 3.

What diagram best describes the accident scene from the perspective of the individual driving vehicle No. 3?

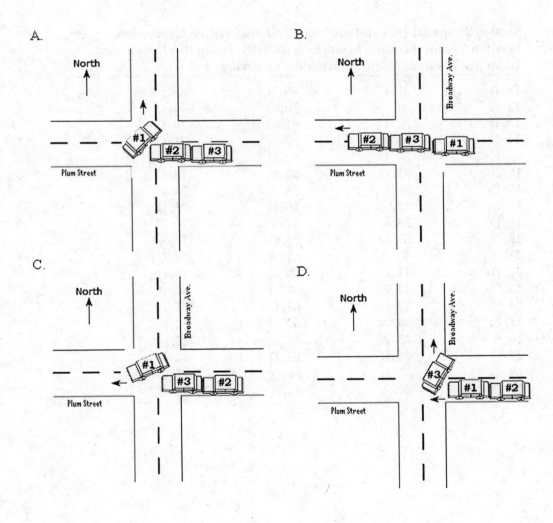

A.

B.

C.

D.

Answer Key

Section 1: Memorization

1. B	**6.** B
2. C	**7.** D
3. C	**8.** D
4. D	**9.** D
5. A	**10.** A

Section 2: Spatial Orientation, Visualization, Written Expression, Written Comprehension, Problem Sensitivity, Deductive Reasoning, Inductive Reasoning, and Information Ordering

11. B	**30.** C	**49.** B	**68.** C
12. A	**31.** A	**50.** C	**69.** C
13. B	**32.** C	**51.** C	**70.** C
14. B	**33.** A	**52.** A	**71.** C
15. C	**34.** D	**53.** B	**72.** B
16. B	**35.** C	**54.** D	**73.** C
17. D	**36.** C	**55.** A	**74.** B
18. B	**37.** A	**56.** D	**75.** D
19. D	**38.** C	**57.** C	**76.** D
20. D	**39.** D	**58.** B	**77.** B
21. B	**40.** A	**59.** A	**78.** C
22. B	**41.** C	**60.** C	**79.** C
23. C	**42.** B	**61.** B	**80.** B
24. C	**43.** D	**62.** C	**81.** A
25. C	**44.** A	**63.** C	**82.** C
26. B	**45.** A	**64.** C	**83.** C
27. C	**46.** B	**65.** D	**84.** C
28. C	**47.** D	**66.** A	**85.** D
29. D	**48.** A	**67.** A	**86.** C

PRACTICE TEST 4

**Similar to the Denver, Colorado,
Law Enforcement Exam**

Answer Sheet

Section 1: Written Skills

1. Ⓐ Ⓑ Ⓒ Ⓓ
2. Ⓐ Ⓑ Ⓒ Ⓓ
3. Ⓐ Ⓑ Ⓒ Ⓓ
4. Ⓐ Ⓑ Ⓒ Ⓓ
5. Ⓐ Ⓑ Ⓒ Ⓓ
6. Ⓐ Ⓑ Ⓒ Ⓓ
7. Ⓐ Ⓑ Ⓒ Ⓓ
8. Ⓐ Ⓑ Ⓒ Ⓓ
9. Ⓐ Ⓑ Ⓒ Ⓓ
10. Ⓐ Ⓑ Ⓒ Ⓓ
11. Ⓐ Ⓑ Ⓒ Ⓓ
12. Ⓐ Ⓑ Ⓒ Ⓓ
13. Ⓐ Ⓑ Ⓒ Ⓓ
14. Ⓐ Ⓑ Ⓒ Ⓓ
15. Ⓐ Ⓑ Ⓒ Ⓓ
16. Ⓐ Ⓑ Ⓒ Ⓓ
17. Ⓐ Ⓑ Ⓒ Ⓓ
18. Ⓐ Ⓑ Ⓒ Ⓓ
19. Ⓐ Ⓑ Ⓒ Ⓓ
20. Ⓐ Ⓑ Ⓒ Ⓓ
21. Ⓐ Ⓑ Ⓒ Ⓓ
22. Ⓐ Ⓑ Ⓒ Ⓓ
23. Ⓐ Ⓑ Ⓒ Ⓓ
24. Ⓐ Ⓑ Ⓒ Ⓓ
25. Ⓐ Ⓑ Ⓒ Ⓓ
26. Ⓐ Ⓑ Ⓒ Ⓓ
27. Ⓐ Ⓑ Ⓒ Ⓓ
28. Ⓐ Ⓑ Ⓒ Ⓓ
29. Ⓐ Ⓑ Ⓒ Ⓓ
30. Ⓐ Ⓑ Ⓒ Ⓓ
31. Ⓐ Ⓑ Ⓒ Ⓓ

Section 2: Basic Skills

32. Ⓐ Ⓑ Ⓒ Ⓓ
33. Ⓐ Ⓑ Ⓒ Ⓓ
34. Ⓐ Ⓑ Ⓒ Ⓓ
35. Ⓐ Ⓑ Ⓒ Ⓓ
36. Ⓐ Ⓑ Ⓒ Ⓓ
37. Ⓐ Ⓑ Ⓒ Ⓓ
38. Ⓐ Ⓑ Ⓒ Ⓓ
39. Ⓐ Ⓑ Ⓒ Ⓓ
40. Ⓐ Ⓑ Ⓒ Ⓓ
41. Ⓐ Ⓑ Ⓒ Ⓓ
42. Ⓐ Ⓑ Ⓒ Ⓓ
43. Ⓐ Ⓑ Ⓒ Ⓓ
44. Ⓐ Ⓑ Ⓒ Ⓓ
45. Ⓐ Ⓑ Ⓒ Ⓓ
46. Ⓐ Ⓑ Ⓒ Ⓓ
47. Ⓐ Ⓑ Ⓒ Ⓓ
48. Ⓐ Ⓑ Ⓒ Ⓓ
49. Ⓐ Ⓑ Ⓒ Ⓓ
50. Ⓐ Ⓑ Ⓒ Ⓓ
51. Ⓐ Ⓑ Ⓒ Ⓓ
52. Ⓐ Ⓑ Ⓒ Ⓓ
53. Ⓐ Ⓑ Ⓒ Ⓓ
54. Ⓐ Ⓑ Ⓒ Ⓓ
55. Ⓐ Ⓑ Ⓒ Ⓓ
56. Ⓐ Ⓑ Ⓒ Ⓓ
57. Ⓐ Ⓑ Ⓒ Ⓓ
58. Ⓐ Ⓑ Ⓒ Ⓓ
59. Ⓐ Ⓑ Ⓒ Ⓓ
60. Ⓐ Ⓑ Ⓒ Ⓓ
61. Ⓐ Ⓑ Ⓒ Ⓓ

62. Ⓐ Ⓑ Ⓒ Ⓓ
63. Ⓐ Ⓑ Ⓒ Ⓓ
64. Ⓐ Ⓑ Ⓒ Ⓓ
65. Ⓐ Ⓑ Ⓒ Ⓓ
66. Ⓐ Ⓑ Ⓒ Ⓓ
67. Ⓐ Ⓑ Ⓒ Ⓓ
68. Ⓐ Ⓑ Ⓒ Ⓓ
69. Ⓐ Ⓑ Ⓒ Ⓓ
70. Ⓐ Ⓑ Ⓒ Ⓓ
71. Ⓐ Ⓑ Ⓒ Ⓓ
72. Ⓐ Ⓑ Ⓒ Ⓓ
73. Ⓐ Ⓑ Ⓒ Ⓓ
74. Ⓐ Ⓑ Ⓒ Ⓓ
75. Ⓐ Ⓑ Ⓒ Ⓓ
76. Ⓐ Ⓑ Ⓒ Ⓓ
77. Ⓐ Ⓑ Ⓒ Ⓓ
78. Ⓐ Ⓑ Ⓒ Ⓓ
79. Ⓐ Ⓑ Ⓒ Ⓓ
80. Ⓐ Ⓑ Ⓒ Ⓓ
81. Ⓐ Ⓑ Ⓒ Ⓓ
82. Ⓐ Ⓑ Ⓒ Ⓓ
83. Ⓐ Ⓑ Ⓒ Ⓓ
84. Ⓐ Ⓑ Ⓒ Ⓓ
85. Ⓐ Ⓑ Ⓒ Ⓓ
86. Ⓐ Ⓑ Ⓒ Ⓓ
87. Ⓐ Ⓑ Ⓒ Ⓓ
88. Ⓐ Ⓑ Ⓒ Ⓓ
89. Ⓐ Ⓑ Ⓒ Ⓓ
90. Ⓐ Ⓑ Ⓒ Ⓓ
91. Ⓐ Ⓑ Ⓒ Ⓓ

Section 3: Police Abilities

92. Ⓐ Ⓑ Ⓒ Ⓓ   126. Ⓐ Ⓑ Ⓒ Ⓓ   160. Ⓐ Ⓑ Ⓒ Ⓓ
93. Ⓐ Ⓑ Ⓒ Ⓓ   127. Ⓐ Ⓑ Ⓒ Ⓓ   161. Ⓐ Ⓑ Ⓒ Ⓓ
94. Ⓐ Ⓑ Ⓒ Ⓓ   128. Ⓐ Ⓑ Ⓒ Ⓓ   162. Ⓐ Ⓑ Ⓒ Ⓓ
95. Ⓐ Ⓑ Ⓒ Ⓓ   129. Ⓐ Ⓑ Ⓒ Ⓓ   163. Ⓐ Ⓑ Ⓒ Ⓓ
96. Ⓐ Ⓑ Ⓒ Ⓓ   130. Ⓐ Ⓑ Ⓒ Ⓓ   164. Ⓐ Ⓑ Ⓒ Ⓓ

97. Ⓐ Ⓑ Ⓒ Ⓓ   131. Ⓐ Ⓑ Ⓒ Ⓓ   165. Ⓐ Ⓑ Ⓒ Ⓓ
98. Ⓐ Ⓑ Ⓒ Ⓓ   132. Ⓐ Ⓑ Ⓒ Ⓓ   166. Ⓐ Ⓑ Ⓒ Ⓓ
99. Ⓐ Ⓑ Ⓒ Ⓓ   133. Ⓐ Ⓑ Ⓒ Ⓓ   167. Ⓐ Ⓑ Ⓒ Ⓓ
100. Ⓐ Ⓑ Ⓒ Ⓓ   134. Ⓐ Ⓑ Ⓒ Ⓓ   168. Ⓐ Ⓑ Ⓒ Ⓓ
101. Ⓐ Ⓑ Ⓒ Ⓓ   135. Ⓐ Ⓑ Ⓒ Ⓓ   169. Ⓐ Ⓑ Ⓒ Ⓓ

102. Ⓐ Ⓑ Ⓒ Ⓓ   136. Ⓐ Ⓑ Ⓒ Ⓓ   170. Ⓐ Ⓑ Ⓒ Ⓓ
103. Ⓐ Ⓑ Ⓒ Ⓓ   137. Ⓐ Ⓑ Ⓒ Ⓓ   171. Ⓐ Ⓑ Ⓒ Ⓓ
104. Ⓐ Ⓑ Ⓒ Ⓓ   138. Ⓐ Ⓑ Ⓒ Ⓓ   172. Ⓐ Ⓑ Ⓒ Ⓓ
105. Ⓐ Ⓑ Ⓒ Ⓓ   139. Ⓐ Ⓑ Ⓒ Ⓓ   173. Ⓐ Ⓑ Ⓒ Ⓓ
106. Ⓐ Ⓑ Ⓒ Ⓓ   140. Ⓐ Ⓑ Ⓒ Ⓓ   174. Ⓐ Ⓑ Ⓒ Ⓓ

107. Ⓐ Ⓑ Ⓒ Ⓓ   141. Ⓐ Ⓑ Ⓒ Ⓓ   175. Ⓐ Ⓑ Ⓒ Ⓓ
108. Ⓐ Ⓑ Ⓒ Ⓓ   142. Ⓐ Ⓑ Ⓒ Ⓓ   176. Ⓐ Ⓑ Ⓒ Ⓓ
109. Ⓐ Ⓑ Ⓒ Ⓓ   143. Ⓐ Ⓑ Ⓒ Ⓓ   177. Ⓐ Ⓑ Ⓒ Ⓓ
110. Ⓐ Ⓑ Ⓒ Ⓓ   144. Ⓐ Ⓑ Ⓒ Ⓓ   178. Ⓐ Ⓑ Ⓒ Ⓓ
111. Ⓐ Ⓑ Ⓒ Ⓓ   145. Ⓐ Ⓑ Ⓒ Ⓓ   179. Ⓐ Ⓑ Ⓒ Ⓓ

112. Ⓐ Ⓑ Ⓒ Ⓓ   146. Ⓐ Ⓑ Ⓒ Ⓓ   180. Ⓐ Ⓑ Ⓒ Ⓓ
113. Ⓐ Ⓑ Ⓒ Ⓓ   147. Ⓐ Ⓑ Ⓒ Ⓓ   181. Ⓐ Ⓑ Ⓒ Ⓓ
114. Ⓐ Ⓑ Ⓒ Ⓓ   148. Ⓐ Ⓑ Ⓒ Ⓓ   182. Ⓐ Ⓑ Ⓒ Ⓓ
115. Ⓐ Ⓑ Ⓒ Ⓓ   149. Ⓐ Ⓑ Ⓒ Ⓓ   183. Ⓐ Ⓑ Ⓒ Ⓓ
116. Ⓐ Ⓑ Ⓒ Ⓓ   150. Ⓐ Ⓑ Ⓒ Ⓓ   184. Ⓐ Ⓑ Ⓒ Ⓓ

117. Ⓐ Ⓑ Ⓒ Ⓓ   151. Ⓐ Ⓑ Ⓒ Ⓓ   185. Ⓐ Ⓑ Ⓒ Ⓓ
118. Ⓐ Ⓑ Ⓒ Ⓓ   152. Ⓐ Ⓑ Ⓒ Ⓓ   186. Ⓐ Ⓑ Ⓒ Ⓓ
119. Ⓐ Ⓑ Ⓒ Ⓓ   153. Ⓐ Ⓑ Ⓒ Ⓓ   187. Ⓐ Ⓑ Ⓒ Ⓓ
120. Ⓐ Ⓑ Ⓒ Ⓓ   154. Ⓐ Ⓑ Ⓒ Ⓓ   188. Ⓐ Ⓑ Ⓒ Ⓓ
121. Ⓐ Ⓑ Ⓒ Ⓓ   155. Ⓐ Ⓑ Ⓒ Ⓓ   189. Ⓐ Ⓑ Ⓒ Ⓓ

122. Ⓐ Ⓑ Ⓒ Ⓓ   156. Ⓐ Ⓑ Ⓒ Ⓓ   190. Ⓐ Ⓑ Ⓒ Ⓓ
123. Ⓐ Ⓑ Ⓒ Ⓓ   157. Ⓐ Ⓑ Ⓒ Ⓓ   191. Ⓐ Ⓑ Ⓒ Ⓓ
124. Ⓐ Ⓑ Ⓒ Ⓓ   158. Ⓐ Ⓑ Ⓒ Ⓓ
125. Ⓐ Ⓑ Ⓒ Ⓓ   159. Ⓐ Ⓑ Ⓒ Ⓓ

Practice Test 4

This test includes 191 questions. The questions are numbered consecutively from 1 through 191. The questions are divided into three groups: Written Skills (questions 1–31), Basic Skills (questions 32–91), and Police Abilities (questions 92–191). Mark your answers on the answer sheet provided.

SECTION 1
WRITTEN SKILLS

This section of the test consists of a three short letters containing numbered sentences. Each letter is followed by questions that must be answered using the information contained in the letters. Select only one answer for each question. There are a total of 31 questions in this section. You will only have 30 minutes to complete this section of the exam. You must get 22 questions correct (approximately 70 percent) to pass this section.

DEAR OFFICER NORBERT:

1   I am pleassed to learn that you have safely returned from your basic training with the military.

2   Your job as a police officer is been kept available until your return.

3   However, you been in Central City for approximately three weeks and have not yet contacted the Department.

4   You have yet to provide the date for which you will be returning to work.

5   This is unacceptable.

6   Both the officers of this department and the citizens of this community relie on your diligence.

7   The City will hold your position open until Monday July 2nd.

8   If you have not contacted this office by that date your employment is terminated.

9   Please contact this office before that date if you have chosen to resign your positon with the City.

10   Thank you for your time and assistanse in this matter.

Answer the following questions regarding the letter provided above.

1. In line 1 of the letter, identify the type of error, if any:

   (A) Spelling
   (B) Grammar
   (C) Punctuation
   (D) No error

GO ON TO THE NEXT PAGE

2. In line 2 of the letter, identify the type of error, if any:

(A) Spelling
(B) Grammar
(C) Punctuation
(D) No error

3. In line 3 of the letter, identify the type of error, if any:

(A) Spelling
(B) Grammar
(C) Punctuation
(D) No error

4. In line 4 of the letter, identify the type of error, if any:

(A) Spelling
(B) Grammar
(C) Punctuation
(D) No error

5. In line 5 of the letter, identify the type of error, if any:

(A) Spelling
(B) Grammar
(C) Punctuation
(D) No error

6. In line 6 of the letter, identify the type of error, if any:

(A) Spelling
(B) Grammar
(C) Punctuation
(D) No error

7. In line 7 of the letter, identify the type of error, if any:

(A) Spelling
(B) Grammar
(C) Punctuation
(D) No error

8. In line 8 of the letter, identify the type of error, if any:

(A) Spelling
(B) Grammar
(C) Punctuation
(D) No error

GO ON TO THE NEXT PAGE

9. In line 9 of the letter, identify the type of error, if any:

(A) Spelling
(B) Grammar
(C) Punctuation
(D) No error

10. In line 10 of the letter, identify the type of error, if any:

(A) Spelling
(B) Grammar
(C) Punctuation
(D) No error

DEAR OFFICER NGUYEN:

1   Congratulations on being selected for promotion to the rank of Seargent.
2   You exemplary work ethic and numerous commendations for service showed us.
3   Also, your skill as an interpreter is highlly valued by this Department.
4   A short ceremony followed by a reception on July 15th.
5   On August 1st you will report to training serrvices for a week of leadership training.
6   Then you will be assigned to the Northeast Station.
7   You duties will include supervising 12 newly commissioned officers.
8   But also 12 veteran officers.
9   In addition, you will be the departments liaison to the Vietnamese community.
10   You will get extra pay for this service and you will retrain on your weapon every six months and you will be issued a car and work for 46 hours every week.
11   I look forward to visiting with you in person at the promotion ceremony.

Answer the following questions regarding the letter provided above.

11. In line 1 of the letter, identify the type of error, if any:

(A) Spelling
(B) Grammar
(C) Punctuation
(D) No error

12. In line 2 of the letter, identify the type of error, if any:

(A) Spelling
(B) Grammar
(C) Punctuation
(D) No error

GO ON TO THE NEXT PAGE

13. In line 3 of the letter, identify the type of error, if any:

    (A) Spelling
    (B) Grammar
    (C) Punctuation
    (D) No error

14. In line 4 of the letter, identify the type of error, if any:

    (A) Spelling
    (B) Grammar
    (C) Punctuation
    (D) No error

15. In line 5 of the letter, identify the type of error, if any:

    (A) Spelling
    (B) Grammar
    (C) Punctuation
    (D) No error

16. In line 6 of the letter, identify the type of error, if any:

    (A) Spelling
    (B) Grammar
    (C) Punctuation
    (D) No error

17. In line 7 of the letter, identify the type of error, if any:

    (A) Spelling
    (B) Grammar
    (C) Punctuation
    (D) No error

18. In line 8 of the letter, identify the type of error, if any:

    (A) Spelling
    (B) Grammar
    (C) Punctuation
    (D) No error

19. In line 9 of the letter, identify the type of error, if any:

    (A) Spelling
    (B) Grammar
    (C) Punctuation
    (D) No error

GO ON TO THE NEXT PAGE

20. In line 10 of the letter, identify the type of error, if any:

(A) Spelling
(B) Grammar
(C) Punctuation
(D) No error

21. In line 11 of the letter, identify the type of error, if any:

(A) Spelling
(B) Grammar
(C) Punctuation
(D) No error

DEAR PRINCIPAL ADAMS:

1   I am honored to have received your gracious invitation to participate in your school's cultural awareness day.

2   As a representative of the Mountain High Police Department.

3   I would be pleased speak with your students about the necessity of becoming bilingual.

4   Of course, they must practice their bilingual a lot.

5   I know the students' don't like to use their books!

6   I will also be promoting the advantages of academic success in English and Math for students who seek to enter the law enforcement field.

7   I unnerstand that the program is to take place from 1 to 4 P.M. on October 14 in the gymnasium.

8   I will bring brochures and a video to share with student's.

9   I look forward to visitting with you and your students.

10   On October 14 at 1:00 P.M.

Answer the following questions regarding the letter provided above.

22. In line 1 of the letter, identify the type of error, if any:

(A) Spelling
(B) Grammar
(C) Punctuation
(D) No error

23. In line 2 of the letter, identify the type of error, if any:

(A) Spelling
(B) Grammar
(C) Punctuation
(D) No error

GO ON TO THE NEXT PAGE

24. In line 3 of the letter, identify the type of error, if any:

(A) Spelling
(B) Grammar
(C) Punctuation
(D) No error

25. In line 4 of the letter, identify the type of error, if any:

(A) Spelling
(B) Grammar
(C) Punctuation
(D) No error

26. In line 5 of the letter, identify the type of error, if any:

(A) Spelling
(B) Grammar
(C) Punctuation
(D) No error

27. In line 6 of the letter, identify the type of error, if any:

(A) Spelling
(B) Grammar
(C) Punctuation
(D) No error

28. In line 7 of the letter, identify the type of error, if any:

(A) Spelling
(B) Grammar
(C) Punctuation
(D) No error

29. In line 8 of the letter, identify the type of error, if any:

(A) Spelling
(B) Grammar
(C) Punctuation
(D) No error

30. In line 9 of the letter, identify the type of error, if any:

(A) Spelling
(B) Grammar
(C) Punctuation
(D) No error

GO ON TO THE NEXT PAGE

31. In line 10 of the letter, identify the type of error, if any:

  (A) Spelling
  (B) Grammar
  (C) Punctuation
  (D) No error

BASIC SKILLS

This section of the exam covers three areas: reading comprehension, vocabulary, and mathematics. There are a total of 60 questions in this section and you must get 42 correct (approximately 70 percent) to pass. You will only be given 30 minutes to complete all three areas of this section.

READING COMPREHENSION

Read each of the following paragraphs and then answer the questions that follow based upon the information contained in the passage. The information needed to answer the questions is contained in the paragraph, but you may need to draw a conclusion based upon the information provided.

One of the most common tasks performed by a patrol officer is stopping vehicles. A lawful stop must be based on factual circumstances rather than a "gut feeling." Clearly, a vehicle may be stopped for a traffic infraction, called a "traffic stop." A vehicle may be subject to a "vehicle stop" when it fits the description of a vehicle involved in a crime.

32. According to the passage, traffic stops are a routine part of police work.

(A) True
(B) False

33. According to the passage, traffic stops can occur whenever an officer gets a hunch that something is wrong.

(A) True
(B) False

34. According to the passage, police can stop vehicles for non-traffic reasons if they can reasonably link the vehicle or occupants to criminal activity.

(A) True
(B) False

35. Failing to signal a turn is lawful grounds to stop a vehicle.

(A) True
(B) False

GO ON TO THE NEXT PAGE

Law enforcement officers are trained to communicate with suspects in a manner that is clear, respectful and easily understood. Following adrenaline inducing situations such as a high-speed pursuit or even a chase on foot, officers will experience emotions ranging from anger to the thrill of a successful capture. Although in these situations the temptation to use offensive or threatening language when speaking to suspects is often very great, such behavior must always be avoided.

36. According to the passage, police are expected to be emotionless.

   (A) True
   (B) False

37. According to the passage, certain situations justify strong language.

   (A) True
   (B) False

38. According to the information provided in the passage, Officer Jeffries should only consider using strong language after a suspect or citizen first uses such language.

   (A) True
   (B) False

Although the United States Supreme Court has generally held that individuals are responsible for educating themselves about their constitutional rights, law enforcement has been charged with informing suspects about two of those rights. In a case involving a defendant named Miranda the Court held that suspects must be warned of the Fifth Amendment's privilege against self-incrimination and the Sixth Amendment's right to counsel. Law enforcement officers as well as the public are often confused about when Miranda warnings must be given. Television dramas have incorrectly taught the general public that Miranda warnings must be given at the time of arrest in order for the arrest to be lawful. In fact, Miranda warnings are only required when a suspect is in custody and subject to interrogation.

39. According to the passage, Miranda warnings are named after a United States Supreme Court Justice.

   (A) True
   (B) False

40. Jerry was arrested after he allowed his car to be searched by police. Although, he took United States Government while in high school, he does not remember much about it. According to the information provided in the paragraph, the search of Jerry's car was illegal because police should have reminded Jerry he had the constitutional right to refuse to permit the search.

   (A) True
   (B) False

GO ON TO THE NEXT PAGE

41. According to the passage, the Miranda warnings include information about:

(A) The fourth amendment protection against searches
(B) The fifth amendment privilege against self-incrimination
(C) The sixth amendment right to counsel
(D) B and C only

VOCABULARY

Read the following 20 vocabulary words, and then select the word from the list provided that most closely describes the vocabulary word.

42. Select the word from the list provided that most closely describes the word DEMEANOR.

(A) Manner
(B) Cruel
(C) Smaller
(D) Reduced

43. Select the word from the list provided that most closely describes the word STIMULUS.

(A) Temperature
(B) Provocation
(C) Kindness
(D) Sting

44. Select the word from the list provided that most closely describes the word INDIGENT.

(A) Unwell
(B) Angry
(C) Deep
(D) Poor

45. Select the word from the list provided that most closely describes the word MUNICIPALITY.

(A) Area
(B) People
(C) City
(D) Court

GO ON TO THE NEXT PAGE

46. Select the word from the list provided that most closely describes the word GIMMICK.

   (A) Function
   (B) Trick
   (C) Noose
   (D) Bird

47. Select the word from the list provided that most closely describes the word DISCRETION.

   (A) Judgment
   (B) Improper
   (C) Ethics
   (D) Secret

48. Select the word from the list provided that most closely describes the word ENERGETIC.

   (A) Happy
   (B) Youthful
   (C) Powerful
   (D) Lively

49. Select the word from the list provided that most closely describes the word IMPETUOUS.

   (A) Friendly
   (B) Spendthrift
   (C) Thoughtless
   (D) Youthful

50. Select the word from the list provided that most closely describes the word VOLATILE.

   (A) Flooring
   (B) Explosive
   (C) Powerful
   (D) Hot

51. Select the word from the list provided that most closely describes the word TENDENCY.

   (A) Method
   (B) Consistency
   (C) Personality
   (D) Inclination

GO ON TO THE NEXT PAGE

52. Select the word from the list provided that most closely describes the word SEGREGATE.

(A) Isolate
(B) Hurt
(C) Punish
(D) Deprive

53. Select the word from the list provided that most closely describes the word RELINQUISH.

(A) Stir
(B) Release
(C) Throw
(D) Return

54. Select the word from the list provided that most closely describes the word DISSEMINATE.

(A) Process
(B) Cook
(C) Speak
(D) Distribute

55. Select the word from the list provided that most closely describes the word INTERVENE.

(A) Periodic
(B) Close
(C) Interfere
(D) Stop

56. Select the word from the list provided that most closely describes the word MASSIVE.

(A) Message
(B) Massage
(C) Huge
(D) Strong

57. Select the word from the list provided that most closely describes the word FLEXIBLE.

(A) Pliable
(B) Breakable
(C) Moveable
(D) Functional

GO ON TO THE NEXT PAGE

58. Select the word from the list provided that most closely describes the word DIRTY.

(A) Rude
(B) Torn
(C) Unkempt
(D) Unclean

59. Select the word from the list provided that most closely describes the word REFUTE.

(A) Rebut
(B) Regale
(C) Return
(D) Reuse

60. Select the word from the list provided that most closely describes the word PROFESSIONAL.

(A) Good
(B) Wealthy
(C) Expert
(D) Faithful

61. Select the word from the list provided that most closely describes the word DENSE.

(A) Fog
(B) Mean
(C) Forest
(D) Thick

MATHEMATICS

Provide the correct answers to the basic arithmetic functions and story problems provided below. There are 30 questions in this area.

62. Add: $817 + 222$

(A) 1229
(B) 1029
(C) 1039
(D) 1129

GO ON TO THE NEXT PAGE

63. Subtract: $915 - 534$

    (A) 381
    (B) 351
    (C) 271
    (D) 251

64. Multiply: 13×8

    (A) 104
    (B) 96
    (C) 112
    (D) 91

65. Divide: $112 \div 8$

    (A) 12
    (B) 13
    (C) 14
    (D) 15

66. Add: $1546 + 397$

    (A) 1843
    (B) 1853
    (C) 1943
    (D) 1953

67. Subtract: $732 - 117$

    (A) 515
    (B) 525
    (C) 575
    (D) 615

68. Divide: $81 \div 9$

    (A) 7
    (B) 8
    (C) 9
    (D) 10

69. Divide: $105 \div 7$

    (A) 12
    (B) 13
    (C) 14
    (D) 15

GO ON TO THE NEXT PAGE

Answer questions 70–73 using the following information.

Exceeding maximum speed limit

  1–10 miles per hour (mph) over the limit, $25

  11–20 mph over the limit, $25 plus $6 per mph over 10 mph over the limit

  21–30 mph over the limit, $85 plus $9 per mph over 20 mph over the limit

  31 and more mph over the limit, $175 plus $15 per mph over 30 mph over the limit

  Fines are doubled for speeding infractions occurring in school zones and construction zones.

Court costs are a fixed fee added to each citation.

70. Officer Maxwell has issued a speeding citation for 45 mph in a 30 mph zone. If mandatory court costs are $50, what is the total cost of the citation?

   (A) $115
   (B) $110
   (C) $105
   (D) $125

71. Officer Maxwell has issued a speeding citation for 55 mph in a 30 mph zone. If mandatory court costs are $50, what is the total cost of the citation?

   (A) $160
   (B) $170
   (C) $180
   (D) $190

72. Officer Maxwell has issued a speeding citation for 64 mph in a 55 mph zone. If mandatory court costs are $50, what is the total cost of the citation?

   (A) $75
   (B) $80
   (C) $85
   (D) $90

73. Officer Maxwell has issued a speeding citation for driving at 35 mph in a 20 mph school zone. If mandatory court costs are $50, what is the total cost of the citation?

   (A) $105
   (B) $120
   (C) $140
   (D) $160

GO ON TO THE NEXT PAGE

Answer questions 74–76 using the following information.

The Super Computer Warehouse stocks the following products:

Desktop computers: valued at $650.00 each
Laptop computers: valued at $850.00 each
Printers: valued at $150.00 each
Flash drives: valued at $50.00 each

74. John has been charged with the robbery of The Super Computer Warehouse. The following items were stolen: two Desktop computers, three Laptop computers, five Printers, and six Flash drives. What is the total value of goods stolen during the robbery?

(A) 5000
(B) 4900
(C) 5250
(D) 5150

75. Further investigation into the robbery of The Super Computer Warehouse has revealed that one laptop computer, one printer and two flash drives were actually found to be missing the day prior to the robbery. Using this new information as well as the information contained in the previous question, what is the actual total value of goods that John stole during the robbery he committed?

(A) 3800
(B) 3500
(C) 3300
(D) 3650

76. The manager reports to the police that flash drives valued at a total of $950 have been discovered to be missing. How many flash drives were stolen?

(A) 14
(B) 16
(C) 19
(D) 21

77. Officer Johnson has 48 gun safety devices to distribute among six different school PTA's. How many gun safety devices will each PTA receive?

(A) 5
(B) 6
(C) 7
(D) 8

GO ON TO THE NEXT PAGE

78. The members of the traffic control unit issued the following citations during a recent seven-day period.

> Officer Maxim issued 36 citations.
> Officer Mendosa issued 107 citations.
> Officer Carosa issued 39 citations.
> Officer Hussein issued 27 citations.

How many citations were issued by the two traffic control officers writing the most citations for this time period?

(A) 143
(B) 75
(C) 134
(D) 146

79. Four items stolen in a recent burglary were valued at $2,432.00. A pawnshop was found to be in possession of three of the items reported stolen in that burglary. Item A is valued at $556, item B is valued at $664, and item C is valued at $763. What is the value of the item that has not yet been recovered?

(A) 349
(B) 399
(C) 449
(D) 499

80. The precinct has hired 16 officers to be equally spread across four police units. How many new officers will each unit gain?

(A) 3
(B) 4
(C) 5
(D) 6

81. Lieutenant Clarice must submit his weekly report of traffic citations issued by his unit. Three officers issued 50 tickets each, three officers issued 30 tickets each, and two officers issued 40 tickets each. How many total tickets were issued by Lt. Clarice's unit?

(A) 120
(B) 320
(C) 270
(D) 170

82. Add: 154 + 397

(A) 554
(B) 421
(C) 551
(D) 454

GO ON TO THE NEXT PAGE

83. Subtract: $72 - 17$

(A) 60
(B) 63
(C) 53
(D) 55

84. Multiply: 8×7

(A) 64
(B) 54
(C) 56
(D) 63

85. Divide: $777 \div 111$

(A) 77
(B) 11
(C) 7
(D) 111

86. The precinct has hired 20 officers to be equally spread across 5 police units. How many new officers will each unit gain?

(A) 3
(B) 4
(C) 5
(D) 6

87. Lieutenant Davies must submit his weekly report of traffic citations issued by his unit. Six officers issued 45 tickets each, four officers issued 40 tickets each, one officer issued 76 tickets, and the final officer issued 74 tickets. How many total tickets were issued by Lt. Davies unit?

(A) 580
(B) 540
(C) 680
(D) 620

88. Add: $692 + 497$

(A) 1099
(B) 1289
(C) 1089
(D) 1189

GO ON TO THE NEXT PAGE

89. Subtract: $3478 - 1107$

    (A) 2271
    (B) 2371
    (C) 2341
    (D) 2241

90. Multiply: 589×15

    (A) 7875
    (B) 6730
    (C) 8835
    (D) 7345

91. Divide: $1020 \div 60$

    (A) 15
    (B) 16
    (C) 17
    (D) 11

STOP. THIS IS THE END OF SECTION 2.

POLICE ABILITIES

This section will begin with a 30-minute study session. On the real exam, you will not be allowed to exit this session early. During this time you will study 12 information items: illustrations, diagrams, maps, documents, and passages. (On the real exam these items are presented on a computer screen.) At the end of the 30-minute study session you will be given 100 fact questions to answer about the information contained in the 12 information items. This section is designed to test your ability to remember facts, read maps, figure out directions, and pay attention to details. You will have 1 hour and 30 minutes to complete this section. You must get 70 questions (approximately 70 percent) correct in order to pass this section.

GO ON TO THE NEXT PAGE

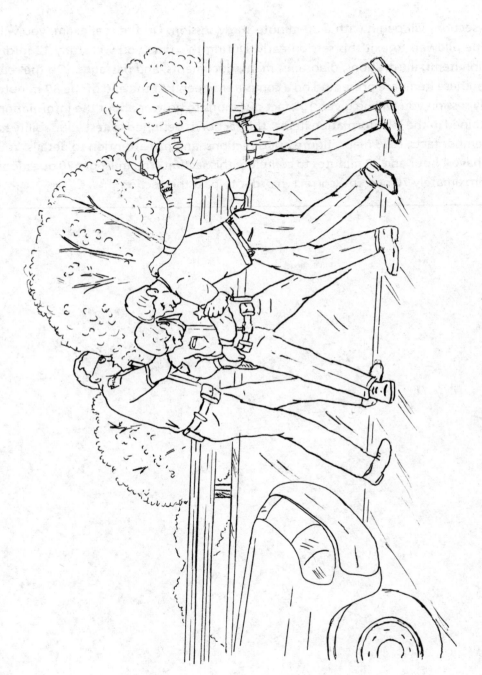

Drawing of struggle with suspect

GO ON TO THE NEXT PAGE

SKETCH OF SUSPECT #1

NAME: Jerry Balducci

Alias: Jason Winters

Age: 23

Eyes: brown

Hair: brown

Height: 5'10"

Weight: 165 lbs.

Identifying characteristics: 1. Missing front tooth, 2. Snake tattoo on left forearm.

Wanted for: Suspected auto theft

KNOCK AND ANNOUNCE RULE

An officer's unannounced entry into a home might, in some circumstances, be unreasonable under the Fourth Amendment. In evaluating the scope of the constitutional right to be secure in one's home against police intrusion, the US Supreme Court has looked to the traditional protections against unreasonable searches and seizures. That Court found that there is historical common law support for the practice of knocking at a suspect's door and announcing law enforcements' intent to enter the dwelling. Until recently that Court used law enforcements' actions of knocking and announcing their presence as a critical factor to be considered in assessing whether a search was reasonable. If a search is found to be unreasonable it will be declared unlawful and all evidence taken during the search will not be allowed to be used against the suspect at trial. Nevertheless, the common law principle of *knock* and *announce* has never been found to be an inflexible rule requiring announcement under all circumstances. Countervailing law enforcement interests – including the threat of physical harm to police, the fact that an officer is pursuing a recently escaped arrestee, and the existence of reason to believe that evidence would likely be destroyed if advance notice were given – may establish the reasonableness of an unannounced entry.

Paragraph about "knock and announce" rule

GO ON TO THE NEXT PAGE

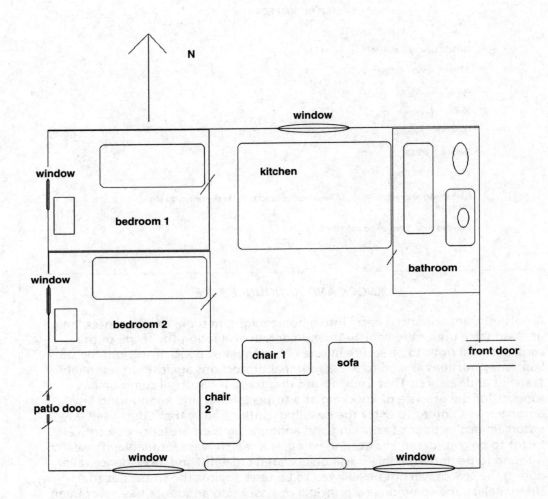

N

window

window

window

bedroom 1

kitchen

window

bedroom 2

chair 1

sofa

bathroom

front door

chair 2

patio door

window

window

DIAGRAM OF THE INTERIOR OF A HOUSE

GO ON TO THE NEXT PAGE

Drawing of a traffic intersection in a typical urban neighborhood

GO ON TO THE NEXT PAGE

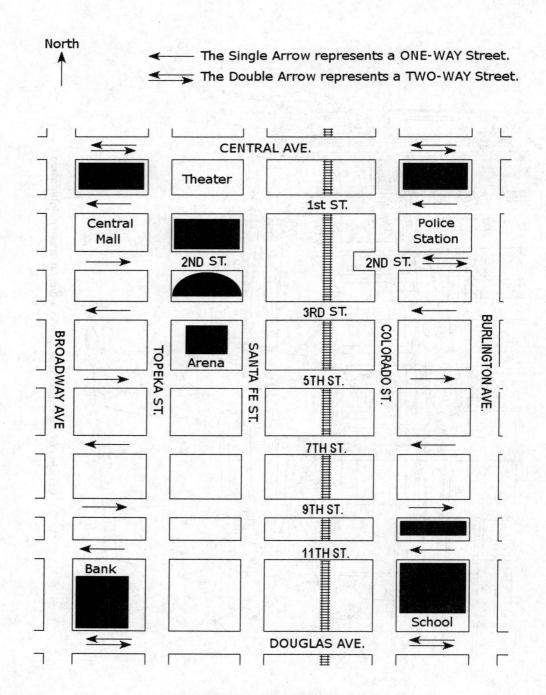

North

→ The Single Arrow represents a ONE-WAY Street.

⇄ The Double Arrow represents a TWO-WAY Street.

CENTRAL AVE.

Theater

1st ST.

Central Mall

Police Station

2ND ST.

2ND ST.

3RD ST.

Arena

BROADWAY AVE.

TOPEKA ST.

SANTA FE ST.

COLORADO ST.

BURLINGTON AVE.

5TH ST.

7TH ST.

9TH ST.

11TH ST.

Bank

School

DOUGLAS AVE.

STREET MAP OF "DOWNTOWN"

GO ON TO THE NEXT PAGE

SAMPLE POLICE REPORT #1

Earl calls for police assistance. When you arrive at the scene you find
Earl clearly upset. He tells you that he was walking toward his car and
carrying some shopping bags with his recent purchases. A man ran up to
him and told Earl that he had better give him the bags or he was going
to hurt Earl "real bad." Earl gave the man the bags containing
approximately $500.00 in new clothes. Earl describes the assailant as
in his mid-twenties, olive complexion, 5'6", 145 lbs, a red sweatshirt,
blue jeans, and a tattoo on his neck. Earl described the clothes as
professional clothing that could be worn to an office environment.
Later you see Fred, a well-known thief and bully, standing outside a
convenience store wearing new clothes matching the description of the
clothes which were taken. You arrest Fred and charge him with robbery.

Scenario labeled "Sample Police Report No. 1"

Standard Arrest Report, Page 1

STANDARD ARREST REPORT			PAGE____ OF____
☐ INITIAL ☐ ADD ☐ MODIFY ☐ DELETE			

☑ ADULT   ☐ JUVENILE   ☐ DOMESTIC VIOLENCE   ☐ RUNAWAY

ARREST

NAME OF AGENCY	AGENCY ORI NUMBER	CASE NUMBER	DATE AND TIME OF ARREST 9/2/06 2200 hours
ARREST TRANSACTION NUMBER	ORI NUMBER	LOCAL NUMBER	CAMPUS CODE

TYPE OF ARREST: ☐ ON - VIEW ☐ TAKEN INTO CUSTODY   DISPOSITION OF JUVENILE ARREST OR RUNAWAY.
☐ SUMMONED / CITED - NOT TAKEN INTO CUSTODY ☐ RUNAWAY   ☐ HANDLED IN DEPARTMENT   ☐ REFERRED TO OTHER AUTHORITIES

ARREST / CONTACT LOCATION: 1500 Pioneer Lane	WARRANT #	DATE

ARRESTEE'S / RUNAWAY NAME   LAST Hastings   FIRST Mary   MIDDLE Sue

ALIASES - MONIKERS

ARRESTEE #

ADDRESS STREET 1500 Pioneer Lane	CITY Lakewood	STATE Colorado	ZIP	TELEPHONE NUMBER (HOME) 720-555-4444

HEIGHT 5'10"	WEIGHT 175	HAIR Brown	EYES Brown	RACE Cauc.	SEX F	ETHNICITY	RES. / N- RES. Res.	AGE 42	DATE OF BIRTH (MM/DD/CCYY) 10-17-63	PLACE OF BIRTH (STATE / COUNTRY) Buena Vista, Co.

HAIR LENGTH Long	HAIR STYLE	FACIAL HAIR	GLASSES	TEETH	EYE APPEARANCE Glassy	COMPLEXION Fair	BUILD	R - L HANDED	SPEECH

SCARS - MARKS	TATTOOS Butterfly on ankle Gang symbols on hands	ARRESTEE/WORE Jeans, T-Shirt	APPEARANCE

DRIVERS LICENSE NUMBER None	D L STATE	LOCAL SECURITY NUMBER 555-55-4444	EMPLOYER / SCHOOL None	

TELEPHONE NUMBER (WORK / SCHOOL)	ADDRESS: STREET		CITY	STATE	ZIP

ARRESTEE INJURIES	MIRANDA: DATE - TIME 9-2-06 2200 hrs	BY #47	ARREST APPROVED BY: #11

ARRESTEE ARMED WITH (MAXIMUM OF 2):   ☒ UNARMED   ARRESTEE BEHAVIOR (ALL APPLICABLE):

☐ HANDGUN ☐ AUTO ☐ SHOTGUN ☒ AUTO ☐ CLUB /   ☒ DRUNK   ☐ RESISTED   ☐ BIZARRE BEHAVIOR ☐ OTHER
☐ RIFLE   ☐ AUTO ☐ LETHAL CUTTING BLACKJACK   ☒ DRINKING ☒ PROFANE   ☐ SUICIDAL REMARKS
☐ OTHER   ☐ AUTO INSTRUMENT / KNUCKS   ☐ INJURED ☒ LOUD   ☐ COOPERATIVE

GO ON TO THE NEXT PAGE

Standard Arrest Report, Page 2

<table>
<tr><td rowspan="3">ADDITIONAL INCIDENTS / CHARGES</td><td>CASE NUMBER</td><td>DATE OF INCIDENT
9-2-06</td><td>STATE STATUTE VIOLATION
CRS 42-4-130(1)(b)</td><td>OFFENSE WAS:
☐ ATTEMPTED
☑ COMPLETED</td><td>CLEARANCE INDICATOR:
☐ COUNT
☐ MULTIPLE
☐ OUTSIDE AGENCY</td></tr>
<tr><td>DESCRIPTION
Driving Under Influence of Alcohol or Drugs
TYPE OF THEFT:
M. ☐ COIN MACHINE   L. ☐ SHOPLIFTING   V. ☐ MOTOR VEHICLE
P. ☐ POCKET-PICKING   F. ☐ THEFT FROM M V
B. ☐ FROM BUILDING   S. ☐ PURSE SNATCHING   O. ☐ ALL OTHER
A. ☐ M V PARTS & ACC.   E. ☐ EMBEZZLEMENT   N. ☒ NOT APPLICABLE
T. ☐ POSS. STOLEN PROP.</td><td>LOCAL CODE</td><td>ADDITIONAL CHARGES   42-4-1413
Eluding a police officer

Speed limit 42-4-1101(f)</td><td>☐ AID / ABET
☐ CONSPIRACY
☐ SOLICITATION</td><td></td></tr>
</table>

(remainder of additional incidents blocks — blank)

CASE NUMBER	DATE OF INCIDENT	STATE STATUTE VIOLATION	OFFENSE WAS: ☐ ATTEMPTED ☐ COMPLETED ☐ AID / ABET ☐ CONSPIRACY ☐ SOLICITATION	CLEARANCE INDICATOR: ☐ COUNT ☐ MULTIPLE ☐ OUTSIDE AGENCY
DESCRIPTION TYPE OF THEFT: M. ☐ COIN MACHINE L. ☐ SHOPLIFTING V. ☐ MOTOR VEHICLE P. ☐ POCKET-PICKING F. ☐ THEFT FROM M V B. ☐ FROM BUILDING S. ☐ PURSE SNATCHING O. ☐ ALL OTHER A. ☐ M V PARTS & ACC. E. ☐ EMBEZZLEMENT N. ☐ NOT APPLICABLE T. ☐ POSS. STOLEN PROP.	LOCAL CODE	ADDITIONAL CHARGES		

CASE NUMBER	DATE OF INCIDENT	STATE STATUTE VIOLATION	OFFENSE WAS: ☐ ATTEMPTED ☐ COMPLETED ☐ AID / ABET ☐ CONSPIRACY ☐ SOLICITATION	CLEARANCE INDICATOR: ☐ COUNT ☐ MULTIPLE ☐ OUTSIDE AGENCY
DESCRIPTION TYPE OF THEFT: M. ☐ COIN MACHINE L. ☐ SHOPLIFTING V. ☐ MOTOR VEHICLE P. ☐ POCKET-PICKING F. ☐ THEFT FROM M V B. ☐ FROM BUILDING S. ☐ PURSE SNATCHING O. ☐ ALL OTHER A. ☐ M V PARTS & ACC. E. ☐ EMBEZZLEMENT N. ☐ NOT APPLICABLE T. ☐ POSS. STOLEN PROP.	LOCAL CODE	ADDITIONAL CHARGES		

VEHICLE

VEHICLE YEAR	MAKE	MODEL	STYLE	COLOR	VIN NUMBER	LICENSE #	STATE	YEAR
1975	Chevrolet	Van	Extended	Green	1GGGG22F3EE444444	Co.	05	

TOWED BY	DRIVER	LOCATION OF KEYS	LOCATION OF VEHICLE	CONDITION
Grady's Tow	Grady			Damaged right front fender

OWNER		ADDRESS		
John Q Summers		1555 Mountain Rd., Loreland, Co.		

RELEASED TO	ADDRESS	DATE	TIME

REPORTING OFFICER	ID#	DATE	COPIES TO:	SUPERVISING OFFICER	ID#
Calvin	144	9/3/06			

GO ON TO THE NEXT PAGE

Standard Arrest Report, Page 3

PARENT / GUARDIAN				
PARENT / GUARDIAN NAME	ADDRESS (HOME)	CITY	STATE	ZIP
EMPLOYER	ADDRESS (EMPLOYER)	CITY	STATE	ZIP
TELEPHONE NUMBER (HOME)	TELEPHONE NUMBER (WORK)	TELEPHONE NUMBER (OTHER)		
PARENT / GUARDIAN NAME	ADDRESS (HOME)	CITY	STATE	ZIP
EMPLOYER	ADDRESS (EMPLOYER)	CITY	STATE	ZIP
TELEPHONE NUMBER (HOME)	TELEPHONE NUMBER (WORK)	TELEPHONE NUMBER (OTHER)		

NARRATIVE / AFFIDAVIT

State of Co., Park _____ County, ss:

I. John Calvin _____ of lawful age, after first being duly sworn on oath, on information and belief states:

On 9-2-06 at. appx. 2200 hrs I saw a vehicle approach an unoccupied intersection, and came to a stop. The vehicle did not move again for several minutes. I then followed the vehicle and observed it cross the center line 3 times. I follow the vehicle for appx. 3 minutes, before I activated my emergency lights and initiated a traffic stop. As the vehicle was pulling over I could hear the transmission gears grinding as the driver had put the vehicle in park as it was still moving. As I approached the driver's side window I could smell a strong odor of alcoholic beverage, and I could see a cell phone lying on the seat with its face light still on. The driver immediately told me she had no i.d. with her, but she told her name was Mary Hastings. When she got out of the vehicle, her eyes appeared glassy and blood shot, and she staggered. She began to question me by asking me the same questions repeatedly.

GO ON TO THE NEXT PAGE

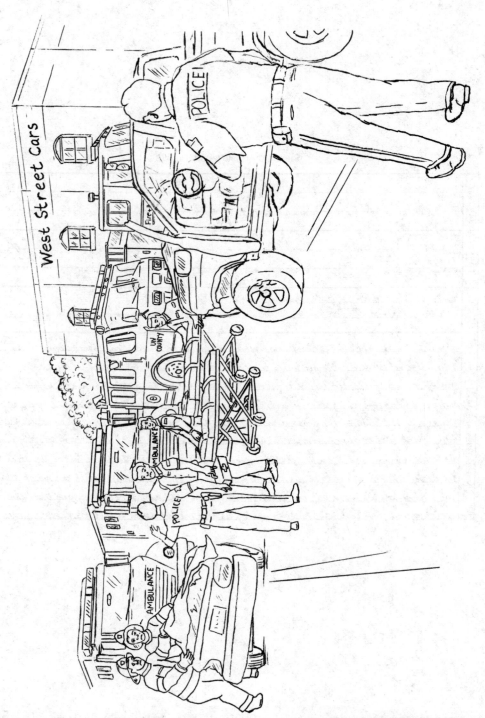

Accident Scene

GO ON TO THE NEXT PAGE

DIAGRAM OF AN ACCIDENT SCENE

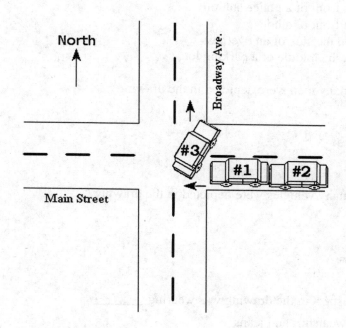

North

Broadway Ave.

#3

#1   #2

Main Street

The following questions are based upon information shown in the drawing depicting several men involved in an altercation.

92. How many of the men shown in the drawing were law enforcement officers?

(A) 2
(B) 3
(C) 4
(D) 5

93. What object were the men fighting over?

(A) Radio
(B) Gun
(C) Car keys
(D) Drug evidence

94. Where was it most likely that this altercation occurred?

(A) In front of a police station
(B) In front of a house
(C) On the side of an overpass
(D) In the middle of a parking lot

95. How many men were depicted in the drawing?

(A) 2
(B) 3
(C) 4
(D) 5

96. How many vehicles were depicted in the drawing?

(A) 0
(B) 1
(C) 2
(D) 3

97. The suspect in the drawing was wearing _____.

(A) Sweatshirt and jeans
(B) Shorts and t-shirt
(C) Heavy winter coat and hat
(D) T-shirt and jeans

98. The suspect in the drawing had _____.

(A) Long hair
(B) Short hair
(C) No hair
(D) Hair under hat

GO ON TO THE NEXT PAGE

The following questions are based upon the police sketch of "Suspect No. 1."

99. The name of "Suspect No. 1" is:

(A) Jimmy Barrachi
(B) Jerry Balducci
(C) Jason Winters
(D) Jeremy West

100. The age of "Suspect No. 1" is:

(A) 18
(B) 21
(C) 23
(D) 30

101. "Suspect No. 1" is known to have _____ identifying characteristics.

(A) 0
(B) 1
(C) 2
(D) 3

102. What is the eye color of "Suspect No. 1"?

(A) Blue
(B) Green
(C) Hazel
(D) Brown

103. How long "Suspect No. 1's" hair as shown on the mug shot?

(A) Long
(B) Shoulder-length
(C) About 1 inch long
(D) Shaved head

104. What alias was "Suspect No. 1" also known by?

(A) Jimmy Barrachi
(B) Jerry Balducci
(C) Jason Winters
(D) Jeremy West

105. What crime is "Suspect No. 1" suspected of having committed?

(A) Rape
(B) Robbery
(C) Battery
(D) Auto Theft

GO ON TO THE NEXT PAGE

106. An eyewitness of a recent auto theft that occurred at 3 P.M. described the perpetrator as about 5 ft 9 in, 155 lbs, Caucasian and wearing a beard. The perpetrator was wearing a tank top and jeans and didn't appear to have any distinguishing characteristics. Based upon the information provided about "Suspect No. 1," which of the traits provided by the eyewitness makes it unlikely that this suspect committed this theft?

(A) Beard
(B) Height
(C) Weight
(D) Lack of distinguishing characteristics

The following questions are based upon the paragraph discussing the knock *and* announce *rule.*

107. What is the *knock and announce* rule?

(A) A rule requiring probation officers to knock and announce themselves prior to entering a probationer's home.
(B) A rule requiring prosecutors to knock and announce themselves prior to entering an interrogation room.
(C) A rule requiring police officers to knock and announce themselves prior to executing a search warrant.
(D) A rule requiring corrections officials to knock and announce their presence prior to entering an occupied cell.

108. In the paragraph discussing the *knock and announce* rule, which constitutional amendment is mentioned?

(A) First Amendment
(B) Second Amendment
(C) Fourth Amendment
(D) Eighth Amendment

109. What law was looked at to help determine the validity of the *knock and announce* rule?

(A) Statutes
(B) Municipal code
(C) Common law
(D) Case law

110. Knocking and announcing one's presence is a critical factor in whether a court finds any subsequent search _____.

(A) Appropriate
(B) Ethical
(C) Reasonable
(D) Moral

GO ON TO THE NEXT PAGE

111. What is a serious consequence of an unlawful search?

(A) All evidence found during the search will be suppressed at trial.
(B) All evidence found during the search will be returned to the suspect.
(C) All charges will be dropped against the suspect.
(D) The suspect can sue the officers for damages.

112. Which of the following circumstances was NOT mentioned as an exception to the *knock and announce* rule?

(A) Threat of harm to police
(B) Fresh pursuit of an escaped arrestee
(C) Possible destruction of evidence
(D) Possible harm to suspect

113. Which court was mentioned in the paragraph explaining the knock and announce rule?

(A) The United States Supreme Court
(B) The state supreme court
(C) The trial court
(D) The United States district court

114. The knock and announce rule is applicable to situations involving

(A) Arrest
(B) Search and seizure
(C) Hot pursuit
(D) Safety and welfare check-ups

115. Officers were preparing to enter a residence to search for guns pursuant to a search warrant. It was approximately 11 A.M. and no lights were on in the house. Officers believed that no one was home and entered the house without first knocking and calling out "police!" According to the paragraph, the search will be determined _____.

(A) Lawful, because there is no point in knocking and announcing when no one is home to notice.
(B) Lawful, because the knock and announce rule only applies after dark.
(C) Unlawful, because the knock and announce rule has no exceptions.
(D) Unlawful, because believing that no one is home is not an exception to the knock and announce rule.

GO ON TO THE NEXT PAGE

The following questions are based upon the diagram of the interior of a house.

116. In the diagram, how many windows were in the house?

(A) 5
(B) 4
(C) 3
(D) 2

117. In the diagram of the house, if you entered the living room through the front door which direction would you be facing?

(A) North
(B) South
(C) East
(D) West

118. If the suspect is known to be hiding in the northwest corner of the house, what room is he in?

(A) Kitchen
(B) Bedroom
(C) Bathroom
(D) Living room

119. How many bedrooms are depicted within the house?

(A) 1
(B) 2
(C) 3
(D) 4

120. How many doors allow entrance of the house from the outside?

(A) 1
(B) 2
(C) 3
(D) 4

121. How many pieces of furniture are shown in the living room?

(A) 1
(B) 2
(C) 3
(D) 4

GO ON TO THE NEXT PAGE

122. If Officer Gutierrez is standing in the living room looking out the front window, his back is to the:

(A) North
(B) South
(C) East
(D) West

123. How many windows were shown in the bathroom?

(A) 0
(B) 1
(C) 2
(D) 3

The following questions are based upon the drawing of a traffic intersection in an urban neighborhood.

124. In the picture depicting a traffic intersection, how many police officers are shown?

(A) 1
(B) 2
(C) 3
(D) 4

125. What is the address of the establishment on the corner?

(A) 122
(B) 137
(C) 147
(D) 156

126. What is the name of the establishment on the corner?

(A) O'Hallahan's
(B) O'Donnell's
(C) Oscar's
(D) Paddy's

127. What type of service did the establishment on the corner NOT provide?

(A) Grocery
(B) Restaurant
(C) Bar
(D) Hotel

GO ON TO THE NEXT PAGE

128. How many people were in the crosswalk with the police officer?

(A) 1
(B) 3
(C) 5
(D) Too many to count

129. What type of hat did the officer in the center of the picture wear?

(A) No hat
(B) Motorcycle helmet
(C) Standard police cap with short brim
(D) Hat with a brim going all around it

130. The car in the center of the picture had a vanity license plate that said:

(A) Broncos
(B) Rockies
(C) Hiker
(D) Nature

The following questions refer to the street map labeled "Downtown."

131. On the map of "Downtown," the names of streets running east and west are primarily named

(A) For trees
(B) With odd numbers
(C) After Presidents
(D) After States

132. On the map of "Downtown," the streets running north and south are primarily named after:

(A) Trees
(B) States
(C) Railroads
(D) Mountains

133. On the map of "Downtown," which way does the railroad line run?

(A) Diagonally across the town
(B) From north to south
(C) From east to west
(D) There is no railroad line shown

GO ON TO THE NEXT PAGE

134. On the map of "Downtown," the police station is located between:

(A) Pine and Ridge Streets
(B) 1st and 2nd Streets
(C) Washington and Lincoln Avenues
(D) Kansas Street and Colorado Blvd.

135. On the map of "Downtown," if you are on Douglas Street and wish to get to 3rd Street, you must head:

(A) North
(B) South
(C) East
(D) West

136. What type of building was located in the Southeast corner of the Downtown area?

(A) Bingo Parlor
(B) Park
(C) Massage Parlor
(D) School

137. Most of the streets running east and west are:

(A) One-way streets
(B) Two-way streets
(C) Equal amount of both one-way and two-way streets
(D) Not designated as either one-way or two-way streets

138. Most of the streets running north and south are designated:

(A) One-way streets
(B) Two-way streets
(C) Equal amount of both one-way and two-way streets
(D) Not designated as either one-way or two-way streets

139. How many named streets are shown running east to west?

(A) 5
(B) 7
(C) 9
(D) 11

140. The Mall, Theater and Arena are all generally _____ of the police station.

(A) North
(B) South
(C) East
(D) West

GO ON TO THE NEXT PAGE

141. The Theatre is at First and Topeka, the School is located at 11th and Colorado. If an officer is called to respond to an incident at the School when he is leaving the Theater, which direction must he drive to reach the school in the shortest amount of time?

(A) Northeast
(B) Southwest
(C) Southeast
(D) Northwest

The following questions refer to information provided in the Scenario labeled "Sample Police Report No. 1."

142. Earl called for police assistance claiming he was approached by a man wearing:

(A) Sweats
(B) Sweatshirt and jeans
(C) T-shirt and jeans
(D) T-shirt and shorts

143. When Earl called for police assistance, he claimed he had been:

(A) At the bar
(B) Shopping
(C) At a restaurant
(D) At home

144. Earl claimed he submitted to the assailant's threats when:

(A) The assailant pulled out a weapon.
(B) The assailant hit Earl.
(C) The assailant threatened to hurt Earl.
(D) The assailant's friends approached Earl.

145. Earl described his assailant as:

(A) African American
(B) Caucasian
(C) Asian
(D) He did not specify a race

146. Earl described his assailant's height as:

(A) 5 ft 9 in
(B) 6 ft
(C) 5 ft 6 in
(D) 5 ft 3 in

GO ON TO THE NEXT PAGE

147. Earl estimated his assailant's weight as:

(A) 145 lbs
(B) 154 lbs
(C) 165 lbs
(D) 184 lbs

148. When you arrest Fred and charge him with the crime against Earl, you charge Fred with:

(A) Robbery
(B) Assault
(C) Kidnapping
(D) Auto theft

149. You suspect Fred of having committed the crime against Earl because he is known to commit these types of criminal acts. However, the only evidence against Fred noted in the report is:

(A) Fred's height matches the description of the assailant's.
(B) Fred's weight matches the description of the assailant's.
(C) Fred's hair, eye, and skin color match the description of the assailant's.
(D) Fred is wearing new clothes that match the description of the items taken.

The following questions refer to information provided on "Standard Arrest Report, Page 1."

150. The name of the person arrested was:

(A) Betty Rae Cinus
(B) Mary Sue Hastings
(C) Sue Ann Clements
(D) Beth Ann Howard

151. According to the information provided on the arrest report, the individual arrested was:

(A) Petite/small
(B) Average height and weight
(C) Above average height and weight
(D) Severely overweight

152. According to the arrest report, the individual arrested had symbols tattooed on her:

(A) Ankle
(B) Hands
(C) Upper arm
(D) Lower back

GO ON TO THE NEXT PAGE

153. According to the arrest report, the individual arrested appeared _____ at the time of arrest.

(A) Injured
(B) Compliant
(C) Unwell
(D) Drunk

154. According to the arrest report, the individual arrested had:

(A) A California driver's license
(B) A Colorado driver's license
(C) A Connecticut driver's license
(D) No driver's license

155. According to the arrest report, the individual arrested was given Miranda warnings:

(A) 24 hours after she was arrested
(B) 2 hours after she was arrested
(C) At the time of her arrest
(D) The report does not note whether she was ever given Miranda warnings

156. According to the information provided on the arrest report, the individual was arrested:

(A) At her place of business
(B) At a local bar
(C) At her home
(D) At a location not associated with the arrestee

157. According to the information provided in the arrest report, the individual arrested was found with:

(A) A handgun
(B) A club
(C) A knife
(D) No weapon was noted on the police report.

158. Which of the following identifying features is the most reliable in future identifications of this arrestee?

(A) Hair length
(B) Hair color
(C) Tattoo
(D) Weight

GO ON TO THE NEXT PAGE

159. What symbol did the suspect have tattooed on her ankle?

(A) Unidentifiable symbols
(B) Heart
(C) Chinese letter
(D) Butterfly

The following questions refer to information provided on "Standard Arrest Report, Page 2."

160. What was the primary offense charged on the report?

(A) Theft
(B) DUI
(C) Speeding
(D) Assault

161. What type of additional charges were listed on the report?

(A) Theft charges
(B) Traffic charges
(C) Misdemeanor criminal offenses
(D) Felony criminal offenses

162. How many additional charges were listed on the report?

(A) 0
(B) 1
(C) 2
(D) 3

163. What model of vehicle was provided on the report?

(A) Pick-up
(B) SUV
(C) Sedan
(D) Van

164. What type of damage was noted to the vehicle on the report?

(A) Damaged right front fender
(B) Damaged right side passenger door
(C) Damaged front bumper
(D) Damaged rear bumper

165. Who took possession of the vehicle following the time of the stop?

(A) Law enforcement impound
(B) Miller's Towing Company
(C) Grady's Towing Service
(D) Vehicle owner

GO ON TO THE NEXT PAGE

166. Who was listed as the owner of the vehicle?

(A) Jerry Petri
(B) John Summers
(C) Evan Matthews
(D) Earnest Miller

167. What day was this report prepared?

(A) August 1, 2006
(B) September 1, 2006
(C) September 2, 2006
(D) September 3, 2006

168. In what state was this vehicle registered?

(A) Colorado
(B) California
(C) New York
(D) New Jersey

169. What was the reporting officer's last name?

(A) Miller
(B) Lewis
(C) Jimenez
(D) Calvin

The following questions refer to information provided in the Narrative on "Standard Arrest Report, Page 3."

170. What driving cue initially alerted the officer to the suspect's vehicle?

(A) Erratic driving
(B) Standing too long at an intersection
(C) Hitting another vehicle
(D) Driving with high beam headlights in traffic

171. How many times did the officer note that the vehicle crossed the center line?

(A) 0
(B) 1
(C) 2
(D) 3

GO ON TO THE NEXT PAGE

172. Approximately how long did the officer follow the vehicle prior to stopping the vehicle?

(A) 30 seconds
(B) One minute
(C) Three minutes
(D) Eight minutes

173. What error did the driver make when attempting to stop the vehicle?

(A) Hit another vehicle
(B) Hit a tree
(C) Slid on the loose gravel on the side of the road
(D) Ground transmission gears

174. What, besides DUI, did the officer believe could have caused the driver to commit the driving infractions that he noticed?

(A) Driving while tired
(B) Driving while dealing with several children
(C) Driving while talking on a cell phone
(D) Driving an unfamiliar vehicle

175. What indicator caused the officer to believe that the driving errors were the result of driving while under the influence of alcohol or drugs?

(A) The smell of alcoholic beverage.
(B) A bottle of beer on the floorboard.
(C) A bottle of wine on the backseat.
(D) An admission of drinking made by the driver.

176. How did the officer identify the driver?

(A) Driver's license
(B) Insurance papers
(C) College ID card
(D) Self identification

177. After the officer asked the driver to step out of her vehicle, which of the following indications of intoxication was NOT present?

(A) Staggering
(B) Blood shot eyes
(C) Fell down
(D) Repeated requests for information already provided

GO ON TO THE NEXT PAGE

The following questions refer to the drawing labeled "accident scene."

178. How many law enforcement officers were shown in the scene?

(A) 1
(B) 2
(C) 3
(D) 4

179. How many vehicles appeared to be involved in the wreck?

(A) 1
(B) 2
(C) 3
(D) 4

180. What type of wrecked vehicle was surrounded by emergency personnel?

(A) Mini-van
(B) Pick-up truck
(C) SUV
(D) Sedan

181. Which vehicle appeared to have sustained the greatest damage?

(A) Mini-van
(B) Pick-up truck
(C) SUV
(D) Sedan

182. How many occupants were still visible within the cab of the wrecked pick-up?

(A) 0
(B) 1
(C) 2
(D) 3

183. How many emergency vehicles were visible within the drawing?

(A) Three fire trucks, one ambulance
(B) One fire truck, one ambulance
(C) Two fire trucks, two ambulances
(D) Three ambulances, one fire truck

GO ON TO THE NEXT PAGE

184. What is the name of the street, based upon the clues within the picture?

    (A) North Street
    (B) East Street
    (C) West Street
    (D) South Street

185. How many people were on stretchers in preparation for transport?

    (A) 0
    (B) 1
    (C) 2
    (D) 3

The following questions refer to the diagram of an accident.

186. How many cars were depicted in the diagram?

    (A) 1
    (B) 2
    (C) 3
    (D) 4

187. How many cars were actually in the intersection according to the diagram?

    (A) 0
    (B) 1
    (C) 2
    (D) 3

188. What was the name of the street running north and south?

    (A) Broadway
    (B) Park
    (C) Main
    (D) Market

189. What was the name of the street running east and west?

    (A) Broadway
    (B) Park
    (C) Main
    (D) Market

GO ON TO THE NEXT PAGE

190. The majority of cars involved in this collision appeared to be traveling on which street?

(A) Broadway
(B) Park
(C) Main
(D) Market

191. Using the designations marked upon each car, which one of the vehicles appears to be guilty of "following too close"?

(A) Car No. 1
(B) Car No. 2
(C) Car No. 3
(D) Car No. 4

STOP. THIS IS THE END OF PRACTICE TEST 4.

TURN TO THE NEXT PAGE

Answer Key

WRITTEN SKILLS

The answer, the sentence referred to from the reading passage, and a correct version (in boldface) for those sentences that contain errors are provided.

1. (A) Spelling
   Line 1 of the letter: *I am **pleassed** to learn that you have safely returned from your basic training with the military.*   Correct Answer: **pleased**

2. (B) Grammar
   Line 2 of the letter: *Your job as a police officer **is been kept** available until your return.*   Correct Answer: **is being kept**

3. (B) Grammar
   Line 3 of the letter: *However, **you been** in Central City for approximately three weeks and have not yet contacted the Department.*   Correct Answer: **you have been**

4. (D) No error
   Line 4 of the letter: *You have yet to provide the date for which you will be returning to work.*

5. (D) No error
   Line 5 of the letter: *This is unacceptable.*

6. (A) Spelling
   Line 6 of the letter: *Both the officers of this department and the citizens of this community **relie** on your diligence.*   Correct Answer: **rely**

7. (C) Punctuation
   Line 7 of the letter: *The City will hold your position open until **Monday July 2nd**.*   Correct Answer: **Monday, July 2nd**

8. (B) Grammar
   Line 8 of the letter: *If you have not contacted this office by that date your employment **is terminated**.*   Correct Answer: **will be terminated**

9. (A) Spelling
   Line 9 of the letter: *Please contact this office before that date if you have chosen to resign your **positon** with the City.*   Correct Answer: **position**

10. (A) Spelling
Line 10 of the letter: *Thank you for your time and **assistanse** in this matter.*　　　　　　Correct Answer: **assistance**

11. (A) Spelling
Line 1 of the letter: *Congratulations on being selected for promotion to the rank of **Seargent.*** 　　　　　Correct Answer: **Sergeant**

12. (A) Grammar (incomplete sentence)
Line 2 of the letter: *You exemplary work ethic and numerous commendations for service showed us.*　　　Correct Answer: **Your exemplary work ethic and numerous commendations for service influenced our decision to promote you.**

13. (A) Spelling
Line 3 of the letter: *Also, your skill as an interpreter is **highlly** valued by this Department.*　　　　　Correct Answer: **highly**

14. (B) Grammar (incomplete sentence)
Line 4 of the letter: *A short **ceremony followed** by a reception on July 15th.*　　　Correct Answer: **On July 15th, there was a short ceremony, followed by a reception.**

15. (A) Spelling
Line 5 of the letter: *On August 1st you will report to training **serrvices** for a week of leadership training.*　　　Correct Answer: **services**

16. (D) No error
Line 6 of the letter: *Then, you will be assigned to the Northeast Station.*

17. (A) Spelling
Line 7 of the letter: ***You** duties will include supervising 12 newly commissioned officers.*　　　Correct Answer: **Your**

18. (B) Grammar (incomplete sentence)
Line 8 of the letter: *But also 12 veteran officers.*　　Correct Answer: **You will also supervise twelve veteran officers.**

19. (C) Punctuation
Line 9 of the letter: *In addition, you will be the **departments** liaison to the Vietnamese community.*　　　Correct Answer: **department's**

20. (B) Grammar (run-on sentence)
Line 10 of the letter: *You will get extra pay for this service and you will retrain on your weapon every six months and you will be issued a car and work for 46 hours every week.*　　　Correct Answer: **You will get extra pay for this service, will retrain on your weapon every six months, and will be issued a car. You will work for 46 hours every week.**

21. (D) No error

Line 11 of the letter: *I look forward to visiting with you in person at the promotion ceremony.*

22. (D) No error

Line 1 of the letter: *I am honored to have received your gracious invitation to participate in your school's cultural awareness day.*

23. (B) Grammar (incomplete sentence)

Line 2 of the letter: *As a representative of the Mountain High Police Department.* Correct Answer: **As a representative of the Mountain High Police Department, I am honored to have received your gracious invitation to participate in your school's cultural awareness day.**

24. (B) Grammar (incomplete sentence)

Line 3 of the letter: *I would be **pleased speak** with your students about the necessity of becoming bilingual.* Correct Answer: **pleased to speak**

25. (B) Grammar (incomplete sentence)

Line 4 of the letter: *Of course, they must practice their **bilingual a lot**.* Correct Answer: **Of course, they must practice their bilingual skills a lot.**

26. (C) Punctuation

Line 5 of the letter: *I know the **students'** don't like to use their books!* Correct Answer: **students**

27. (D) No error

Line 6 of the letter: *I will also be promoting the advantages of academic success in English and Math for students who seek to enter the law enforcement field.*

28. (A) Spelling

Line 7 of the letter: *I **unnerstand** that the program is to take place from 1:00 to 4:00 P.M. on October 14th in the gymnasium.* Correct Answer: **understand**

29. (C) Punctuation

Line 8 of the letter: *I will bring brochures and a video to share with **student's**.* Correct Answer: **students**

30. (A) Spelling

Line 9 of the letter: *I look forward to **visitting** with you and your students.* Correct Answer: **visiting**

31. (B) Grammar (incomplete sentence)

Line 10 of the letter: *On October 14 at 1:00 P.M.* Correct Answer: **I look forward to our visit on October 14 at 1:00 P.M.**

SECTION 2
BASIC SKILLS

Reading Comprehension

32.	(A)	True
33.	(B)	False
34.	(A)	True
35.	(B)	False
36.	(B)	False
37.	(B)	False
38.	(B)	False
39.	(B)	False
40.	(B)	False
41.	(D)	

Vocabulary

42.	(A)	DEMEANOR = manner
43.	(B)	STIMULUS = provocation
44.	(D)	INDIGENT = poor
45.	(C)	MUNICIPALITY = city
46.	(B)	GIMMICK = trick
47.	(A)	DISCRETION = judgment
48.	(D)	ENERGETIC = lively
49.	(C)	IMPETUOUS = thoughtless
50.	(B)	VOLATILE = explosive
51.	(D)	TENDENCY = inclination
52.	(A)	SEGREGATE = isolate
53.	(B)	RELINQUISH = release
54.	(D)	DISSEMINATE = distribute
55.	(C)	INTERVENE = interfere
56.	(C)	MASSIVE = huge
57.	(A)	FLEXIBLE = pliable
58.	(D)	DIRTY = unclean
59.	(A)	REFUTE = rebut
60.	(C)	PROFESSIONAL = expert
61.	(D)	DENSE = thick

Mathematics

62.	(C)	1039
63.	(A)	381
64.	(A)	104
65.	(C)	14
66.	(C)	1943
67.	(D)	615
68.	(C)	9
69.	(D)	15
70.	(C)	$105 (fine $25 + $30 + costs $50 = $105)
71.	(C)	$180
72.	(A)	$75
73.	(D)	$160 (fine $25 + $30 = $55 × 2 for school zone = $110 + costs $50 = $160)
74.	(B)	$4900
75.	(A)	$3800
76.	(C)	19
77.	(D)	8
78.	(D)	146
79.	(C)	$449
80.	(B)	4

81. (B) 320
82. (C) 551
83. (D) 55
84. (C) 56
85. (C) 7
86. (B) 4
87. (A) 580
88. (D) 1189
89. (B) 2371
90. (C) 8835
91. (C) 17

POLICE ABILITIES

92. (B) 3
93. (B) Gun
94. (C) On the side of an overpass
95. (C) 4
96. (B) 1
97. (A) Sweatshirt and jeans
98. (B) Short hair
99. (B) Jerry Balducci
100. (C) 23
101. (C) 2
102. (D) Brown
103. (C) About 1 inch long
104. (C) Jason Winters
105. (D) Auto Theft
106. (D) Lack of distinguishing characteristics
107. (C) A rule requiring police officers to knock and announce themselves prior to executing a search warrant.
108. (C) Fourth Amendment
109. (C) Common law
110. (C) Reasonable
111. (A) All evidence found during the search will be suppressed at trial.
112. (D) Possible harm to suspect
113. (A) The United States Supreme Court
114. (B) Search and seizure
115. (D) Unlawful, because believing that no one is home is not an exception to the knock and announce rule.
116. (A) 5
117. (D) West
118. (B) Bedroom
119. (B) 2
120. (B) 2
121. (C) 3
122. (A) North
123. (A) 0
124. (B) 2
125. (C) 147
126. (D) Paddy's
127. (A) Grocery
128. (A) 1
129. (B) Motorcycle helmet
130. (D) Nature
131. (B) Odd numbers
132. (C) Railroads
133. (B) From north to south

134. (B) 1st and 2nd Streets
135. (A) North
136. (D) School
137. (A) One-way streets
138. (D) Not designated
139. (C) 9
140. (D) West
141. (C) Southeast
142. (B) Sweatshirt and jeans
143. (B) Shopping
144. (C) The assailant threatened to hurt Earl
145. (D) Did not specify a race
146. (C) 5 ft 6 in
147. (A) 145 lbs
148. (A) Robbery
149. (D) Fred is wearing new clothes that match the description of the items taken.
150. (B) Mary Sue Hastings
151. (C) Above average height and weight
152. (B) Hands
153. (D) Drunk
154. (B) Colorado Driver's license
155. (C) At the time of her arrest
156. (C) At her home
157. (D) No weapon was noted on the police report
158. (C) Tattoo
159. (D) Butterfly
160. (B) DUI
161. (B) Traffic charges
162. (C) 2
163. (D) Van
164. (A) Damaged right front fender
165. (C) Grady's Towing
166. (B) John Summers
167. (D) September 3, 2006
168. (A) Colorado
169. (D) Calvin
170. (B) Standing too long at an intersection
171. (D) 3
172. (C) Three minutes
173. (D) Ground transmission gears
174. (C) Driving while talking on a cell phone
175. (A) The smell of alcoholic beverage
176. (D) Self-identification
177. (C) Fell down
178. (B) 2
179. (B) 2
180. (D) Sedan

181. (D) Sedan
182. (A) 0
183. (C) Two fire trucks, two ambulances
184. (C) West Street
185. (A) 0
186. (C) 3
187. (B) 1
188. (A) Broadway
189. (C) Main Street
190. (C) Main Street
191. (B) Car No. 2